SPECIAL EDUCATION SERIES
Peter Knoblock, *Editor*

W9-ADK-906

(Continued)

SPECIAL EDUCATION SERIES, *Continued*

CREATING TOMORROW'S SCHOOLS TODAY

Stories of Inclusion, Change, and Renewal

MICHAEL S. BERRES
DIANNE L. FERGUSON
PETER KNOBLOCK
CONNIE WOODS

Editors

Teachers College, Columbia University
New York and London

Published by Teachers College Press, 1234 Amsterdam Avenue, New York, NY 10027

Library of Congress Cataloging-in-Publication Data
Creating tomorrow's schools today : stories of inclusion, change, and
  renewal / edited by Michael S. Berres . . . [et al.].
      p.   cm.—(Special education series)
    Includes bibliographical references and index.
    ISBN 0-8077-3550-7.—ISBN 0-8077-3549-3 (pbk.)
    1. Mainstreaming in education—United States—Case studies.
  2. Special education—United States—Case studies.   3. School
  management and organization—United States—Case studies.
  4. Educational change—United States—Case studies.   I. Berres,
  Michael S.   II. Series: Special education series (New York, N.Y.)
  LC3981.C746   1996
  371.9'046—dc20   96-9093

ISBN 0-8077-3549-3 (paper)
ISBN 0-8077-3550-7 (cloth)

Printed on acid-free paper
Manufactured in the United States of America

03 02 01 00 99 98 97 96   8 7 6 5 4 3 2 1

Contents

Acknowledgments

This is an extraordinary time to be involved in school change and reform issues. We are witnessing changes in how our nation's schools educate students. This project describing how several school communities across the country practice full inclusion within their larger restructuring work leaves us with much hope and optimism for the future. There are many educators and parents who have shared their stories of school change with us. It is impossible to thank each of them for their support for our work. The authors do wish to acknowledge the following persons for their contributions:

Myrna Zitek and Terri Surratt for their typing and production skills.

The staff of South Valley Elementary School for their ongoing willingness to open their classrooms and school activities to our research and learning.

The staff and parents of Lawton Elementary School for their commitment to making education for every child a top priority in the life of their school.

The staff, parents, and community supporters of Jowonio for their passionate belief and practice of inclusion for the last 25 years.

Our colleagues in the Schools Projects for their support and assistance in both the research and the writing. These include Mary Dalmau, Cleo Droege, Jackie Lester, Diana Oxley, Ginevra Ralph, and Chris Willis.

Gwen Meyer for her assistance in editing the chapters.

CREATING TOMORROW'S SCHOOLS TODAY

Stories of Inclusion, Change, and Renewal

All Children, All Schools

Michael S. Berres

Why restructure schools so that children of all abilities can be active and contributing members of their school communities? This book suggests that the complex process of creating homes within our schools for all children is a worthwhile endeavor, not only for children with disabilities, but for all members of the school community.

AVOIDING MISTAKES

A few years ago, two of us (Berres & Knoblock, 1987) showcased nine American school districts that had successfully increased the amount of contact between general education students and students with moderate and severe disabilities. The intent of that book was to focus on the most current special education trends and to demonstrate that it was possible for schools to achieve more than just mainstreaming if they worked with the current progressive concept of integration. While we were preparing that volume, however, we discovered a very disconcerting fact. In the short time between the beginning of our search for effective mainstreaming programs in schools around the country and the volume's publication in 1987, major changes had occurred. In reality, some of the practices cited in our book as "current" and "innovative" were neither. At best, many of the ideas we put forth could have been described as "transitional"—they were strategies that might help educators move students from separate to integrated programs

Recently, we decided to develop a new volume about today's "current" practice of fully incorporating children with moderate and severe disabilities in general education programs. This effort would take readers beyond "mainstreaming" and "integration" and focus on the concept of "inclusion." We defined "inclusion" as the full participation of students with special learning needs and disabilities in the daily life, curriculum, and learning activities of same-age peers in general classrooms. We asked Dianne Ferguson and Connie Woods to join us in this project. Together we agreed to present to educators what we hoped would be a credible case: that inclusion, as we were coming to understand it, was important for children and schools.

We decided to keep this book relatively free of jargon, to use few citations, and to rely upon the actual stories of people in inclusive schools to make our point. But, as we planned, we began to realize that we were about to make a critical mistake: We were talking about inclusion from a special education perspective and defining it as an external process to provide support to students with disabilities rather than as an integral component of general school restructuring and systemic reform. So, instead of producing yet another book about innovations in special education, we decided to explore the ways in which special and general education are merging as part of the general reform and restructuring of schools to serve all children more effectively.

This book strongly supports the tenet that the inclusion of children with moderate and severe disabilities is only one facet of this restructuring of schools and classrooms. Although the concept of inclusion arose out of the disability rights movement, educators face many of the same challenges with children who speak English as a second language, with children who are "gifted," with children of color, and with children whose families suffer financial difficulties. Accommodation of diversity also includes gender equality in our programs and curriculum.

COMMUNITIES FOR ALL STUDENTS

How are we to create classrooms that welcome and nurture the inquisitiveness and creativity of many different children? We must begin by adopting the language and beliefs of restructuring and systemic school reform. We must not create schools that cater to or favor particular groups of students (e.g., students who are identified as bilingual or "remedial" or "gifted"), but we must make a commitment to welcome and support all our students and all our families. Authors who would share examples of inclusive education through books and articles must look for their stories in schools that include many groups of students with "special needs" as integral members of the school community.

The schools we write about in this book did not restructure simply to accommodate students with disabilities, although sometimes modifying special education services acted as a catalyst for other shifts in practice. Neither did these schools try to redesign special education services out of what the disability rights groups might describe as a "pity or charity model" (Biklen, 1985; Bogdan & Biklen, 1977; Wolfensberger, 1975), where we act because we feel pity or sympathy for a group of people. The educators portrayed in these pages created inclusive schools because they strongly believe that such schools are good for all children and that all students benefit from participating in and being a part of a diverse, vibrant community of learners.

REASONS FOR CHANGE

Why would anyone leave familiar ground for uncharted territory? What motivates people to change their practice? Why do educators adopt new approaches to teaching that add complexity to their work lives? Sometimes change is mandated by state initiative, by the central office, by building administrators, or it comes about under threat of legal action. Many educators work to create inclusion, not from personal choice, but because of external pressures. Sometimes this may be necessary, but as educators with strong relationships in our educational communities we realize that externally motivated change often meets obstacles not encountered when the changes come from within.

Over the years, we have listened to many advocates of inclusion tell their stories about inclusive teaching. These educators see children as individuals and they frame the discussion pragmatically and personally—"Does this make sense for John?" or "Will it help me in my work with Jill?" They are engaged in asking questions, brainstorming, and talking to others for validation and for new ideas.

Thomas Sergiovanni (1994) describes the most powerful change as emanating from a personal commitment to an ideal rather than from administrative decree and defines this engagement as "moral leadership," whereby all stakeholders have the opportunity to debate and then coalesce around site-based ideals for their own school's improvement. We would like to see educators making the choice to open their schools to all children for full participation. It is certainly easier to provide inclusive education when it is part of a school's core philosophy than when advocates must lobby and fight for the changes. Some schools have included students with diverse needs from the beginning. Each school, however, becomes an inclusive community in its own time and manner. Most schools adopt inclusive practices after they have been in operation for some years, or even decades. Change may be initiated in a number of schools as the result of a parent's request, perhaps, or through the concerted action of a disability rights group. In others, a court case or a change in belief by a segment of the staff may create a shift in practice. Situations will continue to arise in which change for children, if it is to happen at all, must be initiated externally, or even mandated, and we must support and encourage those whose participation in inclusion is not of their own choosing.

Among the many influences that motivate people to *choose* inclusion as a practice and as a philosophy, four, we think, stand out. Some people become advocates of inclusive education because of their involvement in other kinds of social and political change. Others' imaginations are captured by curricular innovations (e.g., multiage classrooms or new technology) and the possibilities they offer to children. Still others may be attracted by the shift in how American schools are defining "community" in classrooms and by their inclusion of a wider variety of participants in school decision-making. A fourth influence is a far more personal one—the direct relationship between schools and children and families who for the first time might be experiencing full membership in school life.

The Influence of Political and Social Justice

Educational and social reformers have worked long to diversify our nation's classrooms (Cremin, 1961). Although progressive educators as long ago as the 1870s called for heterogeneity, the real pressure for change was felt most during the turbulent 1960s and 1970s. With the nation focused on "equal opportunity" and with leaders like Dr. Martin Luther King, Jr., and President John Kennedy raising questions about social inequality, education entered a period of intense examination. Three powerful forces behind some of the changes leading to diversity and inclusion were: newly elected legislators joining with other liberal legislators who were bent on reform, parent advocacy groups, and change-oriented caucuses within professional educational associations.

In *Brown v. Board of Education* (1954), the U.S. Supreme Court extended the equal protection clause of the Fourteenth Amendment of the Constitution to children of all races. It was the political, social, and ethical precursor to literally thousands of other legal and legislative decisions supporting the placement of children with widely varying backgrounds and abilities in the same schools and classrooms. Advocates and legal groups agreed that the policy of "separate but equal" was inherently unequal and provided less opportunity to many children. While few battles for equality have been won quickly, the clear trend during the past three decades is that our schools are well on their way to becoming more inclusive communities.

With the media eager for stories about social justice, services for children with disabilities began to change. Burton Blatt's *Christmas in Purga-*

tory (1966), a pictorial study featured in *Life* magazine, showed the degrading conditions in which children and adults—warehoused in our large tax-supported institutions—lived. The concept of "normalization," suggesting that people with developmental disabilities should enjoy the same opportunities and experiences available to people without disabilities, grew in acceptance. With challenges to large institutions such as Willowbrook School in New York state and attacks on more benign forms of segregation—such as separate schools, separate classrooms, and resource programs—educators and parents gave momentum to a strong movement that would continue to champion the educational rights of their students and children. The fight for schooling for students with disabilities, coupled with the turbulence and passion in other political and social movements, has led many educators to become advocates of inclusion and of increased diversity as a critical facet of school restructuring.

The Influence of Innovative Instruction and Curriculum

Sometimes educators are excited by instructional and curricular innovations that provide them with opportunities to embrace diversity in their classrooms. Some teachers attend inspiring workshops that lead them to adopt particular new approaches, while others try new practices that have proved successful for colleagues. Some teachers simply feel dissatisfied with current practice and decide to try something new. Whatever the source, many educators bring a vibrancy or excitement to their teaching through the integration of new strategies into their daily work.

A shift to the "multiage classroom" is one such change. During the 1980s and early 1990s, interest in multiage classes grew among educators seeking "developmentally appropriate" approaches to serving children. Wary and critical of categorizing and sorting children by age and standardized test scores, these reformers contended that multiage groupings formed more natural communities that allowed children to proceed at their own learning pace. Many advocates of inclusion feel supported by research that demonstrates that, although multiage classrooms show about the same degree of academic efficacy as single-grade classrooms, they appear to be more beneficial in the areas of self-esteem, affective development, and the attainment of social skills (Anderson & Pavan, 1993; Goodlad & Anderson, 1987).

A second powerful instructional approach, especially when used in classrooms with a lot of diversity, cooperative learning (Johnson & Johnson, 1984) has shifted the traditional form of classroom management from competition among students to a model of student interdependence. Cooperative learning advocates argue that children learn content when they assist other children in mastering that same content and that children of differing abilities, interests, and learning styles should be placed together in small learning groups formed around common curricular tasks. Advocates of inclusion will agree strongly that heterogeneous working groups help students understand and appreciate that each of them has different skills and abilities in different subject areas. Cooperative learning lends itself nicely to peer and cross-age tutoring, a strategy that, like multiage grouping, dates back to nineteenth-century American one-room schoolhouses.

A third factor contributing to the development of classrooms that accommodate a broader range of diversity is the phenomenal growth of technology. Some of the more creative offerings, such as the Integrated Technology Classroom (ITC), allow students to access technology in every classroom throughout the school day. There is no waiting for lab time, no crowding around printers. Technology is a "means" rather than an "end" and, at its best, allows teachers to have children with wide ability ranges working together in cooperative learning groups.

The Influence of the School as Community

Traditionally, schools have done little to foster family involvement. Parents brought their children to school and transferred full authority to the educational staff. Parents volunteered and participated in or organized "frill" events. The insight and wisdom of parents about their children's learning needs were rarely solicited. In this book, we describe educators who have developed vital partnerships with families and community supporters. They see school decision-making in fundamentally different ways. School governance, once the sole purview of central office administrators and principals, increasingly includes parents, teachers, and community members in site-based councils and teams to address policy matters such as mission statements, hiring, grant development, and program evaluation.

Parents have moved from a peripheral to a more central role in schools. Today, effective classroom management often requires teachers to coordinate the efforts of other adults (e.g., parents, student interns, members of the community, and business volunteers) as they work with students. There is strong evidence that, besides the help provided to children in the classroom, active and visible parent–family participation in a school has a positive impact on student achievement and the "climate" of the school.

Many people now think of schools as centers for *family* education. Where schools used to offer only occasional parent workshops run by PTAs, many schools now reach out to parents through ongoing parent training programs such as "Family Math" and "Talking to Your Child About Sexuality." Many districts sponsor nonprofit "Community Schools," keeping their buildings open after school hours to offer youths and adults low-cost classes ranging from "How to Find a Job" to "Creative Writing." Other schools invite family service agencies to locate medical, legal, psychological, and daycare services in their buildings so that schools become centers of community and family life. The lines of separation between home and school are gradually fading away.

American business has long been involved in education. In the beginning, schools were structured to train children to be workers on the assembly lines, and the competitive style of education focused on the acquisition of lower-level information. The business world now recognizes the importance of giving time and money to local school systems. Companies see a clear connection between our country's future economic success and the ability of beleaguered school systems to produce well-educated, critically thinking adults who are able to collaborate with others and solve problems independently.

Visiting a school that welcomes its families and community members is an invigorating experience. It is exciting to see teachers, instructional assistants, university interns, family volunteers, and business people working together to achieve a common mission. Although some educators feel uncertain, or even fearful, about the rush of the community through the schoolhouse doors, many find these times to be invigorating, hopeful, and even fun! Risking the addition of new adults to decision-making teams makes it easier to accept new children, including those with moderate and severe disabilities. If, as Carl Glickman (1993) writes, the primary goal of our schools is to help children understand and be skilled in the practices of democracy, what a wonderful model we are creating for children. If we include adults who represent a range of diversity, we must also include all kinds of children.

The Influence of Personal Experience

We believe that it is the last of these four influences—the personal experience and contact with children and families and being a part of children's lives—that fosters in us the long-lasting dedication to advocating inclusive schooling. For each of the authors, there is a clear commitment to school diversity that has come from personal experience: from seeing firsthand that separating children into groups based on abilities is both ineffective and unethical and from watching and participating in the lives of children made markedly better because they were included as members in groups and activities—both in and out of school. While this is hardly a surprising statement, given the last three decades of research showing the devastating effects of labeling and separating children, it forced us to confront our own professional practice and biases.

We each began our careers in different places but eventually found ourselves working in special education roles: Knoblock as a professor at Syracuse University and a founder of the groundbreaking inclusion program called Jowonio School; Woods as a technical assistance provider on integration matters in Washington state; Ferguson as a professor at the University of Oregon and the parent of a son with severe disabilities; and Berres as a district special education supervisor and regional compliance monitor in Washington state.

Peter Knoblock's own views on inclusion were formed during the 15 years he worked with Jowonio School, which was founded cooperatively by a group of parents in Syracuse, New York. Originally established as a child-centered alternative to some of the public schools in Syracuse, Jowonio quickly expanded to provide a school home for children who had been excluded from public schooling because of their challenging behavior. One contribution of this remarkable school has been its inclusion of children with all degrees of autism. Knoblock describes a child he worked with in the mid-1970s who forever changed the way he thought about education:

> Gradually, as (Jowonio School's) reputation spread, we began accepting children who were experiencing difficulty in the public schools. One situation is particularly poignant for me. A family contacted us about their 5-year-old daughter who was attending class at the Association for Retarded Citizens (later, the ARC). The parents believed she was capable of doing more; they thought of her as brighter and wanted her challenged. Initially, we worried about her ability to handle our structure—would she run out into the road? We admitted her to the school and began reframing many of the initial questions. Specifically, we now asked ourselves if we could structure a program to meet her needs rather than regard it as a matter of her fitting our program. The experience was wonderful for all of us. She never ran into the road! And we learned that inclusion of a child who seemed so different on the surface was not so difficult once we acknowledged the range of differences and needs at the school. (Personal correspondence, September 1994)

Although he was instrumental in successfully creating a publicly funded, private, inclusive school long before the concepts of integration and inclusion entered the educational conversation, Knoblock's real interest lay in teacher preparation programs. For many years, Syracuse University's teacher education programs, like most other large universities', had been graduating well-trained teachers for an increasing number of specialized settings outside the general classroom. Working with a cadre of other faculty, Knoblock helped reframe the teacher education program into one that prepares teachers to work in inclusive classrooms from the beginning. Rather than working as support staff to general education teachers, Syracuse University's newly prepared teachers *are* general classroom teachers. Questions of "reintroducing" or "contacting" or "integrating" or "mainstreaming" students simply do not arise for these teachers because their students never leave the classrooms in the first place.

When Connie Woods completed her special education degree at the University of Oregon, students in the program were required to complete a practicum with adults with disabilities. Because the only adult programs in Oregon were in segregated environments, she began working in what she now calls a "birth-to-death" segregated school. She later taught in a public high school, where she focused on community-based instruction for her students. When Woods moved to Seattle, she obtained a state-funded technical assistance position to help school districts provide better specialized services for older students with special needs. In that role, she began to meet teachers and families who were seeking inclusive education for their students and children. Seeing and hearing directly from students, parents, and teachers whose lives were forever changed by full inclusion, Woods evolved to her current beliefs about inclusive education. She says, "Once a person has personally felt the power of inclusion, properly understood and implemented, there is no going back to separate education, training, and programming" (personal correspondence, September 1994).

Dianne Ferguson's passions and energies have been directly linked to issues that she and her family have had to confront on a daily basis. She has seen dramatic changes in the field of special education and disability services in the 26 years that she and her husband Phil have maneuvered their way, with their son Ian, through the various service systems. She recalls no early childhood programs for their son until he was 4 years old. What did exist for them were day-long clinic visits every 6 weeks or so at the medical center 60 miles from their home. She recalls how pleased they were when they were finally offered public education services at a regional segregated school 15 miles away, after having been told that their son was not eligible for schooling because he did not have "clean bodily habits" and could not follow simple directions.

When new movements occurred in the field, the Fergusons always seemed to find themselves involved. Ian was among the first in an elementary school—which also served all the district's students with physical and multiple disabilities—to begin attending the Grade 5 classroom for some parts of the day. The Fergusons argued with the principal for "two types of mainstreaming": one type for students who, with a little time and help, could be expected to learn much of what all the other students were learning, and another for students who would not be learning the same things but would benefit from learning other things in other ways. Ian was also the first student who used a wheelchair to attend the neighborhood school (that had recently been renovated to include an elevator and ramps), where he quickly became known among the other students as the only student with an elevator key.

In the end, however, the Fergusons' commitment to what we will refer to here as "systemic inclusion" solidified during the years Ian was in high school. The inclusive activities that Ian enjoyed in high school, such as being included in a drama class and spending time with his developing network of school acquaintances, revealed to the Fergusons the range of possibilities that existed for Ian and other adults with disabilities. They also realized that these experiences were unlikely to be realized without strong advocacy and commitment to change. Creating schools and communities that effectively support all children and youths is a complex task. This struggle must achieve a social place and a growth in competence for each student. This is the challenge that Dianne Ferguson accepts in her work with teachers, schools, and the graduate students who study with her to become teachers. Her commitment is partly a result of watching Ian participating in one special education innovation after another, but never quite becoming a full member of his school community.

My own views on inclusion were formed at Jowonio, a decade after it opened. In 1979, I began a doctoral program in Special Education at Syracuse University, whose reputation for being innovative, even radical, with regard to integration and education in general, seemed just the right fit for my ideals. At Jowonio, children, whose needs and behaviors were similar to children I had seen living in large residential programs in California, Pennsylvania, and the District of Columbia, were going to school and attending general education classrooms for the entire day, doing what "typical" children did. Sometimes these children, diagnosed by multitudes of certified professionals as "moderately or severely autistic," acted out or engaged in self-stimulatory behavior. It was the professional visitors who seemed to feel uneasy over these behaviors. They couldn't understand how "severely handicapped" children could be doing so well in nontherapeutic and unspecialized places. However, Jowonio was very specialized in its own way. The staff succeeded in teaching children with disabilities because of their commitment to talking about every child's progress through the normal developmental stages of childhood.

After a year at Jowonio, I had a discussion with a teacher that allowed me to discover what an inclusive school is all about. As a beginning administrative intern at the school, I was trying to hire staff for the summer program. New York State funds for summer programming were only provided for "handicapped" children, so the "typical" children would not be included in the program. I was having a difficult time finding teachers, and I couldn't understand their reluctance to take a teaching position in the half-day, relaxed, recreational program. Frustrated, I questioned a teacher about her disinterest. She told me, "Summer school is boring! And it doesn't work!" What she meant was that she didn't want to teach in a segregated, artificial environment with a group of very similar children where there was limited chance for modeling and transfer of skills. Jowonio and my experiences there have provided me with a standard for decisions about what is possible for children.

Before my Jowonio experience, disability rights seemed easy to support in theory, and I often discussed civil liberty issues with other special education students and faculty. It took many months of working at Jowonio before my theoretical support for inclusion was balanced by experience as I faced the realities of working with children like Jamal and Justin. It was seeing Jamal successfully participating in a reading group with other 6- and 7-year-olds that grounded me and gave birth to my personal commitment to diversity. Hearing Justin talking about going to a sleepover with his friends touched me more profoundly than reading the newest integration texts or hearing inspiring conference speakers ever did. Personal experience forced me to confront the incompleteness of my theoretical views and encouraged me to find ways to live my new commitment to inclusion.

When I left Jowonio, I moved to the State of Washington and worked for 7 years as a state regulator for special education programs and as the administrator of a district special education program. In those positions, I encouraged districts and schools, through various means, to provide specialized services to their students with disabilities. But my effectiveness in facilitating quality education for children often seemed negligible. Gradually, it did become clear that my job, trying to make special education programs more effective, was really tackling the wrong problem. In 1991, I applied for the principalship at Lawton Elementary School in the Seattle School District, and was hired. Chapter 3 is the story of my work there and the changes we implemented in the school.

Sometimes in my visits to other schools, I encounter a special education classroom that reminds me of past sites: self-contained and nearly always with a small number of children, a teacher, and an instructional assistant. During a visit to one such class, I was told that the children were mainstreamed for small portions of the day "as appropriate" so that they might learn the skills necessary for their eventual reintegration into the school community. I listened politely and felt pain for the futures of these children. If we want children to participate as productive citizens in a society characterized by diversity, they will need to learn together. We cannot expect that "training" done in isolation will mystically transfer to the real world.

ONE CHILD'S STORY—ONE SCHOOL'S GROWTH

The beautiful Skagit Valley in the northwestern corner of Washington state is the home of Tyler Davis and of his school, Centennial Elementary. Tyler's mother, Barbara Davis, is a special educator who, over the years, has established many quality segregated recreational, educational, and social programs for students with disabilities. Davis' story of Tyler's birth in 1986 and of his early years is all too familiar (personal correspondence, December 1994):

> I gave birth to a son, Tyler, who has a variety of labels. These include mentally retarded, visually impaired, and orthopedically impaired. Soon after diagnosis, we began attending our local early intervention program. Tyler had a case services manager, a family services manager, a speech therapist, a physical therapist, and a teacher. In addition he was seeing a neurologist, a pediatrician, a surgeon, two ophthalmologists, a geneticist, a urologist, and an orthopedist. In one year's time, we—as a family—became encased in a cocoon of educators, managers, therapists, and doctors. While they were helpful and well meaning, we felt we were losing control of much of the parenting process in our son's life.

While the Davis family was experiencing a myriad of specialized and separate services for Tyler, they were also experiencing the normal childhood experiences of daughter Megan, who is 3 years older than Tyler. Because of the "wonderfully normal experiences we had with our daughter, we began to realize how isolated and 'label focused' we had become with our son."

The personal events in Davis' life were causing her to reexamine many professional values that she had accepted without question. A conference presentation by parent educator Jeff Strully had a strong impact on her:

> As the parent of a labeled child, he [Strully] described much of what we were feeling and introduced us to a new concept: inclusion. As we sat with tears in our eyes, he described the normal life his teenage daughter enjoyed, despite her many labels. As I reflected on his message, I knew that this was what I wanted for my son. And as I began to think about this dream, I realized that I could want no less for my students, all of whom were labeled in the moderate to severe range of disabilities, than I did for Tyler.

At the end of that same school year, Davis was transferred to the newly constructed Centennial Elementary School in Mount Vernon. In a planning meeting with her new principal, Janice Masten, she raised the issue of an inclusion approach for children then being served in traditional self-contained classes. Masten stopped her in midsentence and stated, "At this school, we do what's best for children, and if inclusive education is what's best, we'll do it." Following the leadership and problem-solving skills of these two educators, Centennial moved quickly into a full-scale kindergarten-through-grade 6 inclusion program. In the first years, there were times when things did not go smoothly: when classroom teachers questioned the amount of work inclusion presented or when the needs of children were not readily addressed in normal classroom operation. But throughout the years, Centennial has never steered away from the philosophy expressed by Janice Masten: "If inclusive education is what's best, we'll do it." The culture of Centennial has been dramatically changed by its commitment to children with special needs. Davis writes:

> We have been asked to put into daily practice values, ethics, and morals that we once only spoke about. Children are now invited to birthday parties by friends they have made at school. No more "mercy invitations" by their friends' parents. They participate in community sports programs, daycares, and scouting activities. And they are learning. Each child is challenged, daily, to be the most that he or she can be, making strides in all areas of development. My son, Tyler, is now a first grader at Centennial. He is doing things we never dreamed he would do and being challenged in ways I never thought to challenge him. Our dream is that the time will come when we no longer have to talk about inclusion because it has become the accepted norm.

Walking through the halls of Centennial, a large school with 650 students, the observer might be able to identify a student who is receiving support because of the student's obvious physical disabilities, but, generally, it is difficult to discriminate between students who are supported and students who are not. The staff does not talk about students that way. The thinking that permeates this school is that all children need help and assistance in learning and that all segments of the school community—parents, staff, and students—help and teach each other. All will attest to the fact that inclusion has positively enhanced the community for everyone.

A ROAD MAP

The following chapters provide a sampling of accounts of successful inclusive school communities. This assemblage does not purport to describe the "best" or the "only" paths to inclusive schooling, but rather to give some insight—and perhaps a glimpse of what is possible—to educators who are presently working to bring about changes in their own schools.

In Chapter 1, Dianne Ferguson reviews the status of inclusionary practices within restructured schools. Her focus is not on special education alone, but on the merging of special and general education to bring about new systems that work for all children, whatever their talents and needs. She describes how these trends in political and social justice changed the field of special education. Chapter 2, by Judy Kugelmass, addresses curriculum design and teaching for inclusive classrooms. Using both a historical review of curriculum reform and examples from classrooms in the Foxfire Network, she provides some helpful ideas for two of the most difficult challenges to inclusion for general education teachers. Kugelmass describes classrooms in which the curriculum and instructional strategies work very well to create inclusive communities and underlines the tenet that it is appropriate for teachers to design curriculum and teaching so that students, although they may learn content in different ways or at different levels, all achieve the same high standards and expectations.

Chapters 3 through 6 visit elementary and high school communities around the country. Chapter 3, by Michael Berres, details the inclusion and restructuring at Seattle's Lawton Elementary School, where the inclusion of students with disabilities was a natural extension of other general education restructuring. Berres describes the political and group-dynamic strategies that led to the creation of this inclusive school and the chapter concludes with some "simple lessons" learned by the whole community as a result of their involvement in growth and change. In Chapter 4, Dianne Ferguson and Gwen Meyer describe an evolving relationship between a rural elementary school and a group of university-based teachers in Oregon. Their account reveals the ways in which both groups came to appreciate the difference between "special education inclusion" and "systemic inclusion" and it serves as an example of the type of partnership that is possible when special and general educators begin to work together.

Chapter 5, by Cheryl Jorgensen and Carol Tashie, describes the creation of Souhegan High School, an exciting and vibrant school in New Hampshire in which all students—including those with moderate and severe disabilities— are included in every facet of school life. Diversity and inclusion were two of the beliefs and operating principles upon which the school was founded, and because chronicles of successful inclusion at the secondary level are rarer, we think this chapter is especially noteworthy.

In Chapter 6, Peter Knoblock expands the typical definition of "community" as it is used in schools. The innovations for community-building created by the Syracuse City Schools provide us with powerful new ways to think about supporting all the children in a classroom. The Syracuse example is important because it is a community support system that atypically serves infants through adults.

In the end, there are no magic or foolproof ways to create inclusive schools and classrooms. Neither is there a "degree" of inclusion toward which we should aspire. Rather, inclusion is a process that continually evolves, requiring the merging of general and special education practice and collaboration among professionals. Though the challenges of inclusion are many and often difficult, the increasing numbers of children with unique characteristics who enter our systems each year require that we do something different. We believe that inclusion makes good sense for all children and that the journey is well worth undertaking.

REFERENCES

Anderson, R., & Pavan, B. N. (1993). *Nongradedness: Helping it happen*. Lancaster, PA: Technomic Publishing.

Berres, M., & Knoblock, P. (Eds.). (1987). *Program models for mainstreaming*. Austin, TX: Aspen Publishers.

Biklen, D. (1985). *Achieving the complete school: Strategies for effective mainstreaming*. New York: Teachers College Press.

Blatt, B. (1966). *Christmas in purgatory*. Boston: Allyn & Bacon.

Bogdan, R., & Biklen, D. (1977, March/April). "Handicapism." *Social Policy*, 7(5), 14–19.

Cremin, L. (1961). *The transformation of the school: Progressivism in American education*. New York: Vintage Books.

Glickman, C. (1993). *Renewing America's schools*. San Francisco: Jossey-Bass.

Goodlad, J., & Anderson, R. (1987). *The nongraded elementary school*. New York: Teachers College Press.

Johnson, D., & Johnson, R. (1984). *Circles of learning: Cooperation in the classroom*. Alexandria, VA: Association for Supervision and Curriculum Development.

Sergiovanni, T. (1994). *Building communities in schools*. San Francisco: Jossey-Bass.

Wolfensberger, W. (1975). *The origin and nature of our institutionalized models*. Syracuse, NY: Human Policy Press.

CHAPTER 1

Is It Inclusion Yet?
Bursting the Bubbles

Dianne L. Ferguson

Marci Richards announced to the class that it was time to read their journals aloud. All the students had written a page about something of interest to them, spelling as best they could, and illustrating their compositions on the facing page. As children raised their hands, Marci called
on them to come to the front of the room. Most of the writings today
reflected their excitement about the Winter Holiday, a week away. The
readings were sometimes clear, sometimes halting, as students tried to
figure out what they had written, to decipher their invented spelling.
Marci commented on each reading

Andy didn't raise his hand, but Marci Richards asked him if he'd
like to read his journal. He immediately stood up, walked to the spot
near the blackboard where the others had stood, and began to read,
holding his journal up in front of his face. There were no words on his
page, only lines of little circles. His picture was of five members of his
family. His words were unintelligible as he "read," and his voice was
very quiet. He paused from time to time, imitating the reading patterns
of the other kids as they had stopped to decipher the words they had
written. The kids listened attentively to Andy. He "read" for a long time,
and when he was done, he turned his journal around to show the class
his picture. He grinned, and Marci said with a laugh "Wow, Andy had
a lot to write today, didn't he?" A couple of kids said "Yeah!" and "He
really did!" As Andy walked back to his desk, he went around one group
of tables showing his journal to the children there, a big grin on his face.

They craned their necks to see his pictures. He sat down at his desk as the next student began to read her journal.

This small slice of teaching life captures one thing we mean to convey about inclusion: Schools ought to be places that incorporate all children and youths, including those with disabilities, as active, fully participating members of the learning community. Andy, like his peers, is learning about writing and communicating. He may not ever accomplish all the same things that many of his classmates will, but he will receive Marci's comments and his peers' reactions, just as every other member of the class does. This is a nice example of the successful incorporation of one special student into a general education classroom and of his true learning membership. Still, inclusion must be about much more than one child, and certainly about more than disability.

The meaning of inclusion has evolved over a very short span of time. What proponents meant by their calls for inclusion as recently as the late 1980s now falls short of the emerging vision. People in schools all over the United States, and in an increasing number of other countries, are somewhere in the process of this evolution of thinking from:

- Inclusion as a *special education reform* aimed at moving students with disabilities, especially those with moderate and severe disabilities, from self-contained classrooms and schools to placement in general education classrooms, with the services and supports needed to achieve effective social and learning outcomes, to:
- Inclusion as a *process of meshing general and special education reform initiatives and strategies* in order to achieve a unified system of public education that incorporates all children and youths as active, fully participating members of the school community; that views diversity as the norm and maintains a high quality education for each student by ensuring meaningful curriculum, effective teaching, and supports necessary for each student.

In this chapter, I briefly detail the evolution of inclusion by first describing some of its historical roots. I illustrate how thinking about inclusion as a *special education reform effort* can result, at best, in "pretty good integration," but not in the kind of inclusion Andy enjoys in Marci Richards' class or that is increasingly envisioned and evidenced by the contributors to this book. Then, I detail some of the general education reform efforts that influence our special education conception of inclusion toward this broader vision. Finally, I describe the features and components of these newly evolving concepts of more systemic inclusion.

A BIT OF HISTORY

As a consequence of compulsory education laws, special education emerged as a field in the twenty years or so spanning the turn of the century. The increasing student diversity that resulted from the requirement that *all* children attend school so challenged teachers, systems, and educational conventions that special education emerged to accommodate those students who did not seem to fit current practices (Ferguson, 1987; Hoffman, 1975; Sarason & Doris, 1979). Special education quickly became a parallel discipline and organizational structure within American public education. Until the mid-1970s, special education was designed to provide adapted curriculum and teaching to students who had either failed, or were likely to fail, in the "mainstream" of compulsory public education. Over time, special education created its own specialized curriculum approaches, which came to support a burgeoning number of subspecialties, each matching curriculum and teaching strategies to ability and performance characteristics of an identifiable group of children or youths. The more unusual the student's characteristics, the more specialized the intervention and the teacher that provided the intervention (Sarason & Doris, 1979).

When compulsory education first emerged, it did not apply to what we now think of as high school. The purpose of secondary education at that time was to prepare a small number of privileged students to enter college where they would continue to pursue the classical studies of philosophy, history, literature, and languages. When pressured to accommodate a much broader range of students—many of whom would leave public education for the workforce—high schools responded (by the 1920s and 1930s) with a system of tracking that sorted out students who might still be preparing for college from those likely to prepare for some specific vocation or just complete high school without a clear postsecondary agenda. Special education eventually became one more particularly separate track, which also happened to free public education administrators from responsibility for its management and administration.

With the passage of comprehensive federal legislation in 1974, the separate, and largely ignored, track of special education finally received full professional legitimacy and procedural power. The landmark Education for All Handicapped Children Act (EHA, P.L. 94–142), reauthorized and updated as the Individuals with Disabilities Education Act (IDEA, P.L. 101–476) in 1990, mandated a free, appropriate, public education for *all* children and youth, regardless of the type or severity of their disability. Until 1975, many potential students with more severe and multiple developmental disabilities had been "excused" from the requirements of compulsory education because they were believed incapable of learning much—if anything at all—believed to require primarily custodial care, and believed to need protection from the eyes and possible taunts of nondisabled or less disabled peers (Berry, 1931; Hoffman, 1975; Kirk & Johnson, 1951; Wallin, 1966). These newest members of the school community, like their more able predecessors early in the century, challenged the current teachers in both general and special education, spawning still more specializations within the field (Perske & Smith, 1977; Thomas, 1977).

Despite the separateness of general and special education, however, both have shared similar fundamental assumptions about students and learning for most of the history of public education in America:

- Students are responsible for their own learning.
- When students don't learn, there is something wrong with them.
- Schools must figure out what's wrong with students with as much precision as possible so that they can be directed to the track, curriculum, teachers, and classrooms that match their learning ability profile. Otherwise, no learning will occur.

Despite periodic challenges, these assumptions have become so embedded in the culture and processes of schooling that they operate as truths rather than assumptions and control even our efforts at reform.

SPECIAL EDUCATION REFORMS

Inclusion, the most recent of the special education reform efforts, is the logical legacy of earlier reform agendas described by the slogans "mainstreaming" and "integration." None of these efforts has yet succeeded in challenging the underlying assumptions of either general or special education in ways that might result in durable and systemic change. Indeed, our first efforts to pursue inclusion as a special education reform have highlighted, once again, the need to rethink some of these most persistent assumptions and recast our efforts from a special education initiative to more "systemic inclusion." In this chapter, then, I refer to "special education inclusion" as the first conceptualization of inclusion that emerged in the late 1980s and "systemic inclusion" as the new emerging vision that we are documenting in this book. But first, a brief review of special education's earlier efforts to reform.

Mainstreaming. This reform effort and accompanying debates stretch back to the 1850s, but only emerged as a substantial effort in the 1960s, as special educators began to question the practice of separate special classes for students with milder disabilities (Dunn, 1968). Mainstreaming emerged, in part, as an argument against separate remediation classes and in favor of "mainstreaming" remediation support into the general education context.

Much of the early controversy regarding mainstreaming resulted in part from the term itself. New legal emphasis on "regular educational environments," combined with emerging references to persons with disabilities functioning "in the mainstream of society," resulted in two misconceptions: first, that mainstreaming meant physical placement in a general education classroom, and second, that mainstreaming should apply only to the appropriately eligible students with mild disabilities. In the service of mainstreaming, thousands of students previously labeled as "educable mentally retarded" were declassified and returned to general education classrooms. In response, educators attempted to restrict mainstreaming to those few disabled students who were "most nearly normal." The confusion and debates about mainstreaming have not been short-lived, nor have they been confined to the United States. Similar discussions about the location of remedial education and the necessary changes in the curriculum and teaching strategies employed by mainstream teachers continue today in several European countries.

What the mainstreaming reform efforts did not address were the underlying assumptions about disability as something that educators need to repair or ameliorate with alternative curricular and teaching offerings. The mainstreaming debate was essentially about where the repair or specialized alternatives would occur and the persons and methods that should be used to accomplish them.

Integration. Integration drew much more on social and political discourse than did mainstreaming. From a democratic perspective, any child has a civil right to public education. For students previously excluded from schooling because they had been considered too disabled to benefit, the application of a civil rights framework accorded them the status of a minority group that had been disenfranchised and discriminated against (Gliedman & Roth, 1980). The essential thrust of integration was to eliminate social discrimination by ending stigmatizing and discriminatory educational exclusion and segregation. Because students with severe developmental disabilities were most often among those excluded and segregated by professional assessments that defined them as having limited or no learning potential, calls for integration promised to result in substantial changes in their schooling experiences.

The negative and deleterious effects of separate education inspired new education policies in countries besides the United States (e.g., Commonwealth Schools Commission, 1985) that were principally focused on democratic ideals of schooling access for all students. In some places, though, the word "integration" seemed simply to replace the word "mainstreaming" with little other change. The concept of integration alone did not define well what exactly was to be done in place of exclusion and segregation and resulted in many different interpretations and examples. Some interpretations emphasized a more political agenda (Booth, 1988), others a matching of provision to need. Most failed, however, to change the segregated schooling experiences of students with significant disabilities and, in fact, increased the overall number of special education students receiving segregated schooling (Fulcher, 1989; Singer & Butler, 1987).

The efforts of educational professionals to address the rights of students to be educated with a highly individualized deficit-remediation or amelioration model of disability most often resulted in educational and other disability services that were delivered along some continuum of *locations*. Students were matched to locations that could provide the services that "fit" the type and amount of deficit and disability they brought with them (Deno, 1970). One consequence of this continuum was that the power of integration was never realized for many of the students or adults it was intended to aid. Integration's promise of a mainstream that at least tolerated, and perhaps incorporated, more differences in abilities remained largely unfulfilled. Even those persons who found themselves physically integrated in general education classrooms did not always experience full membership. This failure to improve the schooling situations of so many students gave rise to a number of analyses of the need for functional, social, community, and organizational integration in addition to simple physical presence.

Renewed concerns about the appropriateness and effects of separate special education classrooms and "pull out" programs, together with the limited numbers of students who had actually been successfully integrated into general education classrooms, led to a series of new initiatives focused on "rethinking" (Wang, Reynolds, & Walberg, 1986), "restructuring" (Reynolds, Wang, & Walberg, 1987), and moving "beyond special education" (Gartner & Lipsky, 1987). While primarily focused on the educational needs and experiences of students with mild disabilities, these initiatives departed from earlier reform attempts in their appreciation of the need for broader structural reform. Special education's status as a parallel service delivery system had not been changed by any previous reform efforts. Instead, each new demand for service or reform had been accommodated by adding a new service, creating a new specialist, and sometimes identifying a new category of disability rather than by challenging either underlying assumptions about students' learning or the established relationship between general and special education (Skrtic, 1987).

Inclusion. As a result of efforts to mainstream and integrate, previously segregated schooling and community services for children, youths, and adults with more severe disabilities were justified anew as appropriate and "least restrictive," giving rise by the late 1980s to calls for educational inclusion. Inclusion, unlike integration, did not depend on segregation in the first place. According to this new initiative, all students would simply be included, by right, in all the opportunities and responsibilities of public schooling. Like integration, early conceptualizations of inclusion focused primarily on students with moderate and severe disabilities, who most often had been placed farthest from general education classrooms and experiences along the continuum of service locations.

As with the movement toward integration, these first calls for inclusion were grounded primarily in the logic and principles of social and civil rights, offering little practical guidance to teachers who were daily engaged in the dynamics of teaching and learning. In the absence of clear direction for achieving learning outcomes in general education settings, especially for students with more severe disabilities, some proponents emphasized the importance of social rather than learning outcomes (e.g., Strully & Strully, 1989). This further fueled debates and challenged the professional roles of both general and special educators in working, with at least some "included" students.

Inclusion in this earliest expression challenged the logic of attaching services to places—in effect, it challenged the continuum of services. Citing regulatory language that stipulated that "as much as possible," students with disabilities should be educated with their nondisabled peers in general education classrooms with necessary supports and services, proponents challenged the educational community to reconceptualize and restructure the continuum so that the full array of services could be available in the general education classroom. The logical outcome of these calls for inclusion would be the separate special education service system being transplanted into the general education classroom.

Inclusion as "Pretty Good Integration"

The special education reform agenda led to a number of practices that were, and continue to be, problematic and unsatisfying. Perhaps the most extreme practice is "dumping," which occurs when students with disabilities are reassigned to general education classrooms, but neither the students nor the general education classroom teachers receive any assistance to ensure successful learning and social outcomes.

Even when students are assigned to general education classrooms and spend most (or all) of their time there with various kinds of special education supports, their presence and participation can still fall short of the kind of social membership the proponents of inclusion envisioned. Even to a casual observer, some students seem set apart—immediately recognizable as different, not so much because of any particular identifiable impairment or disability, but because of what they are doing, with whom, and how. Consider Evan's experience in a physical education class as an illustration:

> Next period starts. Kids come out of the locker rooms. The boys jump quickly into the pool, and the girls use the stairs and tiptoe slowly into deeper water, arms raised above their heads. No one acknowledges Evan who is swimming slow laps. The kids gather at the end of the pool near the teacher and the assistant. When the kids start swimming, Evan does too in the lane on the farthest side of the pool. No one has acknowledged his presence yet. The teacher and Evan's assistant stand at the end of the pool calling out the number of laps to swimmers as they complete each lap. They don't tell Evan his numbers, but each time he finishes a lap, the assistant waves to him to turn around and do another one. When laps are done, the kids go to one end of the pool to practice treading water. The assistant signals Evan to get out of the pool. Evan sits on the side of the pool and watches for about 10 minutes, then the assistant sends him to the locker room. The others have already gone. The assistant comes over to talk to me and explains that Evan will be about 15 minutes late to his social studies class because of the time it takes him to change.

Even though Evan is "included" in swimming class, his experience there seems different for several reasons. The assistant, not the teacher, gives him all his instructions. He swims a little apart from the others and begins before the rest of the class even gets into the pool. The teacher and assistant do not provide the same feedback to Evan that most other students receive (calling out the number of laps completed), even though it seems from this brief account that the number of laps might easily be given him with the wave to keep going. He leaves later than the others even though he might have been able to use the extra locker-room time to get to social studies punctually. There may have been good reasons for the decisions these teachers made about Evan's participation, but if this kind of separation of "included" students happens often, then the vision of inclusion will never be realized.

During a 3-year research project to understand better what happens when students with disabilities are "included" in general education classrooms (Ferguson, Willis, Boles et al., 1993), my colleagues and I saw scenes like this one repeated over and over again in many schools and in many different ways. We saw students walking through hallways with clipboard-bearing adults attached. We saw students sitting apart in classrooms with adults hovering over them to show them how to use books and papers that were different from those anyone else in the class was using. These "velcroed" adults were easily identifiable as "special" teachers, because the students usually called them by their first names while addressing the general education teachers by the more formal "Ms." or "Mr."

These students seemed *in but not of the class*, so much so that we noticed teachers referring to particular students as "my inclusion student." It appeared to us that these students were caught inside a bubble that teachers didn't seem to notice, but that succeeded in keeping other students and adults at a distance. Once again, underlying assumptions about who the student was seemed unchallenged by the reform.

Relocating special education to the general education classroom also relocated special materials, specially trained adults, and special curriculum and teaching techniques. The assumptions remained clear and clearly communicated:

- These students are "irregular" even though they are in regular class.
- These students need special services and materials that the regular teacher is not competent to provide.
- The special educator is the officially designated provider of these special things.

The power of these assumptions, still largely unquestioned as part of special education inclusion, has led to some curious scenes made even more curious by the fact that no one seemed to regard them as out of the ordinary. For example:

The bell rings and all the students start to swarm back to the school. The girl and redheaded boy who have been swinging with Karen yell at her to come with them as they run off to the third-grade room. She starts to follow them, but slows as she sees her special education teacher standing at the door of the special room and heads back toward the swings. The two third graders run back and try to get her to come with them. She keeps playing.

They see the special education teacher and shout, "She won't come!" The teacher tells them it's okay and to go on to class so they run off. Karen gets off the wooden structure and comes into the special room—the last kid off the playground. The teacher tells her to pull out her token card. Karen takes it out of her pocket and hands it to the teacher who tells her that she doesn't earn a penny because she has come into the room too slowly, but that if she hurries she can earn a penny by getting to the third-grade classroom on time.

Karen is not yet completely "assigned" to the third-grade classroom. Her special teacher maintains primary responsibility for managing her schedule and her behavior. As a consequence of this division of labor, the natural efforts of the two peers are not only unsuccessful, but may be discouraged in the future. They may be learning that special adults are the proper ones to let Karen know what to do next. To us, it seems that this adoption of the unquestioned assumptions by peers can doom too many efforts at genuine inclusion of students with disabilities to "pretty good integration" at best. Two more quick examples:

During middle school math class while most of the students work on assignments at their desks, two students spend the period having Evan practice using his new communication board. The students sit with Evan at his desk and point to pictures on his board, expecting him to respond. One boy wants Evan to get his bag off the back of his chair so he can put some papers in it. He has Evan look at the board and the boy points to the words "get" and "bag." Evan doesn't respond, so the boy tells him "point to the words 'get' and 'bag.'" He gives Evan this command five times. No response from Evan, who just stares at the boy. Finally, obviously frustrated by his lack of success, the boy puts the board down and says to Evan, "I need your bag." Evan turns around in his seat to get the bag off the back of his chair. The other boy tells him to put his papers in the bag and to put the bag away.

Another day, the rest of the students in sixth-grade math class are working on their assignments in class. A girl takes some blocks over to Evan and begins stacking blocks on the table in two piles. Then, pointing to the piles, she asks Evan, "Which is more?" She repeats the question five times, with no response. She gets out the communication board and uses it to ask, "Which is more?" by pointing to the symbols for "more" and "blocks" as she speaks. No answer from Evan. She makes more piles of different sizes and appears totally confused about what she's doing. Evan looks confused, too. The girl calls out to the teacher, "When you point to 'more,' he just points to 'more.' He doesn't get it yet, does he?"
The teacher says, "Well, we're working on it. Make one stack of 1 and one of 10 and tell him which is more."
The girl tries hard to teach Evan the concept using the board and the teacher's suggestions. She makes a big stack and a little one, then uses the board to point to numbers and the symbol for "more." She does this over and over. Evan just watches the girl's efforts.

Sometimes special education–initiated inclusion results in students getting into the general education classroom, but still doing all the same "different" things they did in separate places. Even involving peers in the students' separate learning agenda does not result in the kind of full learning–membership inclusion sought to achieve. All too often, the students without disabilities remain puzzled about the students' presence. One student frankly asked, "Why isn't Evan with his own class? He's having a hard enough time keeping up as it is." In another school, we encountered a situation where a group of students from a general education classroom that "included" several students with disabilities decided to borrow the separate special education room to make a surprise banner for their third-grade teacher. As they were adding final touches to their artwork, one of them glanced around the room and said, "Hey, maybe we should let the handicaps sign it, too."

All these examples seem to represent the unquestioning acceptance of the bell-shaped-curve norm that uncompromisingly identifies some students as "inside" and others as "outside." Even when students experience complete structural inclusion—when there simply is no special room anymore to be identified with or sent to—the unchanged special practices continue to set "inclusion students" apart. Special education inclusion can often result in students bringing their special education "bubble" with them.

Of course, the general education environment, organized according to ability labeling and grouping, may not be enough of an inclusive environment even if special educators and their special ideas, materials, and techniques become less "special." An educational delivery system that relies upon ability grouping will only result in students carrying their officially labeled differences into their communities and their lives outside school.

SYSTEMIC INCLUSION

When inclusion is only a special education agenda, it results in pretty good integration at best, but it doesn't achieve the inclusive membership we seek. Special education efforts have taught us that successful inclusion can only be achieved as a joint agenda between general and special education working together to "reinvent" schools that will be more incorporative of all dimensions of human diversity. Neither system alone has the capacity or the vision to challenge and change the deeply rooted assumptions that separate children and youths. Systemic inclusion must organize the purposes and processes of schooling to make sure that all children, regardless of their abilities or talents, are prepared to access and participate in the benefits of their communities, so that others in that community care about what happens to them and value them as members.

Debates on Systemic Inclusion

Systemic inclusion is neither easy nor quick—it is a work in progress that continues to meet with vociferous debate (e.g., Fuchs & Fuchs, 1994; Kauffman & Hallahan, 1993; Shanker, 1993). One of the current debates involves the reconceptualization of the *continuum of services* in special education. Initial interpretations of the continuum tied service to place (a different location in the school or outside the school) and person (the special educator officially licensed to provide the specific service). Calls to eliminate the continuum of services (e.g., Giangreco, Dennis, Cloninger, Edelman, & Schattman, 1993; Taylor, 1988), or at least some locations on the continuum (e.g., Gersten & Woodward, 1990; Pugach & Lilly, 1984), are interpreted by some (e.g., Fuchs & Fuchs, 1994) as a call to discontinue the services themselves. In contrast, others (e.g., Ferguson, Willis, Boles et al., 1993; NASBE, 1990; TASH, 1994) emphasize the need to disassociate the delivery of specialized and support services from *places* and instead to make the full continuum of *services* available to all students, whether they are labeled or not. Systemic inclusion will not mean a loss of services, but rather should encourage groups of teachers with different abilities and expertise to work together to provide more effectively a greater number of services to a broader range of students.

Another aspect of the continuing debates is whether or not *all* students should spend *all* their time in general education classrooms (e.g., Brown et al., 1991; Sailor et al., 1989; Stainback, Stainback, & Moravec, 1992). Some arguments rely largely on extreme examples of inappropriate students: Do you really mean that the student in a coma should be in a general education classroom? What about the student who holds a teacher hostage at knife point? Other arguments seek to emphasize the inappropriateness of the general education classroom: Without one-to-one specialized instruction, the student will not learn and her or his future will be sacrificed. Still others argue that the resources of the general education classroom are already limited: The addition of resource-hungry students will only limit what is available for students already being short-changed.

We believe that these debates miss both the point and the promise of the shift from special education inclusion to systemic inclusion. Some students, for some parts of their schooling, might spend more time than others in some settings, but any child should have the opportunity to learn in many different places, including small groups, large groups, in classrooms, hallways, libraries, and a wide variety of community locations. With more students learning in different locations, with more varied approaches and innovations, the less likely it is that any students will be disadvantaged by not "qualifying" for some kind of attention, support, or assistance, or suffer stigma because of their learning needs, interests, and preferences.

General Education Reform and Restructuring

Fortunately, there are reform agendas within general education that are entirely consistent and supportive of a new vision of systemic inclusion. Many of these agendas are not new, but are tested alternatives. Broadly speaking, there are two strands of reform within general education. At a national and governmental level, there is much discussion aimed at making schools more effective in terms of how many students complete school and how well they do on achievement measures. One specific aspect of this "top down" reform is a call for national achievement standards and tests to measure students by those standards. At the same time, for the first time, there is an effort to establish standards that focus on learner expectations. A growing number of states, and several national organizations, are trying to define what schooling should accomplish for students in order to improve its effectiveness for individual children, and to document better the effectiveness of schooling in general. While some of these emerging learner-outcome systems emphasize curriculum content, others are beginning to explore a variety of process outcomes, like students' abilities to work in groups, communicate effectively, think, solve problems, and produce creative and high-quality work.

Focusing on what students learn and how they use their learning rather than on whether or not they can recall information is a major shift in thinking. Teachers at all levels are redesigning curricula to help students explore topics of interest and relevance in depth, so that students not only acquire some essential information and capacities, but, more important, develop habits of learning that will serve them long after formal schooling ends. No longer is it sufficient merely to cover a large number of subjects and "facts." An important aspect of this curriculum shift is that all students will not need to learn exactly the same things, so that teachers must have the flexibility to design curricula in collaboration with their students rather than in constraint of a rigid scope and sequence lesson plan. More often, students' efforts are measured, not by some arbitrary criterion of recollection alone, but rather by how they can demonstrate their ability to use their learning in novel situations or to explore new topics of interest.

There are, of course, a number of other dimensions of general education reform. One recent examination of the large body of reform literature (Conley, 1993) identified 12 dimensions of restructuring that are either central variables (e.g., learner outcomes, curriculum, instruction, assessment/evaluation), enabling variables (e.g., learning environments, technology, time, school/community relationships), or supporting variables (e.g., governance, teacher leadership, personnel, working relationships). Too often, our efforts to improve schools have addressed only some of these important dimensions.

Although much remains to be done, the seeds of systemic inclusion are well rooted within each of these dimensions. The changes occurring in general education offer rich opportunities for students previously labeled and separated; the challenge to special education is to assist in their nurturance. The promise of integrated curriculum, activity-based learning, developmentally appropriate practices, cooperative learning, and authentic assessment—to mention just a few examples—is a rejection of old ability-grouping and tracking practices that left some students "outside." When the norm is diversity, the extension of range and variety is much easier to accommodate, value, and support. For general education teachers who are experimenting with these kinds of curriculum and teaching reforms, students with disabilities become a difference in degree rather than kind. Classrooms and teachers seriously engaged in preparing students for the future have already expanded and enriched the curriculum to respond to both the demands for broader student outcomes and the different interests, purposes, and abilities of each student.

Features of Systemic Inclusion

Mixed-ability groups of teachers. Throughout schooling history, we have developed a way of working in schools that sets boundaries to what a teacher, or any other adult, can do. General education teachers teach general students—those in the middle of the bell-shaped curve—because they were trained to teach such students. Special education teachers work with special students because such students have some identified disability or fall beyond the middle of the bell-shaped curve. This matching of teachers' work to students' characteristics is best elaborated in some of the specialist areas: Physical therapists work with legs and whole bodies; occupational therapists with hands and sometimes mouths; speech therapists with mouths, sounds, speech, and language. We only do certain things with those students who "fit" our training.

Yet, we are finding that no single teacher, no matter how experienced or gifted, is likely to possess all the knowledge, skills, and judgment required to effectively design curriculum and teaching for the full range of student diversity. Some students with disabilities, for example, might require specialized supports; others with unique abilities in some areas of learning might require creative consideration to make a lesson an effective learning experience.

Teachers involved in the reinventing of schools find their roles shifting from being designated providers of some category of specialized knowledge and service to being more generic teachers of diverse groups of students. In their new roles, they more frequently work in collaboration with other teachers and share areas of expertise and interest to benefit the learning of all students (Ferguson, Ralph, Meyer et al., 1993; Roach, 1993). School reformers are finding that teacher teams that include teachers with *different* abilities and skills can together design effective learning experiences for all children. Some of the teachers on the team need to be skillful at teaching familiar academic content, others at creating imaginative learning activities that offer a wide range of learning opportunities across content areas. Still other teachers need to be able to adapt and expand learning experiences effectively for those students who learn differently, have unique preferences about their learning, or who have disabilities that impede or obviate some kinds of learning in favor of others. Each team will also sometimes need the more specialized knowledge of a variety of other educational personnel who can assist the team in the design and delivery of communication, behavioral, physical, medical, cultural, linguistic, and family supports for those students who require them in order to learn well. Despite previous training, professional experience, or interests, the new role for all adults in schools is that of *teacher*.

Personalized learning and accomplishments. Traditionally, districts, states, and even countries have identified an "official" or "standard" curriculum—a set of things they expect students to know and/or be able to do at various points in their school careers. It is these expectations about content that are translated into learning materials like textbooks, teachers' manuals, and so on. The underlying logic of these approved standard curricula is that a student who learns this content is likely to be able to use it to become an active, contributing member of the community. Historically, this logic has served most teachers and students reasonably well. Many students have learned most of what is contained in the official curriculum and textbooks—those that did not were "ability grouped" into remediation tracks or special education. These students were also effectively "excused" from learning the official curriculum, or from being counted in the achievement test scores that measured a school or district's success at transmitting the official curriculum to its students. Some students were failed or dropped out.

In recent years, the increasing complexity of society and the broadened range of student diversity have made most educators less and less confident that learning the official curriculum has much bearing on the competence with which students will conduct their lives. Increasingly, educators in both general and special education are concerned that students use their learning in ways that make a difference in their lives outside school. The challenge for teachers is all manner of differences that students bring with them and that must be taken into consideration: different abilities, different interests, different family lifestyles and compositions, and different preferences for learning approaches. Students' linguistic background, socioeconomic status, and cultural heritage must also be considered as a part of curriculum and teaching decisions. Finally, some students have different ways of thinking and knowing that can aid learning if teachers design experiences to draw out and use these various intelligences (e.g., Armstrong, 1994; Gardner, 1993).

Teachers in schools that are reinventing themselves are relying less and less on packaged curriculum materials as their primary source for lessons. Instead, they are working together to use a wide variety of educational and other "natural" materials to design teaching that is individually tailored to each student's unique mix of interests, abilities, and learning histories. The resulting personalized learning assures that students learn things that make sense to them and that they can use in their lives.

To some degree, individually tailored curriculum and teaching have always been devised by good teachers. They have always known that teaching and learning were two-way activities, involving transactions between teachers and students that were negotiated anew with each lesson and each new day. What is different about this period of reform is that the emphasis on each student's learning accomplishments is replacing the old "official" curriculum and its underlying logic. Of course, this shift is not without some dilemmas, as noted by Wiggins (1989):

> The inescapable dilemma at the heart of curriculum and instruction must, once and for all, be made clear: either teaching everything of importance reduces it to trivial, forgettable verbalisms or lists; or schooling is a *necessarily* inadequate apprenticeship, where *preparation* means something quite humble: learning to know and do a few important things well and leaving out much of importance. The negotiation of the dilemma hinges on enabling students to learn about their ignorance, to gain control over the resources available for making modest dents in it, and to take pleasure in learning so that the quest is lifelong. An authentic education will therefore consist of developing the *habits of mind and high standards of craftsmanship* necessary in the face of one's (inevitable) ignorance. (p. 45) [Emphasis in original]

Support rather than services. An important consequence of teachers working together to reinvent their curriculum and teaching practices is a shift in the focus of what schools do—from providing services to providing supports. Our history of separating out differences in order to repair them led previous reforms to focus on the most effective approaches and tools. The current reform effort's focus on valuing diversity and difference, rather than trying to change or diminish it, is resulting in the new metaphor of support. This is not to say that educators should discontinue trying to remediate or attenuate the effects of disability or disadvantaged home lives, or whatever else might be interfering with or slowing a student's growth, but rather, that, regardless of the results of efforts to fix or minimize deficits, individuals still can and should be supported as active members of their communities. The opportunity to participate in life must no longer wait until some standard of normalcy or similarity is reached.

This shift from services to supports has several important features. One has already been mentioned: "Support" implies that a student doesn't have to wait to become active in the community. Support also encourages a shift from viewing disability or difference in terms of individual limitations to a focus on environmental constraints. As a result, teachers and others are encouraged to make changes in the environment that might *support* an individual's learning and use of abilities rather than discouraging or constraining them.

Supporting learning necessitates a shift in our traditional individualized assessment and planning procedures from an emphasis on diagnosis and prescription to the provision of options and the encouragement of choices. Finally, a support metaphor for schooling encourages use of the same environments for all students and encourages the employment of both informal and formal supports. For example, many students may find that the most effective supports come naturally from classmates, not teachers. Perhaps the most important feature of the concept of support is that it is grounded in the perspective of the person receiving it, not the person providing it. We can no longer assume that a particular text, activity, or teaching mode will work to support any particular student's learning. The learning enterprise becomes a constant conversation between student and teacher to construct learning, document accomplishments, and adjust supports.

Components of Systemic Inclusion

General and special education reform literatures both include a number of resources that attempt to describe how the kind of fundamental change now being called for might be accomplished (e.g., Center on Organization and Restructuring of Schools, 1992; Roeher Institute, 1991; Sailor et al., 1989; Sizer, 1992; Villa, Thousand, Stainback, & Stainback, 1992). Taken together, these descriptions can be summarized in the following key features (Ferguson, 1992), which may help guide the reading of the different accounts in these chapters.

Students are learning members of their neighborhood school and participating members of the surrounding community. Reinvented schools incorporate all the children and youths in the neighborhood into the daily routines and life of the school. All students acquire the information, thinking skills, and competence that permit them to be active, socially valued participants in the school community and the larger surrounding community. Their learning experiences and activities are rich and varied and occur in different locations in the school building and in the community surrounding the school. The lives of children and youths outside school hours extend and reflect the relationships and learning they experience in school.

Students, families, and community members contribute to the design, maintenance, and effectiveness of the school community. The reinvented school clearly defines ways for family members, students, and other community members to participate in the development of the school's mission and accomplishments and to contribute ideas for the generation and allocation of the school's fiscal, human, and material resources. This broader school constituency contributes to the ongoing life and effectiveness of the school in a variety of direct and indirect ways.

All faculty and staff contribute to the design, maintenance, and effectiveness of the school community. Similarly, reinvented schools actively solicit and systematically use all faculty and staff in defining and managing the school's operations. Faculty and staff participate in developing and using the school's mission and accomplishments to continually improve the effectiveness of the school for both students and adults. Faculty and staff participate in resource generation and allocation as well as the school's operational duties and responsibilities. All faculty and staff contribute, not only in terms of their officially designated roles, but also their specialized work knowledge and abilities and personal skills and interests to enrich the creativity and effectiveness of the school's operation and accomplishments.

Teachers share responsibility for curriculum development, teaching, and problem-solving for all students. Reinvented schools approach teaching as a shared responsibility among teachers and between teachers and students. Teacher teams collaborate on the development of curriculum and teaching plans in solving students' learning problems and in teaching.

Individual students' experiences of the curriculum are age-appropriate and referenced to family and community. The students in reinvented schools experience learning that is tailored to their learning abilities, preferences, and outside interests. Teachers systematically collect information from students and families about their lives outside school and about the way school can support students' interests and competence. Teachers have the time to know students adequately so that learning is tailored and information is shared with new teachers as students move through the school system.

Teaching is creative, varied, effective, and responsive to individual student learning. Teaching in reinvented schools is a flexible, dynamic interaction between the creativity and thoughtfulness of teachers and the eagerness and interests of students. Students are actively engaged, not just in the subject matter, but in the excitement of learning and of exploring new capacities with their peers and with their teachers.

Individual classrooms and the school as a whole are efficiently organized and managed. The operations of the school support the central mission and accomplishments of the teachers and the learning enterprise. People, time, operations, and information are organized for efficient operation without deflecting the attention of either adults or students from the school's central effort.

SUMMARY

Public education is in an exciting period of change, and perhaps for the first time, change in all parts of the system will begin to coalesce. Over the next decade, schools will be reinvented from the bottom up *and* from the top down. There will be shifts in the way teaching and learning occur for both teachers and students, in the experience of work for teachers, and in the distribution of power among schools, communities, and governance structures (Elmore, 1990). Such fundamental changes are arduous, painful, and slow (Fullan & Miles, 1992; Sizer, 1992), in part because the task is so large and complex. Nevertheless, there is an increasing clarity about "what really counts in schools" (Eisner, 1991) and how to achieve this newly articulated agenda (e.g., CASE, 1993; Fullan & Miles, 1992; NASBE, 1990; Noddings, 1993; Oakes & Lipton, 1990; Osborne & Gaebler, 1993). The teachers and students, families and administrators, specialists and assistants in the schools portrayed in this book have accepted the challenge and engaged the task. We hope they will assist you and your schools to do the same.

REFERENCES

Armstrong, T. (1994). *Multiple intelligences in the classroom.* Alexandria, VA: Association for Supervision and Curriculum Development.

Association for Persons With Severe Handicaps, The (TASH). (1994, February). Resolution on inclusive education. In TASH *Newsletter* (pp. 4–5). Seattle, WA: TASH.

Berry, C. (1931). *Special education: Report of the White House Conference on Child Health and Protection.* New York: Century Co.

Booth, T. (1988). Challenging conceptions of integration. In L. Barton (Ed.), *The politics of special educational needs* (pp. 97–122). London: Falmer Press.

Brown, L., Schwartz, P., Udvari-Solner, A., Kampschroer, E., Johnson, F., Jorgensen, J., & Gruenewald, L. (1991). How much time should students with severe intellectual disabilities spend in regular education classrooms and elsewhere? *Journal of the Association of Persons With Severe Handicaps, 16,* 39–47.

Center on Organization and Restructuring of Schools. (1992). Estimating the extent of school restructuring (Brief to Policymakers No. 4). Madison: University of Wisconsin–Madison, School of Education, CORS.

Commonwealth Schools Commission. (1985). *Report of the working party on special education on Commonwealth policy and directions in special education.* Canberra, Victoria, Australia: Commonwealth Schools Commission.

Conley, D. T. (1993). *Roadmap to restructuring: Policies, practices and the emerging visions of schooling.* Eugene: University of Oregon, ERIC Clearing House on Educational Management.

Council of Administrators of Special Education (CASE). (1993). *Future agenda for special education: Creating a unified educational system.* Bloomington: Indiana University.

Deno, E. (1970). Special education as developmental capital. *Exceptional Children, 37,* 229–237.

Dunn, L. (1968). Special education for the mildly retarded—Is much of it justifiable? *Exceptional Children, 35,* 5–22.

Education for All Handicapped Children Act of 1975, PL 94-142 (August 23, 1975).

Eisner, E. (1991). What really counts in schools. *Educational Leadership, 48*(5), 10–17.

Elmore, R. (1990). *Restructuring schools: The next generation of educational reform.* San Francisco: Jossey-Bass.

Ferguson, D. (1987). *Curriculum decision making for students with severe handicaps: Policy and practice.* New York: Teachers College Press.

Ferguson, D. (1992). *The elementary/secondary system: Supportive education for students with disabilities. Module 5b: School development system.* Eugene: Specialized Training Program, University of Oregon.

Ferguson, D. L., Ralph, G., Meyer, G., Willis, C., & Young, M. (1993). *The elementary secondary system: Supportive education for students with handicaps. Module 1d: Individually tailored learning: Strategies for designing inclusive curriculum.* Eugene: Specialized Training Program, University of Oregon.

Ferguson, D. L., Willis, C., Boles, S., Jeanchild, L., Holliday, L., Meyer, G., Rivers, E., & Zitek, M. (1993). *Regular class participation system* (RCPS) (Grant No. H086D90011: U.S. Department of Education). Eugene, OR: Specialized Training Program, University of Oregon.

Fuchs, D., & Fuchs, L. (1994). Inclusive schools movement and the radicalization of special education reform. *Exceptional Children, 60*(4), 294–309.

Fulcher, G. (1989). *Disabling policies? A comparative approach to education policy and disability.* London: Falmer Press.

Fullan, M., & Miles, M. (1992). Getting reform right: What works and what doesn't. *Phi Delta Kappan, 74,* 745–752.

Gardner, H. (1993). *Multiple intelligences: The theory in practice*. New York: Basic Books.

Gartner, A., & Lipsky, D. (1987). Beyond special education: Toward a quality system for all students. *Harvard Educational Review, 57*, 367–395.

Gersten, R., & Woodward, J. (1990). Rethinking the regular education initiative: Focus on the classroom teacher. *Remedial and Special Education, 11*, 7–16.

Giangreco, M., Dennis, R., Cloninger, C., Edelman, S., & Schattman, R. (1993). "I've counted on Jon": Transformational experiences of teachers educating students with disabilities. *Exceptional Children, 59*, 359–372.

Gliedman, J., & Roth, W. (1980). *The unexpected minority: Handicapped children in America*. New York: Harcourt Brace Jovanovich.

Hoffman, E. (1975). The American public school and the deviant child: The origins of their involvement. *Journal of Special Education, 9*(4), 415–423.

Individuals with Disabilities Education Act of 1990, PL 101-476 (October 30, 1990).

Kauffman, J., & Hallahan, D. (1993). Toward a comprehensive delivery system for special education. In J. Goodlad & T. Lovitt (Eds.), *Integrating general and special education* (pp. 73–102). New York: Macmillan.

Kirk, S., & Johnson, G. (1951). *Educating the retarded child*. Cambridge, MA: Houghton Mifflin.

National Association of State Boards of Education. (1990). *Today's children, tomorrow's survival: A call to restructure schools*. Alexandria, VA: NASBE.

Noddings, N. (1993). Excellence as a guide to educational conversation. *Teachers College Record, 94*(4), 730–743.

Oakes, J., & Lipton, M. (1990). *Making the best of schools: A handbook for parents, teachers, and policy makers*. New Haven, CT: Yale University Press.

Osborne, D., & Gaebler, T. (1993). *Reinventing government: How the entrepreneurial spirit is transforming the public sector*. New York: Plume.

Perske, R., & Smith, J. (1977). *Beyond the ordinary: The preparation of professionals to educate severely and profoundly handicapped persons*. Parsons, KS: Words & Pictures.

Pugach, M., & Lilly, S. (1984). Reconceptualizing support services for classroom teachers: Implications for teacher education. *Journal of Teacher Education, 35*, 48–55.

Reynolds, M., Wang, M., & Walberg, H. (1987). The necessary restructuring of special and regular education. *Exceptional Children, 53*, 391–398.

Roach, V. (1993). "Winners all." *Colloquium*, October 18. Eugene: University of Oregon.

Roeher Institute, The. (1991). *Changing Canadian Schools: Perspectives on disability and inclusion*. North York, Ontario: Roeher Institute.

Sailor, W., Anderson, J., Halvorsen, A., Doering, K., Filler, J., & Goetz, L. (1989). *The comprehensive local school: Regular education for all students with disabilities*. Baltimore: Paul H. Brookes.

Sarason, S., & Doris, J. (1979). *Educational handicap, public policy, and social history*. New York: Free Press.

Shanker, A. (1993, September 19). Where we stand: A rush to inclusion. *New York Times*.

Singer, J., & Butler, J. (1987). The Education for All Handicapped Children Act: Schools as agents of social reform. *Harvard Educational Review*, *57*(1), 125–152.

Sizer, T. (1992). *Horace's school: Redesigning the American school.* Boston: Houghton Mifflin.

Skrtic, T. (1987). An organizational analysis of special education reform. *Counterpoint*, *8*(2), 15–19.

Stainback, W., Stainback, S., & Moravec, J. S. (1992). Using curriculum to build inclusive classrooms. In S. Stainback & W. Stainback (Eds.), *Curriculum considerations in inclusive classrooms: Facilitating learning for all students* (pp. 65–84). Baltimore: Paul H. Brookes.

Strully, J., & Strully, C. (1989). Friendship as an educational goal. In S. Stainback, W. Stainback, & M. Forest (Eds.), *Educating all students in the mainstream of regular education* (pp. 59–68). Baltimore: Paul H. Brookes.

Taylor, S. (1988). Caught in the continuum: A critical analysis of the principle of the least restrictive environment. *Journal of the Association for Persons With Severe Handicaps*, *13*, 41–53.

Thomas, M. (1977). *Hey, don't forget about me!* Reston, VA: Council for Exceptional Children.

Villa, R. A., Thousand, J. S., Stainback, W., & Stainback, S. (Eds.). (1992). *Restructuring for caring and effective education.* Baltimore: Paul H. Brookes.

Wallin, J. (1966). Training of the severely retarded, viewed in historical perspective. *Journal of General Psychology*, *74*, 107–127.

Wang, M., Reynolds, M., & Walberg, H. (1986). Rethinking special education. *Educational Leadership*, *44*(1), 26–31.

Wiggins, G. (1989). The futility of trying to teach everything important. *Educational Leadership*, *47*(3), 44–48, 57–59.

CHAPTER 2

Reconstructing Curriculum for Systemic Inclusion

Judy W. Kugelmass

Our understanding of what we see in schools is informed by years of our own experiences as students, teachers, and/or parents. We view these institutions through old lenses that have been shaped by recollections of our childhood and a nostalgia for the past, even though many of these memories may not be positive ones (Meier,1991). As children, we were not aware that our school experiences were guided by long-established beliefs and assumptions of the adults in charge of our lives about how and what we learned, and how and what we should be taught. In order for us to imagine and then create the inclusive systems that have been called for in Chapter 1, we need to understand better what those beliefs and assumptions have been, where they have come from, and how they have provided the framework for a system that has excluded many children. Such an understanding is the first step toward removing the blinders that keep us from expanding our views of teaching and learning to include processes that are quite different from what we experienced in school, but that can enable the creation of inclusive systems.

Before visiting the schools and classrooms I describe in this chapter— classrooms that illustrate instructional processes supportive and enabling of systemic inclusion—it is important to scrutinize the models of teaching and learning upon which they are based. This examination explores the development of approaches to curriculum and instruction that have emerged from the vision articulated by John Dewey early in this century. Specific examples from several elementary classrooms are presented as operational models, which may be useful in the application of these ideas to promote systemic inclusion within a framework of restructured schools.

38

Systemic school restructuring calls into question many aspects of schooling, including the basic structure of schools, the content of curriculum, and the process of instruction. The following questions provide much fuel for current discussions, debates, and research throughout the United States. These questions bear directly on the education of children for whom traditional education has been viewed as inappropriate.

Critical Questions for Systemic School Restructuring

1. How many hours, days, weeks, and years should children be in school?
2. How many children should be in a classroom or school building?
3. What is an optimal yet cost-effective teacher–student ratio?
4. How should funds be allocated to school districts and distributed within schools?
5. In what way should chronological age determine a child's placement and program?
6. For what length of time should a child remain with the same teacher?
7. Should all children in one classroom be expected to learn the same thing at the same time and rate?
8. What are the roles of parents and communities in schools?
9. Is breadth or depth of curricular content coverage more important?
10. What roles do culture, race, gender, and class play in public education?
11. How should we address issues of diversity?
12. How should learning be assessed?
13. What is intelligence?
14. What is it important to teach?
15. What is the role of the teacher?
16. What choices should children have in their education?
17. Who is responsible for answering these questions and running schools?

The answers to these questions have significant political and cultural ramifications and constitute the beginning of the redefinition and reconstruction of public education.

It is, however, beyond the scope of this chapter to address these questions directly. They must be examined at local levels, by all the stakeholders in any given school community. In fact, there are likely to be several different answers to the same questions, depending on the ecology of a school. What matters most is that these questions are being asked, and that the *process* used to answer them is participatory, democratic, and inclusive. Special educators need to join these conversations not only to ensure that a reconstructed system includes the needs of those children with whom they have traditionally been most concerned, but also to bring their accumulated knowledge and expertise to all children. At the same time, they must enter these conversations to learn more about general education from colleagues, parents, and other members of our communities.

Although this chapter focuses on the pedagogical foundations of the general education curriculum and the application of progressive teaching methods within inclusive classrooms, the discussion is not meant to diminish the importance of considering structural, social, or political factors in the establishment of systemic inclusion. Rather, the emphasis on curriculum and teaching is designed to develop an understanding of what needs to take place in general education classrooms to meet the needs of all children. This discussion provides a framework for understanding the classrooms that are described in this chapter and those that follow.

DEFINING CURRICULUM

Before examining some of the pedagogical principles that have shaped general education, it will be helpful to clarify terminology. Special educators often think about educational concepts quite differently from general educators. The development of a separate language, characterized by acronyms (e.g., IEP, IPSE, CSE, LRE, IDEA, ADA, ADHS) and a vocabulary based in medical technology (e.g., diagnostic/prescriptive teaching, dyslexia, sensory integration, phonological analysis, soft signs of neurological impairment), has compounded mis-communication between special and general educators, creating a significant barrier to systemic inclusion.

Many special education teachers define curriculum quite narrowly, thinking only in terms of the content of learning that is required by the school system, that is, curriculum related to the "ends" of the educational process rather than the process itself or the needs, interests, and abilities of the child. This definition is not incorrect, only incomplete. In general education, curriculum is defined in much broader ways. These broadened definitions encompass *everything* the child learns within the school, including extracurricular activities and social and interpersonal relationships (Henson, 1995). The definition of curriculum has been expanded further to include what is known as the "hidden curriculum," or " the tacit teaching to students of the norms, values, and dispositions, that goes on simply by their living in and coping with the institutional expectations and routines of schools day in and day out for a number of years" (Apple, 1979, p. 14).

The many definitions of curriculum reflect the philosophical, theoretical, political, and social positions of the definer, as well as the context in which they are being used. The lack of clarity about the meaning of the term "curriculum" has created a good deal of confusion between general and special educators and has been identified as one of many barriers to systemic inclusion (Stainback & Stainback, 1992). In this chapter, "curriculum" is used in its broadest sense. It includes *everything* the child is learning in school: discipline, specific subject matter, general knowledge, skills, social interactions, learning processes and experiences, and the hidden curriculum.

"Instruction" is a term that is often confused with "curriculum." It is used here to mean the manner in which the curriculum is delivered. The discussion about specific aspects of "instruction" includes teaching "techniques," that is, the specific learning activities designed to achieve certain learning objectives. The "methods" that a teacher uses include the techniques that she or he has chosen because of their compatibility with her or his theoretical perspective and that of the school and/or educational system and the assumptions the teacher holds about the learner. The term "approach" relates directly to process. Here it describes a concept broader than "curriculum," which includes several instructional methods and embraces a wide range of theoretical assumptions (Fantini, 1993).

The Child and the Curriculum: A Precarious Balance

During the years I defined myself as a "special" educator, I viewed the "curriculum" as something that belonged to traditional classrooms. Therefore I believed that curriculum development was primarily the concern of "regular" classroom teachers. Although teaching students to read, write, and calculate was obviously important, my primary concern was the social, affective, and cognitive growth of each child rather than the accumulation of specific bodies of information or academic skills. Like other special educators, I set myself apart to work with "those" kids for whom the curriculum of the general education classroom was not working. I didn't see the teaching of subject matter as my concern. Had I been asked, I would have said that my students were:

> the starting-point, the center, and the end. His [*sic*] development, his growth, is the ideal. It alone furnished the standard. To the growth of the child all studies are subservient; they are instruments valued as they serve the needs of growth. Personality, character, is more important than subject matter. Not knowledge or information, but self-realization, is the goal. (Dewey, 1902/1964, p. 342)

Although I believed that the learning problems exhibited by "special education students" came from the failure of regular education to address their specific needs, I accepted the notion of their "specialness." Because they fell on the outer edges of the normal bell curve, I believed my students needed an education that was different from that of other students. They must be "the starting-point, the center, and the end." They needed special teaching approaches and special educators who were "clinical teachers," therapists, and counselors, and not *just* teachers. Our work was defined in terms of diagnosis, prescription, remediation, treatment, and therapy. Our role was to develop and implement Individual Education Plans, and not curriculum. This isolation and separation from regular education further reified our practice.

It has been only recently, through my work in teacher education, school reform, and restructuring, that I have begun to understand the choices I made as a special education teacher in terms of curriculum. Throughout the twentieth century, many educators had worked with students as I had, not as "special educators," but as educators who saw themselves operating within the tradition of "progressive education." This became most apparent when, several years ago, I came upon "The Child and the Curriculum," a pamphlet written by John Dewey in 1902 and published by the University of Chicago, in which he describes and critiques the approach I had taken as a special educator.

Since long before I began teaching, educators had been struggling to balance the teaching of subject matter and academic skills with the affective, emotional, and social needs of children. In "The Child and the Curriculum," Dewey argued against the either/or debate that was raging between the traditionalists and the progressives at the turn of the century, the former insisting on discipline-specific subject matter as the center of education, and the latter focusing on the child as "furnishing the standard" (Dewey, 1902/1964, p. 342). He believed that neither point of view, by itself, provided the direction for the development of appropriate education, for any child. This debate is central to the issues surrounding systemic inclusion today.

> Abandon the notion of subject matter as something fixed and ready-made in itself, outside the child's experience; cease thinking of the child's experience as something hard and fast; see it as something fluent, embryonic, vital; and we realize that the child and the curriculum are simply two limits which define a single process. Just as two points define a straight line, so the present standpoint of the child and the facts and truths of studies define instruction. It is continuous reconstruction, moving from the child's present experience out into that represented by the organized body of truth we call studies (Dewey, 1902/ 1964, p. 344).

THE EVOLUTION OF A PRAGMATIC–PROGRESSIVE CURRICULUM

The current movement toward inclusive education is the most recent response to the needs of children who have challenged the traditional education system. The curriculum changes that are supportive of systemic inclusion, described in this chapter and book, are the most recent manifestations of the "interactive phases" (MacIntosh, 1983, 1990) in curriculum development and part of a process that has been going on throughout the history of American education. Thinking about change and growth as incorporating previous learning rather than negating it, allows for the integration of prior learning into newly emerging practices. Unlike other discussions of school reform, thinking of change in this way removes the metaphor of the pendulum and points up the importance of exploring the historic precedents of our current practices. Systemic inclusion can then be understood as a phase in an evolutionary process that integrates what we have learned from earlier work in both general and special education.

The development of formal education in the United States can be understood as having evolved over the last three hundred years toward increasingly inclusive practices. Certainly, an examination of the history of public education that is grounded in contemporary values and beliefs will not provide evidence of an educational system based on principles supportive of systemic inclusion. The first American schools were neither inclusive nor democratic. Rather, they were developed to prepare the sons of Puritan immigrants for entrance to the elite college that was to become Harvard University. From a seventeenth-century perspective, however, the development of schools for Puritan men represents a progressive movement. Education in America was moving away from the beliefs that education was only for landed aristocracy, and religion the only subject to be taught.

The first American textbook, developed for use in these schools in 1690, was a blend of religion and morals, and taught both religious doctrine and language skills. By today's standards, the *New England Primer* would be judged as being rooted in an exclusivist model of education, reinforced by a curriculum dominated by religious teaching and relying on methods that used lectures, preaching, and group recitation. However, the introduction of that textbook provided a bridge from religious to secular education. Prior to 1690, the only textbook was the Bible.

It would be almost a century before a more secular textbook was introduced. In 1782, Noah Webster developed his *Elementary Spelling Book*, known until today as the "Blue-backed Speller," bringing spelling and general knowledge into the curriculum as well as moral and nonsectarian religious guidance. Although the content of the curriculum was clearly expanding, instructional methods continued to be centered around the recitation of memorized materials. Failure to remember correctly led to corporal punishment or expulsion (Henson, 1995).

By 1860, half the nation's children were in school; however, the school population still did not represent a true sample of the general population. The majority of children in school were English-speaking, white males who were neither wage earners nor needed for family labors. The curriculum had, however, continued to expand and included content and processes that related more generally to secular life. In 1875, Francis Parker established a school in Quincy, Massachusetts, designed to create a natural learning environment that substituted games and puzzles for recitation and memorization. Play, singing, drawing, reading, and counting objects characterized the curriculum. Children were given real-life problems to solve. Rules and generalizations about life were developed out of these experiences (Henson, 1995).

Known as the "Quincy System," the approach Parker advocated and modeled provided the catalyst for the development of other experiments in public education that were based on "student-centered curricula." His work represented a new phase in American education that evolved from philosophical principles articulated in the seventeenth century by John Locke, emphasizing experience as the basis of all understanding. That idea had been ignored in earlier formal educational practices in the United States. Rather, Locke's notion of the "tabula rasa," that is, that children were born as "blank slates" onto whom the truth needed to be imprinted, had been the cornerstone of formal education.

Locke's ideas had been used previously to support Plato's view of students as passive learners who needed to receive the truth from their teachers. These ideas had shaped formal education for thousands of years. It was not until the late nineteenth century, when industrialization began to alter the conceptions of human experience as solely the expression of God's will, that education began to change dramatically. Parker's ideas of experience-based education came at a time when life in America was being shaped in dramatic ways by the belief that political, social, and economic realities could be created by individual and collective action. These beliefs would lay the cornerstone of what was to become known as the "Progressive Education Movement."

Parker became the head of a normal school that would merge with the University of Chicago, where from 1894 to 1904 John Dewey headed the philosophy and psychology departments (Henson, 1995). Dewey's work in education grew out of the philosophical traditions of "pragmatism." He saw knowledge as arising from the active participation of the individual in the physical and social world. He believed that individuals were driven by their nature to arrive at solutions to problems that were of interest and concern to their lives. Therefore, the role of education was to provide experiences for individuals through which they would develop their problem-solving capacities. The teacher's role was to create opportunities and guide students through their experiences in ways that were growth promoting and therefore "educative" (Dewey, 1938).

The principles of pragmatism provide a basis for understanding how Dewey's ideas can be applied to the development of curricula in ways that meet the needs of very diverse learners. Basic to pragmatism is the notion that no one theory can appropriately explain all human behavior. Context and process are essential to reaching desired goals. William James, the philosopher identified as one of the founders of American pragmatism and a colleague of Dewey's, expressed these ideas in 1907 in his lecture, "What Pragmatism Means." The metaphor of the "hotel" can be applied to an inclusive school.

> Pragmatism unstiffens all our theories, limbers them up and sets each one at work. Being nothing essentially new, it harmonizes with many ancient philosophical tendencies. Against rationalism as a pretension and a method pragmatism is fully armed and militant. . . . But, at the outset, it stands for no particular results. It has no dogmas and no doctrines save its methods. Papini has well said, it lies in the midst of our theories, like a corridor in a hotel. Innumerable chambers open out on it. In one you may find a man writing an aesthetic volume; in the next someone on his knees praying for faith and strength; in a third a chemist investigating a body's properties; in a fourth a system of idealist metaphysics is being excogitated; in a fifth the impossibility of metaphysics is being shown. But they all own a corridor, and all must pass through if they want a practicable way of getting into or out of their respective rooms. (James, 1907/1991, p. 571)

Following the pragmatic tradition, schools should be places where many things are going on at once, where children are learning different things in different ways, according to their interests, abilities, and needs. This idea opens the way for integrating many instructional processes. The principles of pragmatism were extended by Dewey into the creation of what became known as "progressive education." The instructional approaches that followed were designed to create a balance between the child and the curriculum.

Progressive education developed from the integration of ideas that were taking shape throughout the industrialized world, in response to the need for providing educational experiences that would prepare American children for life in the twentieth century. The complexity and change of the late nineteenth and early twentieth centuries and the loss of socializing structures that had existed in the earlier agriculturally based, preindustrialized society required new kinds of educational experiences. Unprecedented numbers of immigrants were coming to American cities. Child labor laws were keeping young children out of the labor market. The recognition that these idle children would create enormous social problems and needed to be prepared as American workers led to the creation of large, urban public education systems (Katz, 1971).

Although there were educators who supported Dewey's ideas, many of those responsible for the development of public education systems did not.

A preoccupation with social control and efficiency took precedence over pedagogy. School systems began to model themselves on the bureaucratic administrative structures and the assembly-line strategies of the factory. These "factory model" schools were designed to ensure an inexpensive and unified system of public education. Their mission was to instill conformity, neatness, and dependence in their students while teaching basic skills (Katz, 1971; Kugelmass, 1987). The curriculum closely followed instructional methods and techniques that grew out of the notion that the teacher's job was to instill the truth in the students, and that students were to be passive recipients of information that the educational establishment had determined to be important.

Dewey and his followers continued to promote the idea that schools should create environments where learning could occur naturally. In these places children could develop their learning capacities more fully and be better prepared to be effective citizens in a democracy. To demonstrate how this might be done and to refine his ideas, Dewey established a school at the University of Chicago, which he directed from 1896 to 1904. Although there is no evidence to indicate that children with severe disabilities were included in Dewey's school, the student population was heterogeneous in ways that made it resemble the public schools of Chicago of that time. Working under the philosophical principles that guided progressive education, teachers had a good deal of autonomy with regard to the curriculum.

The teachers in Dewey's school frequently questioned his faith in children's ability to learn at their own, self-regulated pace and whether the freedom he advocated was appropriate for all children at all times (Katch, 1991). In his later writings (Dewey, 1938), Dewey addressed the issue of children who, because of conditions outside the school, did not initially respond to the approaches he advocated. He called for "common sense" in developing "educative" experiences for children and commented on the issue of inclusion in the following statement: "Exclusion is perhaps the only available measure at a given juncture, but it is no solution" (Dewey, 1938, p. 57). The responsibility for handling situations of noninvolvement or unruly behavior, he believed, belongs to the teachers, and their planning of educational experiences for all the children. This planning must, however, allow for the kind of flexibility in the curriculum that:

> [is] conducive to community activity and organization which exercises control over individual impulses by the mere fact that all are engaged in communal projects.

> [the teacher] must survey the capacities and needs of the particular set of individuals with whom he is dealing and must at the same time arrange the condi-

tions which provide the subject-matter or content for experiences that satisfy these needs and develop these capacities. (Dewey, 1938, p. 58)

The progressive approach to teaching and learning included the beliefs that: learning is a social experience; individuals solve problems in interaction with the physical and social environment; learning must be linked to the real-life experiences of individuals in order to have meaning and purpose and to endure; the historical, intellectual, and artistic traditions of society should be included in education, but must be connected to the present experiences of children; active exploration and creation must include the arts; linguistic and mathematical literacy develop naturally as the outcome of children's physical and intellectual development in concert with their experiences; there is a continuity to experience, with each new development in learning growing out of previous learning; conscious reflection on experience is essential for learning; and social control and rules emerge out of the inherent nature of experiences (Archambault, 1964, 1966; Dewey, 1938; Phillips & Soltis, 1991).

Although there have been periods and situations in American education where these ideas have taken hold, they have not become the dominant voice. Instead, the assumptions that have guided public education are: first, that the content of the curriculum should be fixed and uniform; second, that there is one best way for all children to learn; and third, that all children need to learn the same things at the same time. The reliance of schools on a subject-centered curriculum has required the segregation of those children who did not succeed with the set curriculum.

Dewey himself summarized the beliefs of the "traditionalists," who thought that the curriculum should focus on "stable and well ordered realities" in the following way:

> Subdivide each topic into studies; each study into lessons; each lesson into specific facts and formulae. Let the child proceed step by step to master each one of these separate parts, and at last he will have covered the entire ground. Thus emphasis is put upon the logical subdivisions and consecutions of subject matter. Problems of instruction are problems of procuring texts giving logical parts and sequences, and of presenting these portions in class in a similar definite and graded way. Subject matter furnishes the end, and it determines method. The child is simply the immature being who is to be matured; he is the superficial being who is to be deepened; his is narrow experience which is to be widened. It is his to receive, to accept. His part is fulfilled when he is ductile and docile. (Dewey, 1902/1964, p. 342)

These beliefs have guided special and general education practice. Although the "topics" that are divided into lessons and into step-by-step facts

and formulae may not have been the same in self-contained special education classes as in general education classrooms, the process has been the same.
Step-by-step, systematic instruction and behavioristic techniques have characterized the methods used in special education, in the same way that these
processes have been the norm in general education. Certainly, they have been
appropriate "techniques" for teaching some discrete skills and for shaping
some behaviors and should not be completely abandoned in either setting,
but it is their predominant or even exclusive use in classrooms that is at the
heart of the debate surrounding school reform today.

Indeed, at certain points in the history of general education, special education programs, including my own classroom, were considered to be quite
innovative. As a special education teacher (1967–1973) and school psychologist (1973–1978), I taught and provided supportive services to educational
programs for children identified as having learning disabilities and other
"handicapping conditions" in self-contained special education classrooms in
public school buildings and in nonresidential special education facilities
located away from students' home schools. We were providing individual
programs for children who were failing in the regular classroom setting. In
my elementary level classroom for children identified with learning disabilities, I used all the "latest" special education techniques: multisensory instruction, individually preprogrammed reading and mathematics workbooks,
perceptual-motor exercises, and individual study carrels to minimize distrac-
tions. Whole-group lessons were rare. Instructional methods focused on the
individual learning needs of each student and the development of isolated,
academic skills. The "handicaps" that were assumed to underlie their learning problems were addressed through specific perceptual–motor exercises.
The approaches used for individual instruction were aimed at remediating
deficits while teaching to students' strengths.

Within a few months, most of my students' "disabilities" were, in fact,
remediated. Reversals and inversions of letters disappeared, coordination
improved, motivation increased, and aggressive behavior decreased. The
magic formula: allowing adequate time for students to complete their work;
carefully selecting individual assignments and providing these in individually developed learning modules designed to match students' interests, needs,
learning styles, and skill levels; integrating art, music, and movement with
perceptual–motor exercises.

In spite of my success, I felt that something was very wrong with the
overall picture. Students could decode words, but still weren't readers. They
could do grade-level math when given adequate time, manipulatives, and real-
life problems to solve, but couldn't memorize all the facts needed to keep up
in a traditional fourth-grade math class. The students in my class had learned
how to maintain a balanced aquarium, had studied animals and plants on

numerous field trips, knew about the neighborhood and town where our school was located, but hadn't covered the social studies and science facts that their peers were learning in the "regular" school. These remediated and successful children were still unable to return to their home school classrooms and, in many cases, could not function appropriately in their communities. I had failed to consider the reality of the public school curriculum, as well as the learning and social environments of my students' home schools. The link between the learning of discrete skills and their functional application to their home school curriculum and the real work of their communities had been neglected. They understood little about the communities in which they lived with their families. They had few friends outside our classroom. For some of my students, the abusive cycles in their home life would result in early death.

Hence, in effect, with my students and special education colleagues, I was working on a puzzle with some of its pieces missing, and many of the pieces we did have did not fit. In order to create a picture of a truly inclusive and optimal educational environment, educators from general education with similar goals needed to reconstruct the puzzle. The problems faced today in many American and European schools (O'Hanlon, 1993) are the result of the continuing failure of special educators to understand the culture of public schools and the central role of a general curriculum whose construction rests on the "traditionalist" model.

Clearly, for any individual to function as a mature adult in today's world requires much more than being able to understand subject matter that has been presented in a logical and sequential manner. Our children do not live in a world that is either logical or sequential. To function in today's world requires flexibility, critical thinking skills, and the ability to solve problems in new and ambiguous situations. These attributes will be even more critical in the next century. If current efforts in schools, which involve the creation of inclusive educational settings, are to be successful, curriculum needs to be based on that understanding and the recognition that strict adherence to linear methods of instruction do not meet the needs of any child.

A DEWEYAN APPROACH TO INCLUSIVE CURRICULUM DEVELOPMENT

For the last six years, I have had the opportunity to participate in the conversation about school reform and restructuring taking place among educators throughout the United States. Some are working in restructured settings, while others work toward change in traditionally organized and administered schools. All share a vision of education and a way of thinking about teaching and learning that focus on approaches to curriculum growing out of the ideas articulated by John Dewey and other progressive educators. Through the integrating framework of the "Foxfire Approach," many of these teachers are supported in designing strategies for teaching and learning that involve students in the development of curriculum. This approach provides opportunities for students' strengths and talents to be utilized in academic instruction, while providing experiences that will develop new and emerging skills.

The Foxfire Approach

Foxfire began as a course designed to develop literacy skills and preserve local cultural traditions among rural Appalachian young people through their involvement in relevant, community-based experiences. With the financial support of several large private foundations, it evolved into a national support system. "Foxfire Teacher Outreach" was designed to support progressive educators in the application and refinement of the teaching approach that emerged from its earlier work (Foxfire Fund, 1994). The Foxfire Approach is neither a curriculum nor a specific instructional method or technique. Rather, it provides a framework for teaching, guided by a set of "Core Practices." These have grown out of the experiences of teachers who have been developing their teaching around progressive educational principles. The Core Practices guide the integration of curriculum, instruction, and teaching methods and techniques and embrace many theoretical positions that share the Deweyan, learner-centered philosophy. The Core Practices are neither a recipe nor a formula for teaching, but they assist teachers in creating a balance between the child and the curriculum. The list below summarizes the ideas they encompass:

1. All the work teachers and students do together flows from student desire, student concerns.
2. The role of the teacher is that of collaborator, team leader, and guide, rather than boss.
3. The academic integrity of the work is clear.
4. The work is characterized by student action, rather than the passive receipt of processed information.
5. Peer teaching, small-group and team work are emphasized.
6. Connections between classroom work and the surrounding communities and the real world outside the classroom are clear.
7. There is an audience beyond the teacher for student work.
8. As the year progresses, new activities spiral out of the old.
9. As teachers, we acknowledge the worth of aesthetic experience.
10. Reflection—some conscious, thoughtful time to stand apart from the

work itself—is an essential activity that must take place at key points throughout the work.

11. The work includes honest, ongoing evaluation of skills, content, and changes in student attitude. Students should be trained to monitor their own progress and devise their own remediation plans. (Foxfire Fund, 1991)

It is difficult to describe a *typical* Foxfire classroom. Given the basic premise, that each classroom represents a unique ecology (Kugelmass, 1991), it follows that no two will ever look precisely alike. The children and their teacher(s) shape classroom life through their ongoing negotiations. The structures of the school and community in which they are situated add another dimension. What does characterize all Foxfire classrooms, however, is that children are actively engaged (Core Practice 4) with one another, their teacher, instructional materials, and in shaping the curriculum. They talk openly and knowingly about what they are learning, and about why and how it is being learned (Core Practice 10). Much of their work is done in groups (Core Practice 5) with a good deal of peer interaction. Children's lives and experiences in the world outside the classroom, including their communities and families, are actively and consciously integrated into academic work (Core Practices 3 and 6), as are the arts and aesthetic considerations (Core Practice 9). Assessment is ongoing and integral to instruction (Core Practice 11). Children are asked to reflect upon and evaluate their own learning (Core Practice 10). When applied in classrooms that include students who have been traditionally viewed as having special educational needs, the Core Practices assist teachers in providing educational experiences that address subject-area "givens," while, at the same time, teaching academic, social, and functional skills (Core Practice 3). Teachers engage their students in the creation of a developmentally and age-appropriate curriculum. The process facilitates the creation of a learning community where diversity is valued and all children are provided opportunities to develop their talents. (Kugelmass, 1991). The process used in one fourth-grade classroom in a traditionally structured, rural, upstate New York elementary school offers an illustration of the way one teacher integrated the Foxfire Approach into her classroom. As is true in many of the other elementary and middle school classrooms I have observed, the Foxfire Core Practices were applied in conjunction with cooperative learning strategies and a whole-language approach. That combination enabled this teacher to provide an enriched curriculum for all her students, including those classified as having learning disabilities and multiple handicaps (language delay, cognitive deficits, and emotional disabilities).

When her 25 students entered the classroom in the fall, they found no posters on the wall. Instead, hanging from the ceiling were several sheets of large chart paper containing lists of the curriculum mandates from the state and the school district that were required in fourth grade (Core Practice 3). The teacher explained to the somewhat baffled group of children that these charts represented all the things they would learn that year and that they, as a group and with her guidance (Core Practice #2), would decide how they were to be learned (Core Practice #1). She explained there would be some things that would happen as "teacher's choice" because of her responsibility for their learning and her years of experience as a teacher (Core Practice #3).

This way of beginning the school year was the start of an instructional process that created a balance between the children and the curriculum. Academic expectations were clarified, while a sense of ownership of the learning process and their classroom community was provided for the students. Students would eventually combine academic outcomes in a variety of ways and create group interdisciplinary projects that would develop a wide variety of skills while acknowledging and expanding upon their talents, interests, and strengths.

The next step in the process involved engaging the students in developing guidelines for behavior, classroom norms, and methods of carrying out classroom instruction and assessment. This is accomplished through a series of activities known as "Memorable Experiences" and "Good Teachers/Good Students." In these activities students reflect on positive aspects of their own learning and how these could be put into practice in their classroom. The guidelines for these group activities require the involvement of all students, either through their active participation in decision-making or by considering the needs of those students who might be unable to speak for themselves. Clearly, a good many preliminary skills are necessary for a group of children to be able to accomplish this task. Here, as in all instructional activities, the teacher's judgment is required to assess the group and what particular modifications may be necessary.

CREATING LEARNING COMMUNITIES

Many teachers have been drawn to Foxfire and other progressive approaches through their interest in developing teaching strategies that are student centered, experiential, and linked to the communities and real-life experiences of students. They include educators working at all grade levels and in all subject areas, general education classroom teachers and special educators, teachers and administrators from rural, urban, and suburban communities. These educators recognize and appreciate the impact and depth of current school reform and restructuring on the development of teaching strategies for children who experience special learning challenges. Many are involved in several national, state, and local school reform initiatives. They have struggled through a conscious deconstruction and reconstruction of their learning and teaching experiences as part of their own learning process, thus leading to the creation of schools and classrooms that they describe as "learning communities."

For the two teachers whose classrooms are described in the following pages, structural changes in their schools have supported their work through the creation of learning communities for themselves as well as for their students. School colleagues provide psychological, emotional, and intellectual support based on a shared vision of education and an articulated set of beliefs and assumptions about teaching and learning that reflect Deweyan principles. Their schools have made a conscious decision to examine and restructure the way education is provided through reconceptualizing curriculum and reallocating resources. This work has required constant reflection, assessment, and change.

These teachers have also placed themselves and their practice within the context of several other adult learning communities outside the school, gaining additional support and sustenance for their own learning from national, regional, and local school reform and restructuring efforts. National and regional affiliations have included: the Coalition of Essential Schools (Brown University), Project Zero (Harvard School of Education), the National Center for Restructuring Education, Schools, and Teaching (NCREST, Teachers College, Columbia University), the Northeast Regional Labs and its Prospect Center in Burlington, Vermont, and Foxfire Teacher Outreach.

Although the two teachers live and work in different small cities in different states (Massachusetts and New York), which have different curriculum mandates for the elementary schoolchild, and although they work under different special education structures, it is not surprising that their classrooms look very much alike. The differences in emphasis that exist between these teachers are hardly visible to the outside visitor. It is only through lengthy conversations that these differences begin to emerge. They share more similarities: Instructional methods in their classrooms follow from progressive educational principles; each has created learning environments with their students that are inclusive learning communities where diversity is viewed by teachers and students as offering richness rather than providing an obstacle to learning and where the presence of a child with a disability is seen as an opportunity to create a new perspective for the class (Kugelmass, 1996).

A Multiple Intelligences Classroom

Julie Carter's work has taken place within the context of a learning community consciously committed to school restructuring and to inclusion as a component of these changes. The "school-within-a-school" program at the Fuller School in Gloucester, Massachusetts (the Blackburn Project, funded through U.S. Department of Education, FIRST [Fund for Improvement and Reform of Schools and Teaching] Schools and Teacher Program, CFDA No. 84-211B) has developed a curriculum for kindergarten through Grade 5 built around the theory of multiple intelligences (MI) as articulated by Howard Gardner (1983,1993); and it incorporates instructional strategies consistent with Deweyan principles. Gardner's theory is based, in part, on research growing out of Project Zero at the Harvard School of Education. Project Zero began its work at Fuller with the kindergarten program, "Project Spectrum," focusing on the development of assessment and instructional practices to promote the development of the "full spectrum" of children's intelligences (Gardner, 1993).

Gardner postulates that there are at least seven "intelligences." Depending on cultural context, one or more are valued in a given society and rewarded accordingly. In the United States and most Western countries, linguistic and logical–mathematical intelligences have been selected as those most indicative of an "intelligent" person. The Wechsler and Stanford-Binet tests of intelligence, used throughout the United States in the identification of children for special education, have been designed around that selection. The "traditional" school curriculum is most often organized to develop the attributes and skills associated with linguistic and logical–mathematical intelligences.

Children who do not exhibit strengths in linguistic and/or logical–mathematical intelligences will, therefore, not perform well in traditionally structured schools or on standardized tests, nor will they be provided adequate opportunities to develop their other talents. Having to learn the content of a curriculum that is taught primarily through the written and spoken word often results in failure for these children. When significant discrepancies exist between their primary forms of intelligence and those valued in American schools, they may be identified as having a learning disability or mental retardation. Rather than using the child's intelligence as the entry point for the curriculum, deficit-based remedial approaches used in both general and special education have focused on children's weaknesses.

The information in Figure 2.1 is taken from material designed by the staff of the MI program at the Fuller School, to acquaint parents and other educators with the learning preferences of the students. This information frames nonlinguistic intelligences in a way that promotes their importance in education and enables the creation of an inclusive classroom. The suggested teaching methods and materials are not used in isolation from one another. They are understood to be as central to the curriculum as the specific content being addressed.

Linguistic

Children with strengths in this area have highly developed auditory skills and often think in words. They like reading, poetry, word games, and making up poetry and stories. Teach by encouraging them to see and say words. Read books together. Tools: books, a tape recorder, or typewriter.

Logical-mathematical

These children think conceptually, are able to see and explore patterns and relationships. They like to experiment, solve puzzles, ask cosmic questions. Teach through logic games, investigations, mysteries. Help them form concepts. Tools: computers, games.

Spatial

These children think in images and are very aware of their environments. They like to draw, do jigsaw puzzles, read maps, daydream. Teach through drawing, verbal and physical imagery. Tools: art materials, camera, building blocks.

Musical

These children love music and are also sensitive to sounds in their environments: the chirp of a cricket, the rain on the roof. They may study better with music in the background. Teach by turning lessons into lyrics, speaking rhythmically, tapping out time. Tools: stereo or radio, musical instruments, a metronome.

Kinesthetic

These are children with a keen sense of body awareness. They like moving, hugging, making things. They communicate well through body language. Teach through physical activity, hands-on learning, dramatics. Tools: sports equipment, crafts materials, a teddy bear.

Interpersonal

These children learn through group interaction. They have lots of friends, empathy for others, and are street smart. Teach through group activities, seminars, dialogues. Tools: telephone, personal time, attention from the teacher, puppets, letter-writing materials.

Intrapersonal

These children have a kind of wisdom that comes from being able to tune in to their own feelings. They are intuitive and introspective. Teach through independent study and provide opportunities for introspection. Tools: diaries and journals, materials and activities that allow for creative expression, privacy.

FIGURE 2.1 The seven Intelligences. Developed by the Multiple Intelligences Program at Fuller School, Gloucester, Massachusetts (from Gardner, 1983).

The introduction of Foxfire Core Practices into the MI program provided an additional integrating umbrella for teaching through these intelligences. Julie Carter had been teaching in the program for three years prior to her training in the Foxfire Approach. In her fourth year, she began teaching a combined first- and second-grade classroom in Foxfire fashion: involving the children in establishing the norms for the classroom while building a learning community. She started the year with few materials or decorations visible to the children; instead, she and her students designed the learning centers in the room together. These centers, built around the different intelligences, continued to be developed throughout the year.

Julie introduced the children to the learning centers by explaining that they would be places where work would be focused on each student's becoming Word Smart, Math Smart, Music Smart, Art Smart, Body Smart, People Smart, and Self Smart (Armstrong, 1994). The class brainstormed the meaning of these concepts and then decided which items in addition to the few Julie had brought to class, should be included in each center. Eventually the learning centers became integrated into the thematic projects that the children designed around the program's theme for the year, "Relationships and Connections." Julie and the other teachers in the program collaborated in selecting the theme and met with one another in grade-level teams on a regular basis throughout the year to determine units for its continual development. Subject-specific material, academic skills, and all seven intelligences became integrated into activities that were developed in collaboration with students. Curriculum was understood as a process that unfolds as the children interacted with one another, with their teacher, with the materials, and with the content of their learning.

Carter's first and second graders began the year with a unit on self, home, and family. Their first "assignment" was to draw pictures of their families. This was followed by storytelling and writing. Several days later, the children were asked to bring a box from home that contained objects that represented themselves. The children shared these objects with one another in cooperative groups and then came together in a large group to tell about one another's "symbols." The concept of "symbol" was discussed and concrete examples were provided. Although these activities seem similar to the way many primary classrooms begin the year, there are significant differences in the meaning and purpose of the process used. The activities are designed to introduce specific concepts and processes to the children and to build a classroom community. Children often work in pairs, a first grader with a second grader. The mixed-age grouping of first and second graders provides an additional opportunity for peer teaching and learning that will further enhance classroom community where a wide range of abilities and interests are the norm. Although the initial pairs are chosen by the teacher, the children have opportunities to choose their own partners as they become more skilled in peer teaching.

The pairing, peer teaching, and self-examination that are built into these first lessons are designed to develop the children's intra- and interpersonal intelligences. As partners in learning, the pairs of children select and rotate through each center, working on writing, reading, mathematical, artistic, kinesthetic, and musical activities that they complete at their own individual level of competency and their own rate of learning. The beginning of the school year is consciously designed to teach these young children the specific vocabulary of MI and to develop the norms that will guide the development of this classroom community. As the year proceeds, and the children internalize an understanding of the need to include all intelligences in their activities, the learning centers become more focused on the project-based activities and other aspects of the curriculum.

This teacher was trained in both special and general education. She taught in both segregated special education settings and more traditional general education classrooms. She believes that her special education background prepared her to expect and accept the differences in children's learning styles, behaviors, needs, and abilities that she sees in her classroom. Three children in her class were identified as having learning disabilities. It became clear to both of us, when I visited the classroom and discussed teaching with her, that aspects of her current teaching practice reflect her special education background. Not only does she welcome the challenge presented by students who do not learn in traditional ways, she is also confident of her ability to deal with children whose behavior might be problematic for other teachers. In addition to incorporating a variety of behavioral approaches as both instructional techniques and management strategies, she recognizes the necessity for creating a balance between the child's intelligences, talents, learning styles, and life experiences with skill development and the content of the curriculum.

It is more than Carter's previous training and experiences, however, that has created an ideal situation for the inclusion of children with learning disabilities. The additional framework of multiple intelligences provides a variety of entry points to learning for children with poor linguistic, mathematical, and/or perceptual–motor skills, as well as opportunities for the development of kinesthetic skills. The Foxfire umbrella adds the dimension of student choice to the activities in the classroom, while promoting problem-solving and peer interactions for modeling and reinforcement of growth-enhancing behavior. Working within a school community guided by a philosophy of learning that places diversity at the center of the curriculum provides structural support for Carter's work. In the MI program, curriculum development is seen as an evolutionary process and not as a predetermined "scope and sequence" for teaching a specific subject area. There is a shared and articulated vision for both the process and content of curriculum throughout the program.

An Elementary "Essential" School

Sharon Weaver's second-grade classroom offers another example of curriculum development in a classroom that operates within the context of a collaborative school culture dedicated to achieving systemic inclusion. The Belle Sherman Elementary School (kindergarten through Grade 5) in Ithaca, New York, is one of 22 elementary schools that have recently joined the Coalition of Essential Schools. Following the work of Sizer (1984), Coalition Schools develop their educational programs and school culture around a set of common principles. These principles are focused on the purpose and organization of schools and were originally designed for the restructuring of secondary schools. The following list presents a revised and summarized version of the "Coalition Principles" that reflects an adaptation to the elementary school.

1. The school should focus on helping students to use their minds well.
2. The school's goals should be simple: that each student master a limited number of essential skills and areas of knowledge. The aphorism "less is more" should dominate.
3. The school's goals should apply to all students, while the means to these goals will vary as those goals themselves.
4. Teaching and learning should be personalized to the maximum feasible extent.
5. The governing practical metaphor of the school should be student-as-worker rather than the more familiar metaphor of teacher-as-deliverer-of instructional-services.
6. Students should be expected to provide evidence demonstration of mastery for graduation—an "Exhibition." The emphasis is on the demonstration that they can do important things.
7. The tone of the school should explicitly and self-consciously stress values of unanxious expectation, of trust and of decency.
8. The principal and teacher should perceive themselves as generalists first and specialists second.
9. Ultimate administrative and budget targets should include provisions for reduced student–teacher ratios, substantial time for collective planning by teachers, competitive salaries for staff and an ultimate per pupil cost that does not exceed the traditional school by more than 10 percent. (Coalition of Essential Schools, 1992, p. 168).

These principles have been adapted at Belle Sherman in support of a commitment to the achievement of educational excellence for all children. Teachers see themselves as responsible for every student. Neither teachers nor students are viewed as "special." The adoption of a "blended services" model has provided the structural support for that perspective. Through the elimination of all its special education classrooms and "pull out" programs (see Sizer, pp. 225–227), the school has been able to realize Coalition Principle #9—reducing student–teacher ratios and providing opportunities for collaborative planning through teaming. Funds for all support services have been pooled and "specialists" included as team teachers in general classrooms. Weaver's teammate is a teacher of English as a second language. Teachers who have had training in special education serve as consultants to other teachers on their grade-level teams when issues arise that relate to their specific areas of knowledge and experience.

The blended services model has addressed one of the greatest problems faced by general education teachers using a "progressive" curriculum approach in classrooms where students identified for special education are included, but where the schools have not redesigned the way they provide support. In these more traditionally structured schools, teachers often find themselves in situations where pull out programs interfere with building the sense of community that is essential to the development of a collaborative classroom environment. In instances where the general classroom teacher receives the support of a special education resource teacher working from a consultant model, but operating under a behavioristic framework, conflicting paradigms and priorities interfere with real collaboration. Under these circumstances, it is often difficult to include "labeled" students in ongoing, interdisciplinary class projects because of the pressure put on the general classroom teacher and special educator to demonstrate the achievement of specific, predetermined behavioral goals as listed in an Individual Education Plan (IEP). In these situations, general classroom and special education teachers are working in schools that attempt to address parental and legislative pressures for inclusion, but still operate within a paradigm guided by the deficit model that has traditionally characterized special education.

In Weaver's classroom I observed a well-developed community of learners actively involved in shaping their own educational experiences. Although there are some differences, there are more similarities between how this second-grade class and Julie Carter's first- and second-grade classroom operate. Weaver does not talk about multiple intelligences with her students and has not identified Gardner's (1993) work as guiding her practice. However, the integration of and appreciation for visual art, music, kinesthetic, and intra- and interpersonal intelligences are evident in the work the children do every day. Student choice, active learning, appreciation for diversity, and authentic approaches to assessment characterize this classroom much as they do classrooms that follow a MI curriculum.

Weaver's students are all second graders; however, this is the second year that most of these children have been in her classroom. She believes that multiple-year placement with the same teacher builds a stronger classroom community and provides continuity of instruction and the time for her and her students to build strong relationships with one another. Her second graders were able to jump into the school year familiar with the collaborative and learner-centered approach of the classroom. Visiting during the second week of school, I found the students diligently writing short stories, individually, but seated in the clusters of four that make up their five base-groups. Occasionally, children would turn to one another for help or for brief conversation. The children in this class bring a wide range of interests, abilities, socioeconomic backgrounds, races, cultures, and languages to the group. Among them are three children identified as having learning disabilities.

A whole-group lesson that began with Weaver reading a story to the class provides an excellent example of her approach to curriculum. It also illustrates the teacher's natural manner of including issues that are particularly relevant to students with learning disabilities, as well as to all young children. The story reading activity will "spiral" into other lessons that include reading, writing, math, and social studies and will explore the diversity of the families and communities represented by the children in the class.

The story, *Don't Forget the Bacon* by Hutchins (1989, p. 1), tells of a boy who is asked to go shopping for:

- six farm eggs,
- a cake for tea,
- a pound of pears,
- and don't forget the bacon.

After reading this first page, Weaver asked the children, "What does this mean?" This question provided the opportunity for a child with strong linguistic skills to explain what the words implied. After he explained that it was a list of the things the boy was asked to buy, she asked the children to identify and count the number of items on the list. This question pushed the children to sort out the words and to describe the items. They debated whether or not "six farm eggs" constituted one item or six; and the items were counted several times by the group. The story proceeded with the boy in the book repeating these words to himself as he walked to the store. He confused words and substituted others, however, a situation that all the children in the class could relate to and one that provided an opening for those children identified as having learning disabilities to talk about their learning difficulties in and out of school. A short discussion about being confused with words and forgetting things ensued, with Weaver facilitating the children's sharing of personal stories.

The story moved to a discussion about the usefulness of lists as organizers and helpers for remembering things. Weaver then guided the class to share with one another the ways in which they had seen lists used outside school. They talked about how writing the items beneath one another made them easier to remember. The discussion became an entry into a writing lesson in which the children were asked to develop their own lists for things they would like. She suggested that they write each item underneath the preceding one, but this was not required. Every child then worked on producing a list that was unique in both form and content.

In this whole-language classroom, the inability to spell a word correctly does not keep any child from participating. If a child wants assistance, he or she asks another child or calls on one of the adults to write the word into his or her personal dictionary. Weaver later explained that she did not ask the children to draw pictures of the items on their lists because she knew that they all were capable of writing something. (She felt that offering the option of drawing would have kept the less able writers from pushing themselves: "I often use art as an entry point into writing. I'll use whatever brings all the children into an activity. However, I know that, sometimes, kids need a push to do things that are hard for them.")

For this teacher, Deweyan principles are integrated into how she thinks about her teaching on a day-to-day basis through her application of Foxfire Core Practices. These are woven into minilessons, group activities, and classroom design, facilitating the development of an inclusive classroom. Interdisciplinary and/or thematic class projects designed by students and guided by the teacher to meet general learning goals and specific academic objectives take place frequently. Although projects offer an impressive showcase of the children's work, it will be the process students engage in throughout the year that provides the more significant aspects of students' learning. Certainly, participation in class projects by "special" children is not unique to this classroom. Projects are frequently used in more teacher-directed settings as a strategy for "mainstreaming." Unlike this classroom, however, they do not often involve everyone in the overall development of a project in an authentic way.

RESTRUCTURING FOR AN INCLUSIVE SOCIETY

In 1938, Dewey wrote *Experience and Education* in the hope of moving away from the battle that had developed between those who identified themselves exclusively as either traditional or progressive educators. He saw the debate as an attempt to resolve an either/or conflict that was both misguided and unresolvable. It also provided a distraction from addressing the larger issues confronting education and American society. Relying upon his pragmatic roots, he called for a balance between the best ideas of both traditions. The lines being drawn today, between special educators calling for inclusion and those who believe that "traditional" special education practices can best meet the needs of children with disabilities, reflect a similar either/or debate.

All educators should examine the assumptions and theories upon which their teaching methods rest. Skrtic (1991) believes this kind of "critical pragmatism" to be essential in coming to a workable resolution of the differences between those who want to hold on to traditional special education practices, which they believe have been proven effective, and those who want to move children into newly evolving, inclusive educational settings. Because the history of general and special education provides many examples of how unexamined practices have had negative consequences, even the most well-intended practices must be carefully examined.

Moreover, special educators should examine critically instructional practices, the effectiveness of which they have regarded as "proven," in the same way they examine innovations. The ascendancy of behaviorism as the method of choice for students with special needs during the late 1970s and 1980s and the use of prepackaged learning programs have, however, been supported by outcomes that are frequently measured by standardized tests, behavioral assessments, and computer-managed IEPs, but not necessarily by the life experiences of students. The teaching of predetermined skills in isolation from the context of their application in the experiences and lives of children limits the functional application of those skills. Educators who support the continuation of these methods as the dominant instructional approach in special education believe that they represent an enormous leap forward in educational practice (Kauffman, 1993). In fact, these methods reflect a belief system that is thousands of years old.

Including children in general education without a critical examination can also result in the failure to meet the included child's needs and promote her or his development. Dewey was very clear in his belief that teachers have the responsibility to develop the kinds of environments that provide growth-enhancing—not growth-inhibiting—experiences. The placement of a child with a disability in a classroom that has not been designed to facilitate positive social, emotional, physical, aesthetic, and intellectual experiences or that does not offer the resources and supports the child needs may provide experiences that are, in fact, "mis-educative" (Dewey, 1938, p. 37).

The teachers profiled in this chapter have examined their beliefs and assumptions as a component of their preparation for implementing an inclusive curriculum. Reflection is a well-established habit that guides their practice. At times, when they determine that a child—whether identified for special education or not—needs one-on-one, teacher-directed instruction to assist in developing specific skills, they may use traditional teaching techniques, including behavior management strategies, direct instruction, and drill. Without this kind of assistance, a student may not get the full benefit of the classroom environment. However, they use these methods and techniques within a framework of learning principles that reflect a different understanding of how children learn and develop than those that have guided either general or special education in the past.

Their classrooms and others described throughout this book apply instructional approaches that emerge from a relatively new paradigm of learning. Dewey's ideas have found support in the theories of both Jean Piaget and L. S. Vygotsky (Phillips & Soltis, 1991). Both emphasize the importance of children's social interactions in education and believe that learning is a natural, social process that occurs as individuals interact with the environment. Constructivist models of learning that have developed out of Piagetian theories have led to the development of teaching methods and instructional approaches that are based on the understanding that process and content are of equal importance in the curriculum. These ideas promote students' active engagement in developing curriculum with each other and with their teacher out of their experiences, questions, and suppositions (Brooks & Brooks, 1993). Vygotsky's work has most recently provided the strongest support for inclusion by acknowledging the importance of the context in which learning occurs. He has demonstrated that our understanding of any content is inseparable from the context in which it is learned (Vygotsky, 1962, 1978).

Although both traditional and progressive educational approaches have been supported at different times by many school reform movements of the twentieth century, traditional ideologies have provided the dominant framework for the structure of schools. Such a basis required the alteration of progressive approaches to fit them within a primarily hierarchical, authoritarian, and content-focused system. Their structures created contexts for learning that have failed to serve the needs of many students. If left unaltered, schools will not evolve into institutions that provide educative experiences for all students, leaving many poorly prepared for the unanticipated challenges of the coming century. We must foster the evolution of educational systems that are based on reconceptualized models of how we understand the world and that facilitate inclusive teaching and learning (Skritic, 1991). We hope that the examples provided in this chapter and those to follow will provide operational models to assist in the creation of such systems and that their evolution will incorporate the best of what we have learned during the last two thousand years.

REFERENCES

Apple, M. (1979). *Ideology and curriculum*. Boston: Routledge & Kegan.

Armstrong, T. (1994). *Multiple intelligences in the classroom*. Alexandria, VA: Association for Supervision and Curriculum Development.

Archambault, R. D. (Ed.). (1964). *John Dewey on education*. Chicago: University of Chicago Press.

Archambault, R. D. (Ed.). (1966). *John Dewey on education: Appraisals*. New York: Random House.

Brooks, J. G., & Brooks, M. G. (1993). *The case for the constructivist classroom*. Alexandria, VA: Association for Supervision and Curriculum Development.

Coalition of Essential Schools (COES) (1992). *The common principles*. Providence, RI: Brown University.

Dewey, J. (1938). *Experience and education*. New York: Macmillan.

Dewey, J. (1964). The child and the curriculum. In R. D. Archaumbault (Ed.), *John Dewey on education* (pp. 339–358). Chicago: University of Chicago Press. (Originally published 1902)

Fantini, A. E. (1993). Focus on process: An examination in the teaching and learning of intercultural communication competence. In T. Gochenour (Ed.), *Beyond experience: An experiential approach to cross-cultural education*. Yarmouth, ME: Intercultural Press.

Foxfire Fund (1991). The Foxfire approach: Perspectives and core practices. *Hands-On: A Journal for Teachers, 41*, 3–4.

Foxfire Fund. (1994). *Annual report, 1992–1993*. Mountain City, GA.

Gardner, H. (1983). *Frames of mind: The theory of multiple intelligences*. New York: Basic Books.

Gardner, H. (1993). *Multiple intelligences: The theory in practice*. New York: Basic Books.

Henson, K. T. (1995). *Curriculum development for educational reform*. New York: HarperCollins.

Hutchins, P. (1989). *Don't forget the bacon*. New York: Mulberry Books.

James, W. (1991). What pragmatism means (Lecture 2). In J. E. Miller, Jr. (Ed.), *Heritage of American literature: Civil War to the present* (Vol. 2, pp. 569–571). New York: Harcourt Brace Jovanovich. (Originally published 1907)

Katch, J. (1991). John Dewey's school. In K. Jervis & C. Montag (Eds.), *Progressive education for the 1990s*. New York: Teachers College Press.

Katz, M. (1971). *Class, bureaucracy and change: The illusion of educational change in America*. New York: Praeger.

Kauffman, J. M. (1993). How we might achieve the radical reform of special education. *Exceptional Children, 60*, 6–16.

Kugelmass, J. W. (1987). *Behavior, bias, and handicaps: Labeling the emotionally disturbed child*. New Brunswick, NJ: Transaction Books.

Kugelmass, J. W. (1991). The ecology of the Foxfire approach. *Hands-On: A Journal for Teachers, 42*, 14–20.

Kugelmass, J. W. (1996). Educating children with learning disabilities in Foxfire classrooms. *Journal of Learning Disabilities* (in press).

MacIntosh, P. (1983). *Interactive phases of curricular re-vision: A feminist perspective* (Working Paper No. 124). Wellesley, MA: Wellesley College, Center for Research on Women.

MacIntosh, P. (1990) *Interactive phases of curricular and personal re-vision with regard to race* (Working Paper No. 219). Wellesley, MA: Wellesley College, Center for Research on Women.

Meier, D. (1991). The kindergarten tradition in the high school. In K. Jervis & C. Montag (Eds.), *Progressive education for the 1990s.* New York: Teachers College Press.

O'Hanlon, C. (1993). *Special education integration in Europe.* London: David Fulton.

Phillips, D. C., & Soltis, J. F. (1991). *Perspectives on learning.* New York: Teachers College Press.

Sizer, T. R. (1984). *Horace's compromise: The dilemma of the American high school.* Boston: Houghton Mifflin.

Skrtic, T. M. (1991). *Behind special education.* Denver, CO: Love Publishing.

Stainback, S., & Stainback, W. (Eds.). (1992). *Curriculum considerations in inclusive classrooms: Facilitating learning for all students.* Baltimore: Paul H. Brookes.

Vygotsky, L. S. (1962). *Language and thought.* Cambridge, MA: MIT Press.

Vygotsky, L. S. (1978). *Mind and society.* Cambridge, MA: Harvard University Press.

CHAPTER 3

A Parent's Request:
Creating Diversity for All Children

Michael S. Berres

This chapter tells a story of change in a Seattle elementary school. Inclusion was not one of the first changes; it occurred only after a number of other curricular and decision-making reforms had taken root in the school. In fact, it was a simple parent request that brought inclusion to our attention. This chapter begins with an account of that request, then describes the broader school reforms that made inclusion possible, and, finally, recounts how inclusion succeeded and what it taught the school community.

THE REQUEST: CREATE A SCHOOL FOR ALL CHILDREN

In some schools Mrs. Johnson's request might have been received as unreasonable or as another "idealistic-but-not-practical" expectation from the community, but at Seattle's Lawton Elementary School, the request to create a fully inclusive school for all children made sense. More important, it fit with the direction and context of an elementary school undergoing rapid and systematic restructuring.

While many view inclusion as a major departure from practice-as-usual—sometimes generating intense political scrutiny—the notion arrived at Lawton more quietly and with much less public fanfare. Its impetus grew from one parent's request: "Can you build a program here at Lawton so that kids can go to school with their friends?" The next week this mother's son was scheduled to return to the third grade at a school 8 miles from their Seattle home. He would be 1 of 10 students who had very challenging special needs. Most of the 10 were boys with major behavior problems—as is too frequently the case in special education classrooms or schools. Mrs. Johnson's son also qualified for special education because of his moderate-level autism.

This parent wanted to know if I, as the incoming principal, would build a program at Lawton for children who were being sent to schools apart from their siblings and friends. Having attended some summer planning meetings with me, her request was prompted by an awareness of my interest in promoting diversity in my new school. She wasn't making the request for her own son, who would remain in his current school for a variety of reasons, but for other children not yet in school, who would benefit by attending the same school as their friends and siblings. Her unease about what her child had missed with his separate, distant education prompted her to want something different for upcoming students. I promised to consult with the appropriate groups and keep her briefed on the matter.

As the school year commenced, I began to learn more about the Lawton community and its 400 children. The students presented a rich array of cultural and economic backgrounds. Fourteen different primary languages were represented by the children and their families. Like other elementary schools, we had children who had experienced every possible economic and social support as well as those who were homeless, those whose parents were in jail for physical and substance abuse, and those who had never even been to a beach while living in this city surrounded by the ocean and lakes.

I also began to learn about the staff. Deemed a "veteran and seasoned" staff by one district observer, it was also a group described by another as "nondefensive," "open to change," "focused on children's needs more so than their own needs," and a "staff that had not yet reached its own potential." As I came to know my new colleagues, I found the second district observer's descriptions to be accurate, and, in part, it was this set of qualities that eventually made the restructuring of Lawton for all students possible.

A SCHOOL IN CHANGE THROUGH SIX BROADER REFORMS

Inclusion worked at Lawton. I don't think that any of the staff members or parents involved ever questioned that it would work. While we understood that it would take effort, patience, and planning, it never seemed to be an innovation in danger of not working. The reason for this optimism lay not so much in special education practice but rather in the interconnected changes rippling through the entire school. Although there have been many factors playing a role in Lawton's move towards inclusion, six are most important:

1. Creating classrooms of diversity
2. Establishing the classroom as each child's learning community

3. Using multiage groupings and developmentally appropriate practices
4. Promoting cooperative learning
5. Providing technology support throughout the day
6. Ensuring site-based involvement in a community school

Notice that none of the six factors is normally considered to be a special education reform or innovation. Rather, the six are standard fare in changing classrooms across the country. Furthermore, although they are the elements that our school selected for its restructuring journey, other schools may select others. There are enough educational innovations for any school to select a set that meets its own agenda while still allowing for greater student diversity. Most important for Lawton was that our particular reform efforts and beliefs made inclusion a feasible, desirable, and logical outcome for the school.

Creating Classrooms of Diversity

Lawton's 400 children are drawn mainly from two areas of Seattle: the largely white and middle- and upper-income Magnolia community and the largely minority and lower-income Central area. The ethnic and cultural mix provides a diverse population for each classroom. Rather than creating these heterogeneous groupings to benefit any single population (e.g., bilingual students), we encourage heterogeneity because we believe diversity is good for all. We see the classroom as the best learning place for all children. For example, when specific groups of children leave the classroom for "advanced" classes, both the groups leaving and the class lose an important dimension of true diversity, affecting inclusion and educational excitement. One outcome of this philosophy is revealed through the staff's effort to make each classroom incorporate practices that support and challenge students with stronger abilities. Individualized learning plans, project-based curricula, integrated themes, hands-on activities, intensive technological opportunities, cooperative learning, and an energetic focus on teaching through inquiry and questioning approaches provide strong programming to all of our students—even those categorized as "Highly Capable" by traditional testing standards.

Lawton has a large number of children whose parents choose to have them tested each year for placement in the district's Highly Capable options at other schools, but, generally, after the assessment is completed, parents elect to keep their children at Lawton. Parents whose children have attended Highly Capable sites increasingly return their children to Lawton. In some schools, this might be considered an additional burden for teachers, but at Lawton, this is viewed as a positive challenge.

Another example of the school's growing diversity is our bilingual program. For many years Lawton served an English-speaking population. When the school moved to its new site in 1991, additional classroom space became available. With Seattle schools serving children from over 80 different language backgrounds, the district routinely seeks new buildings to fill the classroom gap. So, with little advance notice and virtually no training, 30 bilingual or non-English-speaking students came to Lawton midyear, with another 30 arriving during Spring semester. The move angered teachers, who felt devalued by their lack of participation in the district's decision-making. Despite their frustration, staff members gradually made the program work for these new children. By the end of the children's first school year at Lawton, they had become an important part of the community's fabric. Now, Lawton staff would resist assertively any effort to remove the bilingual program from the school. Although staff members willingly admit to the difficulties and weariness they felt as they stretched their teaching repertoires to accommodate so many student needs, they never spoke against the value of having many different cultures represented in their classrooms.

A third example, though not directly classroom based, has been the School Programs Involving Community Elders (SPICE) at Lawton. About 100 community elders participate in a range of educational, social, and recreational activities in the school's SPICE center, 50 of them on a regular basis and another 50 less frequently. In addition, SPICE members participate in many intergenerational activities such as tutoring relationships, joint arts projects, and mentoring roles. We view this partnership between SPICE and our children as another thread in the fabric of the school. For different reasons, including transiency and changes in family structures, many of today's children do not have older people as part of their lives. The SPICE center—a partner in our children's and our community's education—provides an easy and natural way for the different generations to work and learn together.

A commitment to a heterogeneous school and diverse classrooms is an essential requirement for supporting practices such as the inclusion of children with different learning needs. By actively inviting many different groups to join the school community, from Highly Capable students to bilingual children, to community elders, to typical children and children with disabilities, we create an ethos that gives everyone a valued place in the life of the school.

Establishing the Classroom as Each Child's Learning Community

Lawton historically served children with special needs through an array of "pull out" options, such as bilingual classes, special education resource rooms, remediation support classes or LAP models, Highly Capable programs, and social and friendship skills support groups. Given academic reports, anecdotal information from other schools, and our increasing discomfort with pull-out models, during the 1991–92 school year we tried to rethink how we served children with different needs. The only constant we found in our search was the following sort of reasoning: "We've always served children with academic problems in the resource or remediation support classes," or, "That's just how it happens here."

All support staff from categorical, itinerant, and family support programs joined to determine where we had been and where we might want to go. By asking, "Which service models are best for children?" rather than, "Which models are most convenient for adults?" we generated a very different set of assumptions for support services. We decided to end pull-outs-by-history and replace them with models that kept all children together in classrooms. We proposed to the rest of the staff that adults follow children to their home classes rather than children following itinerant and support staff to pull-out rooms.

Throughout these discussions, we also understood that there might be times when some children should receive some service or support outside the classroom. What was different in our proposal was that a child's needs would dictate that decision and not our tradition or convenience. For example, a child receiving a specific bit of articulation instruction might need to be in a quiet room away from the noise and tumult of active classrooms, but whenever possible we would pull out other children with that student to create a mixed group so that all the children might benefit from the opportunity to practice and generalize their learning.

This change meant new or enhanced team teaching roles for many staff members. For some staff this was difficult. A few felt intimidated teaching alongside other adults in a partnership. Generally, however, staff felt that it was a positive change, because it diminished the isolation from peers that so many classroom teachers feel. As one member of our staff expressed it, "I talk to children all day long, but seldom get to talk to another adult except during lunch." Staff also appreciated the tremendous advantages in having support staff work in the classrooms. By learning the specialists' routines they could teach those skills when the specialists were not present.

Today at Lawton, bilingual and remediation staff work mostly in team teaching or support roles. The remediation teacher teaches math or reading content as an integral part of the primary and intermediate teams so student–staff ratios are lower. Likewise, bilingual staff provide most of their support to children in the general education classroom. The only routine use of pull-out is for children newly arrived in this country in order to provide them with a bit of extra social support from other children who, from the vantage point of a different language and culture, have learned to navigate the school's norms and practices. Social skills groups, previously provided on a pull-out basis, are now offered to entire classrooms through special social-skills or classroom meeting formats.

Reducing pull-outs has strengthened our commitment to the classroom as each child's rightful center of learning. It has also reinforced the priority of children's needs over the needs of the school's adults. It has not resulted in teachers having the answers for every difficult instructional problem, but it has redoubled our efforts to reshape our classrooms in response to children's needs more effectively than we might have in the past.

Using Multiage Classes and Developmentally Appropriate Practices

The third element of change at Lawton involves the move from single-grade to two- or three-grade multiage classrooms. Students in a traditional Grade 4 classroom might read at levels that range from first to seventh grade, and their understanding of math concepts might span a similar range. The single-grade classroom encouraged curriculum and instruction geared to a narrow range of student abilities, and it did not allow us to respond to the diversity of needs presented by the children. We studied the issue, and, after visiting many schools and districts in the Seattle area, felt that the multiage configuration was a more reasonable option for our children's needs. It was not an easy choice because we had to confront two major concerns. The staff was initially concerned that multiage classrooms would require more planning and work. Second, some parents believed that having an older child in a multiage class, for example, a third-grade student in a class of second and third graders, implied that the student was less skillful or would face a less challenging curriculum than he or she would if placed in a class of third and fourth graders. The teachers' concern about increased work dissipated as they realized that, if their classrooms truly responded to the breadth of student diversity, there was an enormous amount of planning required no matter what the classroom configuration. We understand now that the second concern is simply one that will require parent education and is an issue that, in the words of one staff member, "never goes away."

The benefits of multiage grouping have been dramatic. Children generally stay with the same teacher for two years in a row (unless the match has outgrown its effectiveness), thus eliminating the need for the several-week period in September and October when teachers and students get to know one another. Children returning to the same teacher in September serve as role models and "interns" for other children, who are just learning the routines and expectations from the teacher. Teachers actually see the fruits of their labors rather than sending their students off after a nine-month association. We have greatly expanded the number of classroom options for children and parents. For example, from one year to the next, we changed the offerings at second grade from two second-grade classrooms to five multiage classrooms (1/2, 1/2, 1/2, 2/3, 2/3), providing more possibilities for finding strong teacher–student matches during the student-assignment process.

Expanded classroom options combined with an acknowledgment of and response to diversity in age, background, and culture have been a boon to our inclusion efforts. By looking at children in terms of their own individuality instead of what the "average fourth grader" or the "average second grader" should be learning, we can better support the needs of our students. At Lawton, multiage classes don't *guarantee* individualized programming—but they certainly support it.

No matter how much effort we expend on teaching, some children will still perplex us. No matter what funding we receive through grants to hire additional staff, we still have between 27 and 30 children in every classroom. No matter how clearly a teacher integrates social–emotional and affective content into class routines, the full needs of urban children exceed what can be realistically offered in a school. Although we know that most of the needs of any child can be accommodated in the general classroom, we have also tried to accept some of the limitations we face—our own limitations and those of the district and our urban environment. Our struggle is a constant one of seeking ways to become a developmentally appropriate school without burning out staff and the community in the search.

Promoting Cooperative Learning

Along with multiage classes and our efforts to respond to diversity in the classroom, we have made a strong move toward cooperative learning. Virtually every facet of the curriculum—from the writing process to artistic endeavors to mathematical analysis—lends itself nicely to this instructional strategy. Much of a child's class time is spent with classmates in the pursuit of answers—and further questions.

Cooperative groups allow us to create learning situations where every child plays dual roles, as learner and as teacher. Each child, regardless of skill level, has the opportunity to take leadership and facilitative roles in cooperative learning groups. Some students with disabilities have more limited leadership roles, but they nonetheless fill those roles to the extent of their ability. As children become used to working in small diverse groups, it does not seem awkward or unusual for a child with a serious disability to be working along with children with stronger skills. Questions such as "How can the group process accommodate a child with a disability?" surface only for adult visitors to the school; children don't think in those terms.

The struggles that have historically occurred when student groups with no prior experience together are joined (e.g., early integration of black and white students; girls entering math, science, sports, and other males-only disciplines; students being "mainstreamed" from special education), seem *not* to be issues for students experienced in cooperative learning. From their first kindergarten days, children are systematically taught cooperative and joint problem-solving skills. As fifth graders, by the time they leave for middle school, they have developed sophisticated cooperative working skills. They assume that a group with diversity is a natural context for learning.

Providing Technology Support Throughout the Day

Over the last six years, Lawton's curriculum has shifted toward a project-centered, integrated approach supporting children's active and inquiry-based learning strategies. Systematic infusion of new technology has been a cornerstone of this work. Rather than creating a technology program as an *end*, we sought to infuse technology as a *means* throughout each child's day. We call our technology approach "transparent," that is, it is not distinguishable from other parts of the curriculum.

We studied various technology models and elected to implement the Integrated Technology Classroom (ITC) model. This meant that technology had to become a vital, living part of each classroom's content, and that each teacher would be able to pursue a love for, or confront his or her phobia for, technology all day, every day. With the disassembling of the intermediate computer lab and the dispersing of its equipment to classrooms throughout the school, it also meant that technology was available to help support every part of Lawton's move toward classroom diversity.

Technology has fostered cooperative learning projects. Though Lawton has a large number of computers and other technology available, we insist that children use the equipment in pairs, trios, or small groups to encourage the collaborative decision-making process in all activities. As children learn to use the technology, we use their struggles to teach them problem-solving skills. Their journey to answers or solutions is usually as interesting as their arrival: Cross-age tutors work together to fashion multimedia presentations on Pacific Ocean salmon. Teams of Lawton key pals from different classrooms experience traveling the planet via Internet to communicate with their key pals. Fourth and fifth graders produce and direct the daily, in-house television newscast, *The KLAW News*, which features interviews with local leaders, such as Seattle's mayor, and stories read by primary students with Down syndrome. With social studies and language arts content about Pacific North-west Native American tribes, heterogeneous groups of students use comput-ers to design banners displaying tribal themes, which they then sew with the help of a fabric artist-in-residence.

Technology has given us an infinite number of ways to approach math-ematical concepts, social studies dilemmas, language arts productions, and artistic designs. When faced with the powers of technology, staff have found that they are, along with the students, learners and inquirers about curricu-lum. No one knows everything about any problem. For some staff, this is an uncomfortable position. For others, it is a welcome relief. Learning with tech-nology is a humbling experience and helps us appreciate what it is like for children to struggle with content. Technology has allowed our curricular practices to become far more responsive to individual student needs than we ever imagined they could be.

Ensuring Site-Based Involvement in a Community School

For many years, Lawton functioned as a reasonably successful, tradi-tionally managed school. The principal made most of the decisions, with input and participation from the staff on selected issues. Parents and the commu-nity participated in the usual parent support activities (e.g., PTA fundraising and classroom volunteerism) but rarely in school policy matters. Students and community groups were a part of the decision-making process only so far as individual teachers allowed it; there was no norm for or expectation of participation. When I first came to Lawton, one parent described it this way: "It's a nice enough staff, but we're not really asked for our opinions." A staff member said that she "knew that staff at other schools were more a part of how things were run, but we haven't taken those steps here." A com-munity observer noted: "It's *their* [the staff's] school."

Over the past several years, we have changed this picture. Lawton is the community's school. I serve as steward of the community's vision of what ought to happen for children and families. It is my job to keep all citizens in our community moving toward ever-increasing degrees of self-management and self-direction. For some staff, parents, and students, self-management is comfortable and feels right. For other community members, self-management is stressful or causes fear. We all approach leadership in different ways. It matters little that community members are in different stages as long as all work to improve and increase their own participation in the decisions that affect them. We are creating, for all, the vision that "it is our school."

Following several years of tension and in-fighting, and a subsequent period of healing, we began to bring school constituencies—staff, parents, students, community members—into the management of school life. As a result of all-school meetings and the establishment of task forces, several decisions were made.

The Lawton School Council, composed of parents, community members and staff, was established to co-manage policy decisions along with staff and the PTA board. This group meets monthly over a potluck dinner and delves into anything it thinks might improve school life for children. Initially hesitant to intervene in matters that were thought to require "professional" guidance, the group has come to feel its own power and now addresses, with the district, issues such as class size, staffing support to the bilingual program, and managing tensions among school groups. Lawton has been designated as one of 10 Seattle schools to operate free of many administrative decrees from the central office, with the School Council taking a lead role in school operation.

Along with the School Council, parents have been encouraged to become actively involved in school life and to take new roles, individually, and through the PTA. The PTA plays an assertive and constructive role in promoting its views about children's education and family rights, and staff have supported its emerging role.

While families with greater economic resources who live near the school have easily risen to this challenge of participation, it has been difficult to involve families experiencing economic pressures, who live greater distances from school or whose culture or background is different from that of the Anglo, middle-income neighborhoods surrounding Lawton. We have initiated many outreach efforts toward these families. We have created positions, funded by grants, to support them. We have established support groups (e.g., family-to-family support groups for children from Vietnamese families) and parent-education training programs. We routinely provide interpreters at major school functions. We have set up one-to-one family relationships between nearby families and central area families so that outreach occurs on an individual and personal level rather than on an organizational one. Through a relationship with a nearby university, free child and family counseling is available to the community at school. We have made overtures to the 40 school families living in nearby military housing, who frequently find their lives disrupted due to mid-school-year reassignments. We want Lawton to feel like a center of community life for our families. Although we have not yet succeeded in changing every parent or guardian's view of their role in school life, we have seen clear improvements.

Another move toward site-based management is that staff now largely run their professional lives. Though we still complain about some aspects of school life that we can't control fully (e.g., class size, bus transportation routes, etc.), we can establish our own educational direction without major interference from the district. One irony of this changing culture is that it has become difficult to use the excuse, "The district won't let us." Now the reason we don't do something to benefit children is that we haven't fully exercised our power. Staff involvement—achieved by rotating facilitation of meetings, a consensual decision-making process, participation on school committees, and the like—is increasing in all areas of school life every year. What feels like a risky or overwhelming issue this year becomes routine the next. It is a growth process for all and there is no going back.

Another focus of restructuring has been children's involvement in decision-making. We no longer believe that just knowing math facts or the capitals of the 50 states adequately prepares children for the social and occupational worlds they will enter as adults. The question we usually ask at meetings of incoming kindergarten parents, to prepare them for a school emphasizing academic, social–emotional, and self-management skills is: "What sorts of skills do you think your children will need to participate successfully in a profession when they are the age that you are tonight?" That is, what will they need to know and understand in the year 2011 or 2022 or . . .? Framing this question in terms of one's own children makes the entire debate about the purpose of education a personal and understandable one, free of much of the rhetoric of public debate. Parents want their children to be able to make sound decisions on the basis of good information sources and to be able to work successfully with lots of different people. They want their children to be happy and to manage their own lives competently.

In this context, it makes sense for children to participate in school and district policy through a Student Council or their classroom meetings, to teach children how to help one another resolve conflicts through our Conflict Helper program (typically called "Conflict Managers," "Peer Helpers," etc. in other schools) and to change our assessment practices so that students chart their own progress using portfolios, goal-setting meetings with their teachers, and, at the intermediate level, student-led conferences with their parents and teachers. Instead of just talking about student self-direction, we now provide real opportunities for practicing decision-making.

The problem with widespread involvement in decision-making is that participatory communities take more time and energy over decisions. There are times when a weary staff would just as soon drop out of a decision-making role and let me make the decision solo. There are also times when I would prefer not to have community input on yet another decision.

The positive impact of restructured decision-making, however, clearly outweighs the weariness and other hazards. If we believe that participation produces greater "ownership" in school life, then we must persevere and minimize the backsliding due to tiredness or cynicism. Our belief is strong that children are our highest priority and that we need to model and practice self-management as part of our teaching them. If we believe in greater family and staff participation in school life, then we also, by definition, believe in expanding diversity through such specific efforts as inclusion.

In light of the six elements of change and Lawton's strong commitment to embracing diversity, Mrs. Johnson's request made intuitive sense. The following account chronicles the first year of inclusion as it was incorporated, along with these other schoolwide changes, and examines the interpersonal and political dynamics of the change process.

THE REQUEST IN CONTEXT: THE CHILDREN'S FIRST YEAR

Lawton had had only a minimal history with special education. A small, part-time resource program, taught by itinerant staff housed in other schools and serving two or three students, was largely unnoticed and had no building-wide impact. Because the emphasis was placed on the general classroom as the site of instruction for all children, and because there was an instructional assistant funded by grant money in each primary classroom, Lawton had not needed the resource option. As a result, there was no negative special education baggage: no prior history of "contacting," "mainstreaming," "integration," or other uniquely special education activities. There was no resistance to changing practice as a result of the turf and ownership problems that special educators frequently impose on themselves. Lawton could approach inclusion with a clean slate.

During my first November at Lawton, I met with our three kindergarten teachers, Carol McKinney, Carol Anderson, and Dorothy Jacobsen (later replaced by Kas Baker) to discuss Mrs. Johnson's request informally. Under normal circumstances, ideas for change were brought to the entire staff and, later, to the PTA Board and School Council. In this instance, I approached these three teachers first, seeking their feedback on a proposal that would create an inclusive program, starting with kindergartners and adding new kindergartners each successive year until the program spanned kindergarten through fifth grade. They agreed to think about the proposal and meet again.

Their interest rose during the next two meetings. While they felt that we could offer a quality program to children who had formerly been excluded from the general program, the teachers were more interested in the overall positive impact that such diversification could have on our entire school community. At the time, none had training or classroom experience in special education. One had a nephew with Down syndrome attending an inclusive school in Massachusetts, and she spoke glowingly about his experience.

We looked at the pros and cons of presenting this proposal to a staff and community that have a difficult time saying "no" to new endeavors. We looked at our own values for children and at our district's track record on innovation. We considered the cynicism that some Lawton staff expressed toward our district's inability to support prior innovation areas. In the end our values for children took precedence over skepticism or reservations about "our plate being too full to take on another school focus."

Because of our uncertainty as to how the district would respond to such a major change in service, we decided to test the less manageable political waters outside our school. To reassure our own staff, we knew that we needed strong central-office and influential outside-of-district allies. Dan LeFebvre, a new district special education coordinator, had just come from a state position in Connecticut and was searching for a school or schools in which to pilot integrated forms of serving children. Our complementary political agendas were readily apparent. LeFebvre joined us with unbridled enthusiasm and valuable negotiating skills.

Connie Woods, the project manager for the Washington State Systems Change Project, was responsible for locating school districts and schools in state that were willing to become inclusive and also for assisting them in the change process. Although she had been successful finding sites in the area surrounding Seattle, the state's largest and most influential district, she had not located a school within the Seattle District itself. She needed our school; we needed her facilitative skills and the legitimacy and influence that she could provide.

By January, the six of us were meeting regularly to create a proposal, one we knew would be incomplete because it was the product of six enthusiastic people and not of an entire community. We moved at a pace somewhere between a planful strategy, and one referred to in some business circles as "Ready, Fire, Aim" pace.

The initial plan called for bringing a few kindergartners with disabilities into our three kindergarten classes. We would make a commitment to a "no exclusion" policy; that is, any child who lived in the neighborhood and, therefore, was eligible to attend Lawton would be accepted as a student. We also had out-of-neighborhood parents of children with disabilities requesting that they be admitted to Lawton. We hoped to keep the number of children with moderate and severe disabilities low so as not to create an unnatural proportion of special needs children in our school. We would not develop a parallel "special education curriculum," but we would provide a developmentally appropriate curriculum to all children and decide how to use those practices to support each student. Most important, we resolved to talk about the children in normal developmental terms and never to use the state disability labels.

While LeFebvre was our advocate for the proposal with the district management, a group that might be resistant to a change in delivery models, the rest of us initiated conversations in the school community. During a two-month period that included four discussions, the staff decided to press forward with the plan. Though the plan was modified, the majority of the staff followed the kindergarten teachers and decided to endorse it. In anticipation of gaining district approval, we agreed to monitor the pilot program on a yearly basis to see if it continued to merit support. Yet, during these discussions, it was clear to almost everyone that this was, in reality, a 6-year commitment to these children.

As in other large urban districts, timelines for each school are often driven by a centralized student assignment process. Because it was already spring and the assignment process was underway for the coming year, we moved very quickly. LeFebvre worked with Student Assignment to locate those families in our catchment area with children attending special education-type preschool, hospital, or mental health programs. A list of eight children resulted. We found their families keenly interested in exploring the new option for the children.

Juggling several agendas at once, including dealing with district procedural matters, initiating outreach and orientation to families, training and planning for involved staff, and gaining consensus from parent groups such as our PTA Board, we moved ahead with seven new children.

Six children arrived the first September morning of the new school year, two by taxi, two by district special education van, and two with their parents. The seventh student came two days later. We put aside our irritation ("Not another special education bus!") and we focused on welcoming our new children. Two of the children seemed fearful as they gazed at their new school and its hordes of older and larger children. One of these students walked behind his mother clutching her dress for security, two other students ran into the building leaving their parents to introduce us to phantom children, and two students followed their new teachers to their classes—the typical range of responses from new kindergartners.

Our seven new students were placed in three classes. The descriptions that accompanied them ranged from "developmentally delayed" (a Washington State term implying less severe disability, such as "learning disabilities" for children younger than 6) to moderately–severely disabled (with Down syndrome and/or behavioral challenges). These seven children would teach us a great deal about our belief that "children are more alike than different." Publicly committed to vague ideals, we all had private concerns about what might happen during the children's first weeks at school: What if Jonathan had violent outbursts? What if Denise, with orthopedic impairments, fell down the stairs? What if we couldn't understand Donnie's verbal approximations of "I want go bathroom"?

As the days turned to weeks and then to months, we found that the children did present many challenges. But we also learned that most of these challenges could be met through brainstorming and trial-and-error interventions. We began to understand that the outbursts, the fear of change in routine or of unpredictable events such as fire drills, or the resistance to requests demonstrated by the children were the same as those we confronted in *any* group of children. Perhaps the severity and frequency of these children's responses made the instances more visible, but the causes of the problems, and their solutions, were really no different.

That first year, we slowly learned that viewing a child in normal developmental terms, even children with more intense needs, made sense. We began to track the challenges presented by the seven children and found that those challenges were often not any more frequent or severe than the challenges presented by other "nonlabeled" children. We validated what we had always preached: that any classroom has students with a range of needs that require an effort for accommodation. We worked hard not to distinguish these seven children from others simply because they came to us with handicapping labels. We also learned that the 200-plus years of accumulated teaching wisdom represented by our staff was quite sufficient to tackle almost any problem posed by a 6-year-old. In short, there wasn't much that any of the new children could do that we hadn't seen and responded to in other teaching circumstances.

Teachers did make some accommodations for the children, but never swayed from their expectations that each child would participate fully in the classroom experience. Cooperative learning, especially at this early age, proved to be the most effective strategy for encouraging achievement and mastery for students with different skills during the same lesson. In spite of the fact that each of the seven children needed some development in the area of social skills, they all became part of their classroom's social fabric. As the months passed, so did the use of terms such as "inclusion students." At different points throughout the year, most staff and students stopped seeing "special" or "inclusion" students and simply saw unique members of their own classrooms. They differed little from any other students who needed some form of additional support.

The Supporters

In the context of the schoolwide restructuring, the new inclusionary process seemed a logical extension, an integral part of current practice. At the same time, the addition of new and challenging students to a school that was already filled to capacity, whose staff was not totally comfortable with disability issues, and in an environment in which the educational media viewed inclusion as controversial, the changes we were attempting to institute became topics for discussion that sometimes gave the move toward inclusion an identity as a separate process altogether.

I had hoped that this wouldn't be the case, that each staff member would see and experience the change as no different from anything we did for any of our other children. That thinking was naive. What became clearer over the years was that each staff person came to understand and support inclusion in his or her own way and, to some extent, at his or her own pace. We allowed people to move at their own pace, as long as that pace was in the general direction of supporting inclusive practices. Had we done differently, we would have risked experiencing the organizational sabotage that disrupts so many mandated educational innovations.

To continue the story, we have identified four significant groups involved in the changes: the children, the staff, other district observers, and the families. We describe the part each group played in the implementation of the plan, beginning with the children.

The new children and their friends. After reading the volumes of information we received from the special education agencies, we anticipated some problems with transitions for the seven children. Indeed, some problems did arise. Denise became separated from her class during one transition and ended up crying in the office. Donnie did well in class, but threw himself on the hallway floor several times during transitions. Jonathan burst into tears and verbally threatened other children when he didn't get his way.

As we came to know the children as people and not as their written case histories, we discovered that virtually every issue or challenge they raised could be effectively addressed from the perspectives of general education or typical child development rather than from special education. For example, Denise, who had some physical limitations, moved more slowly through hallways than did her peers. She would find herself at the end of the line, then trailing behind, and finally she would panic. The solution: Denise and a few classmates would leave class 2 minutes early.

Donnie's hallway tantrums were more difficult to understand. Several brainstorming sessions resulted in strategies that proved to be unsuccessful at ending his outbursts. It finally struck us that Donnie, who was having difficulty expressing his needs to unfamiliar adults, had succeeded in gaining an enormous amount of attention from several adults every time he had a tantrum. Flailing his arms and legs and screaming in the hallway was a wonderfully logical strategy. As we learned more about Donnie, we taught other children to ignore the behavior. At the same time, we tried to provide positive support to Donnie just prior to transitions. The outbursts diminished.

During the first few weeks, Jonathan, a student who had experienced severe deprivation in his home life, frequently burst into tears and threatened children near him if he thought he might lose something. Kas Baker provided primary support to him, sometimes having to hold him back from hurting himself or others. Like Donnie, Jonathan needed to feel that he was getting his fair share of attention and opportunities (e.g., computer time, snacks, one-on-one time with adults). Trying to look at the world from Jonathan's vantage point, his anxiety about the possible loss of objects or opportunities made sense, and this understanding made it easier for us to decide upon our responses. We would give him more individual cues just before he would be asked to share objects and we would coach him more in expressing his needs to classmates.

Two months into the year, we realized that every strategy we were using with Donnie, Denise, and Jonathan was simply a retooled teacher's "trick-of-the-trade" that one or more of us had employed in situations with non-labeled, general education students. The only difference with Donnie, Denise, and Jonathan was that we were using the strategies more often than we usually did with other children.

As we approached the end of the first year, the "inclusion" students had become simply Lawton students. Despite individual issues (e.g., Jonathan's continuing, though less frequent, outbursts), the children had strong, positive images as members of their classes and of the school. While peers were aware of their special needs (e.g., for emotional support to help with anger management or physical support in the case of orthopedic impairments), they seemed to view these needs as unique characteristics of the child, in the same way they viewed other children's individual traits (e.g., "James doesn't like art" or "Darnell loves computer stuff"). Our students were beginning to show us that our dreams were not only possible, but very achievable.

We watched the formation of friendships over the year. They mirrored the relationships of other children. Sometimes, the interactions were positive: Denise eating lunch with her friends, working with her computer partners on beginning word processing, attending birthday parties and sleepovers, and learning to use a jump rope. At other times, the interactions were a bit spicier: "Denise, stop pulling my hair!" or "Jennifer and Denise, you need to stop interrupting the group or we'll never finish."

At times, we had to change what one parent termed the "mother hen syndrome." We wanted each of the seven students to navigate successfully through the school day. Although each required support at times, we wanted them to depend on their own increasing competence and the school's ethos of "help one another." We did not want any of our students to interact with the new children from a "pity" or "charity" model.

In the first and second years, we found the classmates of these children often demonstrating two patterns in relating to them. The children who didn't have experience with people with disabilities and couldn't comfortably relate to them distanced themselves, but with time and shared experiences, the barriers and hesitations quickly vanished, and students came to see their new classmates as peers and not as labels. Other students found it difficult to forget that their friend(s) had special needs. Erika felt she *had* to help Donnie find his way through the crowded hallways; Tanisha *had* to show him how to do things on the playground. The children, perhaps confused about the notion of cooperative learning, were unintentionally moving our seven children toward a more subtle form of dependency.

To the friends of Donnie, Denise, and Jonathan, we posed the same questions we would pose to any staff member: Is what you are doing encouraging Denise's independence or is it something that will eventually get in her way? In conversations during classroom meetings (which were structured to help every student in each class find positive solutions to the inclusion–exclusion issues that each one of them faced, whether they bore a label or not), we found that students, even our younger primary children, could see the distinction between cooperative interactions and interactions that fostered dependency. We also found that children were able to generalize this distinction to other activities: for example, working in pairs on computers to increase their collaborative efforts or using a writing process format to develop their written language skills and to encourage them to give help to and receive help from their peer editors. We found that children's desires to help their friends—and sometimes to help them too much—became a very good learning opportunity for the entire school.

The children grew substantially during their first year. We had the same general expectations of them as we did for any student in the school. We believe that much of their growth can be attributed to that fact and to their participation in classrooms that support *all* children, although it is a struggle to provide quantitative proof. The children who entered Lawton as timid, uncertain, and shy young learners finished the year as confident (sometimes a bit overconfident) and proud school members.

Staff values, hesitation, and ownership. As they had with other major policy changes, Lawton staff had listened carefully to the proposal to include children with special needs. At first, they reacted with caution, then with haste. Spending very little time thinking about the challenges inclusion might present, the staff had seen it as an opportunity to promote and practice the accommodation of diversity, which we so easily professed in theory. Seeing similarities between inclusion and bilingual infusion, our more talkative staff saw inclusion as a civil rights issue. They began talking about how "wonderful" and "great" it would be for our school to become Seattle's first full-inclusion model.

The kindergarten teachers and I had tried to slow down the discussion. We knew that we weren't hearing from everyone and that it would be easier for intermediate teachers to agree with the discussion because they would not be impacted by actual implementation for a few years. We also knew that it was one thing to take a pro-civil rights position in public but another to make the practical adaptations required in each classroom.

Two additional meetings resulted in a "let's do it!" approach. We hoped this enthusiasm would carry us through the difficult and wearying moments. Some staff had concerns about potential problems: "We already have large classes." "What about the time it will take away from other students?" "I don't have any training in the area. . . . Will there be support for me?" "We've already shut our pull-out options and brought in kids that used to go out of Lawton for gifted programs. . . . Don't you think this is moving too quickly?" "What about waiting a year and studying the issue?"

Connie Woods attended the second meeting and addressed the hesitancy. Rather than challenging the uneasiness or brushing aside the concerns, Connie acknowledged that inclusion does take work, planning, and energy. Although the majority of the staff clearly were proponents of inclusion, it was reassuring to note that others felt comfortable voicing their concern or opposition. In the end, those who had been opposed decided to support the proposal—or at least, not to undermine it. We agreed that it was acceptable for each staff member to feel differently about inclusion and concluded that, if inclusion worked at Lawton, it would be through our support of one another.

The first year proved the importance of this mutual support. There were many instances in which we questioned ourselves, worried about whether our students were achieving adequate growth, and doubted our ability to attend one more problem-solving meeting. The moments of doubt, however, became the vehicle that allowed us to discover our greatest source of power. Staff were forced to team together to resolve issues, to lift one another's spirits, or just to laugh together. Some staff described this growing trust and passionate caring about one another as an unanticipated, but wonderful, consequence of having the new children come to our school. The sharing of support and the collaboration have continued through each year of the program, from the first year of changes in kindergarten to the current year's efforts in the more challenging intermediate curriculum areas.

We learned another lesson—to be patient with ourselves. We might not find the most effective response to a problem the first day, or the first week, or even the first month. Good intent is no guarantee of pedagogical success. Patience, when coupled with the ability to laugh at ourselves, helped us understand that success doesn't come quickly. Some issues were resolved quickly. Others, like Donnie's hallway tantrums, required much longer periods of brainstorming before we solved them.

We learned also that we had placed greater pressure on ourselves with our newly included students than we had with the majority of our other students. Because of our intense desire to demonstrate to observers—parents, other staff, other district administrators—that inclusion "worked," we initially expected the children to make more rapid progress than was reasonable. Because these children are no different from others in their patterns of plateaus and valleys, we often doomed the realization of our initial hopes to failure, or, at the very least, experienced feelings of inadequacy to the task.

When we stopped viewing the children as "pilot" children or "inclusion children" and thought of them as we thought of other children, much of the apprehension we had unwittingly brought upon ourselves dissolved. During this same year, I gave a number of workshops to staff in other schools that were initiating inclusionary practices. It was striking how frequently teachers and other educators held themselves to unrealistic and, therefore, unattainable, standards for the students' growth, thereby generating despair at their lack of success.

At the end of the first year, we finally realized that the students who had entered Lawton as "pilot" children had shown dramatic growth and that we truly had not done anything different for them than we had for any other children. We had met. We had planned. We had reached consensus. We had implemented. We had evaluated. If a strategy worked, then we institutionalized it. If not, then we went back and started the cycle again. Our belief in our own efficacy was finally grounded in a year of success—not just theory. Even though staff members had succeeded with other experiences of change (e.g., working with non-English-speaking students and parents), we had been skeptical of our own skills until we had actually created a working model.

Other district observers. That other district staff and observers had an interest in Lawton's inclusion effort was evident from the beginning. We knew we had to succeed, not only for our own students, but also to demonstrate to the larger school community that inclusion can work.

Many inclusion advocates suggest the importance of gaining a clear board of education policy in favor of the practice. With Seattle moving into a period of site-based decision-making and knowing that we had support from key central administrators for our inclusion work, we did not see a need to pursue board policy. We also knew that pursuing such a policy would require an extraordinary amount of work that would have to be diverted from building the program for children. Moving into a period of site-based decision-making, we felt that it was more important to do what we wanted. We have basically maintained that we will do what we need to do on behalf of children without stopping to check every possible ramification with the powers-that-be. Since no upper-level administrator, from the superintendent to the special education managers, acted to oppose our work, we proceeded on our own authority.

In the 1992–93 school year, Frosyne Mensendick came to Seattle as our special education director. Coming from a comparable position in Alaska, where integrated services were frequently the norm rather than the exception, she welcomed our young inclusion program as a way to highlight other programs that kept children together in their neighborhood classrooms. Given the political nature of her position within her new district, however, she could not show undue partiality toward the Lawton effort, especially in her first year in Seattle. And since the entire district was trying to pull itself out of a long history in which schools often seemed to be pitted against one another for resources and reputation, her quiet support was the best stance for her to take.

The Lawton pilot project clearly put pressure on the midlevel special education managers, educators with many years of service supporting current district service options, as they were confronted by a school that wanted to do something entirely different. The issues we raised called into question the formal organizational systems to which these managers had dedicated their professional lives. Some managers worried privately, others publicly, about whether or not quality service could actually be provided to all children in general classrooms.

While they raised both personal and professional doubts, they were also very much aware of the changing political climate. Parent advocacy groups, legislative and courtroom actions, journal reports, dissatisfaction on the part of the current teaching staff, and stories from a number of districts just outside Seattle that had embraced inclusion—all put pressure on managers to reexamine their perspectives on inclusion.

In the end, these managers generally came to support our work. Some were enthusiastic about our work; others were ambivalent. No one appeared to be actively opposed to inclusion. One supervisor said, while visiting our classrooms, that she had always been philosophically opposed to the theory of inclusion but had changed her mind after seeing children who had formerly been placed in self-contained special education classrooms faring successfully with their typical peers on a full-day basis.

The related services staff—communications disorders specialists and physical or occupational therapists—often had difficulty with our inclusion format. We maintained that there was very little need to pull children out of their general classrooms for "therapy." We wanted related services to be provided in the general classroom within heterogeneous groups of children. This would ensure that the new skills would generalize and be reinforced by other children during the greater part of the week when the therapists weren't in the classrooms. We clearly stated our preference for students learning skills that would be useful and functional in any general education classroom rather than being able to demonstrate a set of esoteric skills in a small, specialized therapy room. We wanted students to learn skills that anyone, especially parents, could easily identify and reinforce at home. To make matters worse, we all wanted to be involved in deciding which skills were taught.

Some therapists made the transition to the inclusion model with relative ease. They found a school community in which teachers and other staff eagerly sought their expertise to implement instructional programs in class-rooms. In many instances, therapists were surprised by the interest of the teachers who wanted to use their skills and perspectives with other groups of children who might benefit but were prohibited from receiving assistance because they didn't carry state handicapping labels. Others perceived us as a rather difficult, and sometimes cantankerous, group and were never able to leave their medical or "deficit" models behind. While we endeavored to show respect for the many different therapists working with us, we also maintained our philosophical position. While we sought commonalties, there were times when the discomfort between Lawton and the district special services staff could not be muffled. The solution was, generally, for the therapist in question to go to other schools where the belief systems were a better match.

Given our district's history and dynamics, I was particularly aware of the wide variety of opinions about inclusion held by one other group—my fellow principals. Some were moving toward their own versions of inclusion in systematic ways. Others were practicing it without calling it inclusion. Some principals, given the mind-boggling array of cultural–language–economic–ability needs they were already trying to support, were steadfastly opposed to any further diversification of their student bodies. Many princi-pals, given the priorities in their schools, simply were not concerned about inclusion. In the buildings of many of this group, special education options were managed and directed by central office managers rather than by build-ing and community people.

We were careful to talk about our inclusion program only in terms of how it had positively impacted our community. We avoided saying publicly that other schools ought to move in this same direction, because we know that this choice must be made by each school community. We wanted to provide one working example of inclusion in Seattle so that interested schools might explore it as an option as they sought the best ways to educate their students.

Our families. The first families to take part in the program came from a variety of early childhood special education programs and community-support networks. As their children reached school age, a common worry for these parents was over "the public schools"—their size, the number of their students, their sensational side presented by the frequently hostile local media. Because these families were already facing issues of exclusion or separation from school, our overtures to join an inclusive school community were warmly received. They were generally surprised by our invitation.

The most troubling thought for the families was that inclusion might lead to a dilution of services for their children. Coming from medical, mental health, and clinical programs, they were used to a myriad of professionals giving full attention to their children. Although they were, on the one hand, uncomfortable with the separateness of such services, there was also, on the other, a comforting element in that intense level of attention. Our promise, "We'll provide everything your child needs in her class," didn't always reassure these families. After many conversations, assurances, and meetings during the early months and the first year, we agreed with families and staff that we would closely monitor services and not hesitate to raise concerns.

Our families' anxiety was evident at the beginning of the year during an informal luncheon for families and for the staff who would serve their children. We began with introductions, then ate, and then moved to discussion. I commented that the luncheon was unusual in that it would be very rare for this particular group to be convened in the future. I explained that we didn't see a need or have a desire to schedule events only for parents of children with special needs, and that from now on, any parent–family meetings or gatherings would be "kindergarten" or "primary" or "all school" parent-family meetings. Their surprise turned to relief when they understood the implications: "Yeah, going to a meeting without having to focus on my daughter's Down syndrome would be a relief." (A few meetings of these parents only were held during the program's third year, when district staffing levels were threatened and the parents felt that it would be useful for them to work as a subgroup of the Lawton community to lobby in support of stronger staffing levels.)

This reasoning surfaced numerous times during inclusion's early years at our school. Groups such as the PTA Board or School Council would list "inclusion" briefly as among the possible topics for parent education workshops only to quickly delete the topic from the list because it artificially separated some children from the rest of their peers. We knew that many schools held special meetings about inclusion; we simply could not see the utility of such an event.

I remember my bewilderment one Saturday morning during the third year of the program when a number of parents and I were placing the last ceramic tiles of an 1,100-tile seascape on an exterior school wall. One parent introduced himself to the parent next to him on the scaffolding this way: "Hi, I'm _____. I'm _____'s dad. She has Down syndrome." That sort of introduction and labeling hadn't taken place in school since the awkwardness of our initial parent luncheons. I told him that it was surprising to hear him describe his daughter in terms of her disability. He replied that he had only made the comment out of his own social shyness of the moment and that he, too, realized how limiting such a descriptor was.

The early meetings began to cement a vital part of the support system for our children with special needs. Parents, initially hesitant about large public school offerings and battle-worn from their efforts to procure services from social service agencies, came to see Lawton as "our school" rather than as a discrete organization with which they would have to struggle.

The partnerships that arose between Lawton staff and parents of included children were not always easy. We all realized that resolving issues of educational support—what types of support would be provided, how much support was necessary, and under what conditions—was critical to the success of these children in their classrooms. Just as inclusion brought together our teaching staff in ways they had not been able to predict, so inclusion brought many of our parents into the central fold of a school community in ways they had not imagined possible. Lawton, with all of its strong and weak points, was their school to help mold and improve. The public examples of this were very evident: one parent becoming a voting member of the school's first Site Council and another becoming copresident of the PTA. Yet, it was the less public roles, the ease in approaching staff with concerns, the lack of hesitancy in advocating for or volunteering to help a child, that were more important. What we experienced through the development of active partnerships with parents of our included children was the evolution of empowered parents. Unlike the posturing or lobbying that parents often have to do for their children in specialized settings, the empowerment of these parents was felt in *all* facets of Lawton life. There were many school issues, such as supporting our bilingual staffing allocation and making progress toward a multiage class structure, in which these parents took active and vocal leadership roles.

Staff and parents knew that they spent far more time developing working agreements about these children than they did about the majority of our other students, and there were times when they resented the level of detail and amount of time required. But, generally, these staff resentments were born of weariness from the demands of teaching itself. Given time to reflect and weekends to rebound, we found that our real resentment was that we didn't know how to give *every* child that sort of thoughtful partnership. Rather than being angry over the time demanded by the inclusion component, we learned to direct our anger toward an educational system that ought to provide that same quality time for every child. Many future restructuring efforts at Lawton, therefore, became efforts to provide teachers such time and consultation for the needs of all children. The children of inclusion taught the Lawton staff and families the real meaning of school collaboration.

Simple Lessons

Inclusion came to Lawton and, within the context of our school's more comprehensive restructuring efforts, taught us nine simple and logical lessons about how a school ought to work. We would not have learned these valuable lessons if we had tried to institute inclusion as an isolated process.

Lesson 1:   Inclusion for children is a values-based decision.
Lesson 2:   Inclusion is a community restructuring issue.
Lesson 3:   "We are all experts."
Lesson 4:   Provide time to talk.
Lesson 5:   Keep it simple and understandable.
Lesson 6:   Expect and honor differences of opinion.
Lesson 7:   Focus on class size and support, not on weighted student formulas.
Lesson 8:   Inclusion becomes transparent.
Lesson 9:   Assume the authority to make decisions.

Lesson 1: Inclusion for children is a values-based decision. At Lawton, decisions are based on the following priorities: children's needs first, staff needs second, and community needs third. We brought inclusion to Lawton because it fit within our priorities and values. We did not have all the technical experience or training often considered requisite for such a change. We did believe, however, that we could provide a nurturing and challenging environment for children who would normally have been sent away from their neighborhood schools. We felt that we could construct a learning community to benefit all children and staff.

Had we done a lengthy and full analysis of all possible pros and cons related to this move, we might have backed away from the commitment. If we had based our school improvement decisions on a different set of priorities, such as staff needs and/or working conditions first, we might have approached the process very differently. Specifically, if we had decided that we could not ask the staff, already burdened with exhausting work and short on time for planning, to give additional time to make this happen, we might have diplomatically answered the initial parent request for inclusion with the following response: "While we appreciate your concern, we are already addressing too many other issues."

Instead, we considered the request in light of our values. At this point, there was really only one approach we could take—to honor the request and make the change work in spite of our already full agenda. Children, all children, have a right to be educated in their neighborhood schools. Although we might occasionally complain about the additional time and energy it would require, it was our job to change the school to fit the needs of children rather than to exclude children because they didn't fit the school. As a result, a diverse group of children and families have accompanied us on our journey. Even though there are areas that still need improvement, we have succeeded in creating the community we envisioned. Strong commitment to our values made the decision a simple one.

Lesson #2: Inclusion is a community restructuring issue. Inclusion at Lawton was successful because it was instituted within the context of general school restructuring, which included: increasing the diversity of our students, using general classroom support models rather than pull-outs, establishing multiage and integrated technology classrooms, making extensive use of cooperative and peer–cross-age tutoring, working with children in ways that were developmentally appropriate, and inviting the full community into school governance matters. Attempting to become an inclusive school in the absence of these changes would have made the struggle much more difficult.

We sought ways to involve all students in the life of their classrooms. Teaching children to use cooperative learning skills while working with computers and video cameras created structures in which children with widely varying characteristics could find success within the same tasks. Providing children with skills to help the group accomplish its task rather than focusing on individual achievement allowed children to understand that they needed to help one another throughout the day. Continual reinforcement of the notion that we are all teachers and learners allowed our students to see that working in diverse groups is natural way to proceed with learning.

Lesson 3: "We are all experts." A frequent explanation for resistance to inclusion is that general classroom teachers lack sufficient training or expertise in special education. At Lawton, we believe that we all have the expertise required for including students with special needs in classrooms, because we all have expertise in *child development and teaching*. From person to person, the degree of expertise and the level of comfort with problem-solving may differ, but we have all had experience helping children learn.

The "special education" issues we anticipated when the children who were to be included arrived at Lawton turned out to be mostly "typical child development" issues. As we mentioned earlier, the included children displayed no behavior that we hadn't seen in other children. What we lacked most was confidence in our own expertise and insight. The labels that accompany special education students, even those who are included, often undermine the confidence and dim the extraordinary insight that most teachers have about children. At Lawton, we learned to value our expertise in many challenging situations: working with children whose families speak another language, or enriching the program for very creative children who are bored with school activities, or supporting the development of communication for children who are frustrated because they are unable to express themselves clearly to others.

Lesson 4: Provide time to talk. Merely affirming the values that guided our restructuring, our commitment to diversity and our belief in our own expertise, is not enough. Without time to talk and plan, the values cannot be lived. In many schools, innovations are often planned and coordinated by staff at the end of long, exhausting days, in miniconferences in the hallways or standing over copier machines. As I conduct workshops for teachers and administrators, I seldom find staff opposed to the idea of inclusion, but I do consistently meet educators who resist adopting the practices because they don't believe their districts will give them the time to do a quality job.

Staff need time to talk, to support one another, and to solve problems associated with children's needs. At Lawton, we have attempted to provide staff with the time to meet with one another during the school day. Grant funding provides every teacher with at least weekly consultation times, and we've used available nonclassroom staff to provide coverage for such meetings. Other grant moneys provide additional paid meeting time beyond the contracted day for staff to plan children's programs. Although these measures still don't provide enough time to do all the necessary planning, they make a solid start. They also help to build a sense among staff that their time and abilities are honored.

Scheduling time to talk is not always easy for teachers. At first, several teachers at Lawton felt uncomfortable about taking time from the instructional school day. Eventually they realized that the time they spent planning allowed them to structure their teaching time more effectively and that the needs of their students really required a shift to some combination of direct teaching and consultation–facilitation work. It is a trade-off in which the advantages outweigh the disadvantages.

Lesson 5: Keep it simple and understandable. Much of the discussion about inclusion in the media and in journals uses special education jargon. Labels for syndromes and character traits replace descriptions of what children really *do*. These discussions can intimidate individuals or groups of people contemplating a move toward inclusion.

We found that talking about children in terms of their behavior and class-room needs was more direct and clear for parents. We decided to avoid terms that parents didn't understand and that were useless to our problem-solving work. "Passive–aggressive behavior," "Down syndrome," and "range of mo-tion" are terms that don't help most people understand a child's needs. Our staff asked related services personnel to rewrite IEPs, if they were written in lan-guage that was not readily understood by parents. We insisted that IEPs and other planning documents be written around activities that have direct, func-tional application to real classroom and home life rather than around activities or skills that can only be implemented in highly specialized "therapy settings."

We believe that the labeling of students, whether the term describes them as "normal," "included," or "advanced," has little or no value in helping us plan for a child. Children are more complex than the educational labels we use to sort them by for legislative convenience.

By talking about a child's behavior, we can energetically engage staff and parents in the discussion about those parts of the lives of their students and children to which they can immediately relate. Their interest in conver-sations about abstractions, which have little linkage to their own experiences, diminishes quickly—especially at the end of the day.

Lesson 6: Expect and honor differences of opinion. Inclusion at Lawton was sparked by a parent's request. That spark was fanned by a small group into a flame, which symbolized the endorsement of the entire school com-munity. All of the community members came to inclusion, as they did to every other part of our restructuring, with their own perspectives, their own levels of comfort, their own skills, and their own willingness to move ahead, and the degree of acceptance varies at each of these levels.

For a brief moment at the beginning, those of us most involved with the idea of Lawton as an inclusive community unrealistically hoped that we would find 100% of the school energetically supportive of the concept. We forgot that consensual decisions don't require 100% participation. The best philo-sophical base and well-supported theories can't assuage the worry that some feel about adapting their classroom activities to meet the needs of all chil-dren and enable them to be successful participants. Our decision-making continues to require open dialogue about each person's level of acceptance and concerns about the issues. This honesty can be particularly difficult to maintain, because some staff are not as comfortable in expressing their views as others are. While most staff strongly endorsed inclusion, a few were hesi-tant, but willing to support the commitment of their colleagues.

Lesson 7: Focus on class size and support, not on weighted student formulas. Working conditions within schools frequently frustrate educators. Sometimes, this frustration is vented on children with special needs—particularly when the students have been placed in classrooms without the unforced consent of classroom staff. "You can't possibly expect me to teach her! If she's placed in my room, I want a full-time aide." "He's worth three of my other students." "How am I supposed to teach the rest of my class if I'm always having to attend to . . .?" These statements reflect the attitudes teachers often adopt when they are required to implement inclusion by administrative decree.

We found that inclusion had little to do with tired or stressed staff. Inclusion does take much time and planning, but we know that the main factors impacting working conditions at Lawton are *class size and the harsh social conditions faced by many children on a daily basis.* Our included children certainly bring challenges to classrooms, but we generally find that we are less concerned about the support and planning we can provide them than we are about the support we can provide many other children in our school. When we ask educators to name the children whose needs they feel are unmet, thereby causing the educators stress, they most often mention the nonlabeled, high-risk children who are not identified or supported by any categorical or school-intervention process. The public cry when inclusion goes wrong is that children are placed in classrooms without any support, when, in fact, included children often bring support with them to the classrooms in which they are enrolled.

At Lawton, class size ranges from 26 to 31 children. Although many districts and states would consider such numbers as fairly low, we believe they are too high, even under the best of circumstances. With grant-funded aide support for our teachers, we may tinker with the numbers, but we know that the answer does not lie in minor alterations, but rather in a structure that allows teachers classrooms of 20 to 24 children. With fewer students, they can more easily attend to the variety and complexity of the children they teach.

We avoid any discussion of "weighted student formulas," because we believe that this numeration makes scapegoats of "included," or "bilingual," or "highly creative," or "homeless" or "————" children, when issues of class size and support should relate to *all* children. Today, teaching means working with conditions of diversity and complexity. Solutions to challenging working conditions must be addressed systematically and not focus on specific groups of children.

Lesson 8: Inclusion becomes transparent. In this chapter and throughout this book, we have referred to groups of children with special needs as "included children," or we have used similar terms. For the purposes of this chapter, these terms serve as a way for the reader to identify the children of whom we speak. The reality at Lawton is that there is no "inclusion program" and no "inclusion students." There are simply students. In the classroom, Denise is a student member of her class. The "inclusion program" is essentially transparent. It exists only so that the school district can follow its funding and legal requirements.

In our school, the saying, "Label Jars, Not People," makes sense. Because we believe that we understand every child, labels serve no useful purpose and only get in the way of describing children's needs. They also inhibit high expectations for every student. We believe that the best inclusion program—like the best bilingual programs, the best Highly Capable programs, the best of any kind of programs—is no inclusion program. Indeed, the best learning opportunities are provided children who learn in their own classrooms with their peers.

Lesson 9: Assume the authority to make decisions. Inclusion made sense for Lawton, not because of district or state politics, but because we felt it contributed to, and was a part of, our restructuring. The school community has learned to use its power base for positive change. We used to believe that we couldn't make many of the changes we wanted—because of district or state regulations, union contracts, historical practice, or financial constraints. We now challenge that thinking and find creative ways—sometimes in collaboration with other district or community allies—to establish new practices. We tried to keep the impetus for change within ourselves, rather than granting it to external forces or organizations.

We don't always feel comfortable in taking leadership in roles that, in the past, resided with those outside the school. Sometimes we do fall back into patterns of trying to predict what others will think of our initiatives before we have even figured out how our own community will respond. Yet, we also see definite improvement in our leadership skills. Issues that we would have deferred to others a few years ago are ones that we now chose to address. Issues that today make us feel nervous in addressing will probably seem routine in future years as we become more accustomed to managing our own affairs.

In a period of restructuring and site-based decision-making, it is logical for schools to make these decisions. We know that the reality of systems in our district or state will, on occasion, cause us to alter or even cancel our initiatives, but these situations have been rare. In most instances, people have been willing to support our work after hearing our rationale for changes. This has certainly been the case with inclusion. We have had to make some accommodations to the district; the district, however, has been willing to make *major* accommodations in its practice in order to support a school that is moving in a new direction. By establishing clear goals, reaching out to potential allies, and acting with constructive authority, we found that we no longer had to engage in confrontational or "hard ball" politics. We have learned to make values-based decisions for ourselves.

THE OUTCOME OF THE REQUEST

Children with many types of learning needs, interests, and backgrounds come to work and play together in our classrooms. This is good for *all* our children. Our teaching is challenged by such diversity, but our teaching is also better for *all* children because we have had to find effective ways to involve everyone.

The initial parent's request on behalf of other children with disabilities fit into our school's move toward change. In another context, we might still have made the move, but it would have been much harder to accomplish. That parent's simple request and our successful effort to include previously excluded children have made our school a richer and more enjoyable place in which to work and learn.

CHAPTER 4

Creating Together the Tools
to Reinvent Schools:
A School/University Partnership

Dianne L. Ferguson and Gwen Meyer

Like a lot of partnerships, we don't remember exactly when this one formed. Probably it grew slowly over time from a small agreement to something much more complicated and multifaceted. We are on the faculty at the University of Oregon (as an associate professor and a research assistant). Three years ago Dianne stood next to the overhead projector in a fifth-grade classroom at South Valley Elementary School to invite the faculty to participate in an ongoing research project.

Funded by the U.S. Department of Education, the project was in its third year of investigating ways to facilitate the inclusion of students with severe disabilities in general education classrooms. There were several strands to this rather large project, which already included 15 different schools. Some efforts focused on careful measurement of teachers' use of a set of procedures for making decisions about how students with disabilities might be included, what they might learn that related to their Individual Education Plans, and what happened to students' learning and social relationships when teachers used these strategies and tools.

The focus of the study we invited South Valley to join was much more open ended. We wanted to know "what happened" when schools included students with severe disabilities who had previously attended school elsewhere. We asked the South Valley faculty if we could spend time informally visiting their classrooms and talking to them about events. Our interpretivist research project sought to understand rather than to prescribe. We explained that we would talk to people about things we noticed, interview everyone who was willing to give us time, and ask what people thought about how things were proceeding. In fact, we promised to write an account of what we saw over the course of the year and share it with faculty and staff the following summer. We also offered to help when asked, but made it clear that our help was not a condition and our ideas could be safely ignored or rejected. We promised as much discretion, fairness, and open-mindedness as we could muster.

The invitation must have been reassuring, perhaps even complimentary, or maybe just nonthreatening and easy to accommodate. In any case, the faculty and staff agreed to allow three of us to begin visiting, watching, and listening to what happened when South Valley became the first school in the district to "take back" students with severe disabilities. Keith Noble, South Valley's principal, viewed our proposal as a way to gather the information he needed to report the results of a state-funded school improvement project already underway at South Valley as well as to collect information on this new effort to "include" students previously excluded from Green River School District classrooms. Both initiatives were supported by a state 2020 Grant for school improvement.

What none of us realized was that understanding "what happened" at South Valley would take longer than one school year and would change much more than what happened to a small number of students with disabilities. We didn't write the promised case study in the summer of 1992; somehow we didn't know enough. We had had many discussions about the pages and pages of fieldnotes and interview transcripts we had collected, but what it all signified still eluded us. So we kept visiting, watching, and listening. Our connections grew more varied, and our roles changed gradually. We visited first as researchers, but soon after as practicum instructors supporting student teachers from our graduate teacher preparation program. As educators who might have some useful ideas, we were invited to planning meetings about students and projects. We invited South Valley teachers to our university classrooms to help us teach our aspiring student teachers. Our relationships with South Valley and its faculty changed and changed us. Our fieldnotes and interview transcripts were being supplemented by meeting minutes, practicum instructor observations, cooperating teacher observations, graduate student portfolios and assignments, lecture notes, classroom activities, course evaluations, and many, many conversations both among ourselves and with various personnel at South Valley. This chapter represents our effort to organize and analyze these various records into a chronicle that captures the changes in ourselves, in the school, and in what we are trying to accomplish collectively. Of course, three years is hard to capture in a single essay. We emphasize a few stories and events that seemed, then and now, to be formative and instructive for all of us. Perhaps they will be for you as well.

THE PARTNERS

South Valley Elementary School

With a student population of nearly 500, South Valley Elementary School is the largest of the five elementary schools in Green River School District. The District serves mostly small agricultural and logging communities, of which Salmon Lake is the largest. The flagging of the timber industry continues to threaten the economic base of this eastern edge of the southern Cooper Valley. The year South Valley was completed, *Newsweek* featured Green River School District as one of the first in the nation to close schools because of lack of funds. Always a fiscally conservative community, not a single school levy had passed on the first attempt since 1912 and, in 1976—the year that South Valley opened—there was simply no reserve to keep the schools operating from before Christmas until the levy finally passed in January.

South Valley began with the faculty from three recently closed rural schools and by the early 1980s had earned a reputation as a "tough" school where student discipline was a problem and the members of the faculty were, as a group, somewhat unfocused and not well organized. One teacher who remembered those early days reported that when she was transferred to South Valley, she cried for three days.

When Keith Noble arrived as the new principal in 1987, he found that, although the staff was accustomed to weekly faculty meetings, and a few small groups of teachers met together for planning at other times, there was really no cohesiveness among the faculty as a larger group. The last two principals had served for one and two years, respectively, which compounded South Valley's problems and clouded its image with inconsistent leadership. Although recently, some strides had been made, some faculty members felt that the safety and productivity of everyone continued to be threatened by the lack of discipline and that more than a few parents enrolled their children in the school reluctantly. Teachers also remember that the staff at South Valley was ready for a change, and some of the teaching staff were excited about the possibility of reform or restructuring in response to a growing state interest in creating 21st Century Schools. One of the first whole-school efforts was to work with faculty from the University of Oregon to address the school's discipline problems.

By the time we began to get involved with South Valley, four years later, a lot had changed. Under Principal Noble's leadership and the growing leadership of the new school Site Council, South Valley had received three consecutive school improvement grants. This participation in the Oregon Department of Education's 2020 Program provided the resources to turn around the "tough school" reputation, thus creating a newly positive and increasingly supportive climate for both students and staff. Soon after, teachers organized into grade teams and began to meet regularly. By 1989, teachers were shifting their school improvement efforts from managing student behavior to thinking about changes in curriculum design and teaching practices that might result in better student learning.

Of course, not all the faculty felt comfortable with some of the changing norms, and a number of teachers transferred to other schools or opted for early retirement. As replacements were hired, the median age of the faculty dropped, further changing the overall climate of the school community and generally increasing the incidence of pregnancies, request for job shares, and family leaves.

Over the course of the next three years, a substantial number of changes occurred in school structures, the culture of teacher work, and the number and types of curriculum and teaching experiments. The following list summarizes South Valley's efforts by the spring of 1990, when a new set of changes involving students with disabilities brought the school to our attention.

Emerging Reforms

- Chapter 1 Elementary and Secondary Education Act services merged into general education classrooms.
- Chapter 1 teachers were replaced with more educational assistants.
- Two educational assistants were assigned to each grade team.
- Additional time was generated so assistants meet weekly with teacher teams.
- The Site Council, originally formed in 1988, began to manage more and more school operations and decisions.
- Pupil Assistance Team met to problem-solve with teachers about challenging students.
- There was more involvement in community issues and projects by school faculty and students.
- Kindergarten teachers experimented with "developmentally appropriate practices."
- Curriculum–teaching experiments by Grade 1 team began in response to new group of kindergarten graduates.
- Some teachers combined classrooms and team-teaching units.
- Discussion took place about creating some "schools-within-school," using nongraded and mixed-age–ability groupings.
- Discussion arose about including parents on curriculum committees.
- Exploring new student assessment options was discussed.

Summer 1990 initiatives. Prior to fall 1990, students eligible for special education services in Salmon Lake received support in one of three ways. Students with learning difficulties were typically "pulled out" to Learning Resource Centers (LRCs). South Valley's LRC, for example, staffed by 2 full-time special educators and 2 educational assistants, provided this kind of out-of-classroom remediation for about 65 students in a typical week. Students with moderate and severe disabilities, as we've already mentioned, were bused to a self-contained classroom in a nearby city that was operated by an Education Service District (ESD). At least, this had become the practice soon after the passage in 1975 of the Education for All Handicapped Children Act (EHA). Initially, the district tried to assign these more disabled students to South Valley, the largest and newest elementary school, with what seemed at the time the most appropriate facilities and resources. Efforts to "mainstream" a few more significantly disabled students had been unsuccessful. Teachers who recalled the stories reported that, although faculty had been generally supportive of the idea, there was little assistance and support and teachers felt unprepared and inadequate.

Students from Green River District with "mild" disabilities, who were not considered "learning disabled," had for some years attended a self-contained district classroom housed at South Valley. The teacher, two educational assistants, and the small group of students had kept to themselves over the years; the staff reported to the district special education supervisor, but did not really involve themselves in the life of the school or its changes. During the middle 1980s, the teacher had tried, with only limited success, to secure involvement of these Room 3 students in field trips and other essentially "social" events.

A new superintendent during the 1989–90 year had brought a number of new central office staff and initiatives to Green River. One of these was a commitment to making Green River one of the first Oregon districts to respond to growing calls for school reform and restructuring, formalized in the 1991, Education Act for the 21st Century (1991, House Bill 3565). Within special education, the Oregon Department of Education identified the implementation of supported education as one of seven major goals in the state plan. This initiative called for local school districts to move away from a separate, segregated system of special education service delivery toward a flexible and creative array of supportive education services that would provide free appropriate public education to students with disabilities in their home schools and communities.

School year 1990–91 initiatives. During the 1990–91 school year, the district created a supported education leadership team, the members of which attended three 2-day workshops in Portland, sponsored by the Oregon Department of Education. One of the South Valley teachers was on this team. In addition, the district sent a team of educators to a summer institute focused on inclusion in Montreal, Canada.

South Valley's 2020 Grant of 1991 included specific objectives aimed at integrating special education students into general education classrooms as well as objectives concerning improved teacher collaboration to accomplish this and other initiatives. The students everyone envisioned integrating, however, were the students currently being "pulled out" to the resource center and maybe some of those from Room 3—eventually. No one really anticipated the swift and dramatic changes that would bring students with quite significant disabilities into South Valley's general education classrooms even before the resource room students returned from pull-out.

During spring 1991, Green River District officials decided to stop sending elementary-age students with moderate and severe disabilities out of district. Instead, beginning in the fall, one student at a time would return to South Valley's Room 3. While South Valley was not the neighborhood school for all these returning students, its history as the district "special education school" led to the choice of Room 3 as the first stop on the students' educational journey toward inclusion.

Concerned about these new demands on Room 3 staff, Noble engineered the departure of the teacher in order to hire one with specific expertise in teaching students with the more severe disabilities. The district special education supervisor, who doubled as the principal of a neighboring elementary school, approached us, inquiring about new graduates from the teacher preparation program who might be prepared for the challenge of taking on Room 3—and then trying to retire it by helping other teachers to include these students in their classrooms. Later that summer, the new Room 3 teacher we had recommended, Joni Fox, Educational Assistants Meg Adams and Lucy Balter, Principal–Special Education Supervisor Art Duffy, new Special Education Supervisor–elect Kelly Jenkins, and Grade 4 teacher, Beth Gibson, who had all agreed to "include" the first returning student, participated in a 3-day summer institute on inclusion offered by the Schools Projects, our program at the University of Oregon. None of the remaining special education staff at South Valley attended or seemed involved in the "supported education" project.

Schools Projects, University of Oregon

The small group of faculty that comprise the Schools Projects had been active since 1985, developing ideas and materials to support improved educational experiences for students with severe disabilities. This focus on people with severe disabilities is a long-standing one at the University of Oregon and has generated research and development activity directed toward a range of community issues, including employment, community living, and the experiences of families, in addition to schools and education.

In 1991, we were in the middle of our research project on inclusion. We had also just initiated a new project that would offer summer institutes to assist teachers in forming ongoing work groups to implement ideas about and strategies for the inclusion of students with disabilities. We also took responsibility for coordinating the University's master's degree and certification programs within the Division of Special Education and Rehabilitation.

Most important here is the fact that everyone at the Schools Projects was a special educator. Our values and ideas regarding inclusion of students with disabilities emerged from our experiences as teachers and, for Dianne Ferguson, as a parent of a son with severe disabilities. Our research, by that summer, was forcing us to ask some new questions. We realized that effecting inclusion of students with severe disabilities would be complex, but our special education backgrounds had not helped us to anticipate the breadth and depth of that complexity.

Throughout the schools participating in our research, we were noticing a common phenomenon (discussed in Chapter 1) that we came to call "bubble kids," or "velcro kids." In more than a few classrooms where students with severe disabilities were "included" they still seemed set apart—immediately recognizable as different—not so much because of any particular individually identifiable impairment or disability, but because they were doing different things from the other students, using different "stuff," often working with different people. Too often students who seemed to have joined were not really included as members of the classroom.

We needed to understand better why this was happening. Our experience with the team from South Valley at our Summer Institute on Inclusion prompted us to seek their participation in our study. We reasoned that their new effort to include students previously sent out-of-district would provide a rare opportunity to watch and understand what happened from the beginning. Would students join or become members? Would there be "bubbles"? If there were, could we understand why? Could we draw people's attention to them and burst them?

Creating Together

Now, three years later, much has changed, both at South Valley and at the Schools Projects. We next describe these changes in terms of achievements and lessons, struggles and supports. Finally, we hope we can draw a portrait of a partnership between a school and one of its many resources (which happens to be a university program). Together the partners are not only working to build an elementary school whose mission statement is becoming more reality than vision, but their collaborative efforts are also broadening the knowledge of the university faculty and providing inspiration for the creation of new projects that are even more comprehensive in vision and scope.

We think many schools face the challenges, make the mistakes, and achieve the successes of South Valley, though not all have exactly the same resources or do it in the same way. Although they speak with pride about the changes that have occurred at their school over the past three years, the faculty would tell you that reinventing the school has not been easy. They will also tell you, with humility, that they don't have it all figured out yet and that it is still a work in progress. Still, we think South Valley's faculty have much to teach others. For three years they have not lost sight of their vision as they struggled to assume the new responsibilities of teaching and leadership, even at times when it has appeared that they might never achieve it.

We have organized our portrait into three snapshots, each one capturing one of the three years. Each depicts the main events, struggles, and lessons from that year, and is summarized by a phrase drawn from South Valley's mission statement: "Creating together the tools to build our dreams: Respecting Diversity, Realizing Potential, Building Futures."

YEAR 1: RESPECTING DIVERSITY

Joni Fox began her new job with six students who had attended Room 3 the year before, and Crystal, the first returning student. Before school had even begun, all seven students were reassigned to five different classrooms. One of the Grade 3 and one of the Grade 5 teachers (Teresa Lester and Mary R. Crane) took two students each. Crystal, the first of the more "severe" students to return, was assigned to Beth Gibson's Grade 4 class.

Asta Thorsdottir, one of our new master's program students, had been teaching elementary grades in Iceland for more than 15 years and wanted to learn about including students with all kinds of disabilities. She was the first general educator we had ever admitted to our special education master's degree program. At least we thought of her that way. Asta had also completed a graduate certificate in special education in Iceland, but had worked far longer as a "regular" grade teacher.

It was an eventful year. Joni had worked for many years for a variety of disability-related organizations, but this was her initiation as a classroom teacher. Asta was shy about speaking English, certain she had a lot to learn, and not sure if her experiences as a teacher would help or hinder her efforts.

Kelly Jenkins and Art Duffy wanted the supported education project to succeed. It had taken a lot of talking and learning to get to the point of "bringing students back." It had to succeed. Changing Room 3 was only one of several ventures being launched at the school. We were anxious to help and document whatever happened in Room 3, certain that we would learn things that might help other schools follow the same path toward including students with disabilities.

False Start

The plan was to reintroduce students slowly. As each student's transition and adjustment to the new school was successful, more students would follow. As South Valley's staff demonstrated that the district could provide appropriate schooling for students with special learning needs, a new set of transitions could begin from South Valley to the students' neighborhood schools.

Even though they knew little about Crystal, Joni and Beth worked closely together. They involved her at the beginning of the day for community circle, "Where we all get together, talk, and get the day started as a community." Crystal also joined writer's workshop, recesses, physical education, lunch, and music. In the beginning, things went well. Beth reported: "Crystal was able to work with assistance really well—doing what the rest of the class was doing. She watched and really wanted to do exactly what everybody else was doing. We were all learning together." During the second week of school, however, Crystal began to present some challenges. Beth provided this interpretation: "Crystal didn't have the background information that the other kids brought as far as experiences, or she didn't remember or want to talk about them. So writing broke down and her behaviors started. She would spit and hit as she walked through the room."

The troubling behaviors occurred in other parts of the building as well. Due to his concern about the safety of other students, the stress teachers were experiencing, property damage, and the success of the Room 3 project, Keith called a meeting to rethink Crystal's assignment to South Valley. Joni, although stressed and frustrated, was determined not to "give up on Crystal" and planned to try some "heavy-duty advocacy" to secure additional resources.

Not all the teachers at the meeting had experienced Crystal's most challenging behaviors, yet all joined in the brainstorming discussion that resulted in a decision to hire a third classroom assistant for Room 3 the very next morning. Joni also identified some university faculty who could help in developing a more focused behavior support plan. Crystal's mother, who was not at the meeting, was concerned about Crystal's behavior, but was relieved to learn that staff seemed willing to keep trying.

Two weeks later, nothing had really changed except that frustrations and emotions were running higher. A second, "pre-IEP" meeting was scheduled and began with Joni reporting: "We've tried everything and I'm at my rope's end. I don't know what else to do." Although she said that "as a professional and a teacher," she was still "not ready to give up," her conflicting feelings were quite evident when shortly afterwards she also said: "I hate to give up on this kid, but personally I and my staff are tired and don't want to be spit on anymore." She offered an even longer list of additional supports and resources that she wanted to have put in place. Keith heard the conflicting emotions and spoke to the "big picture," saying, "The most successful place for Crystal isn't here. A more restrictive setting would give her the structure she needs." Discussion ensued, ending when Art called for a roll call vote. Six of the staff voted for Crystal to stay. Joni was "on the fence," and Keith thought Crystal should return to special education. Last to speak, Art declared, "She should go back to Ducktown. We're not emotionally ready for her." His declaration, although it didn't coincide with the vote count, was restated as the "decision of the team."

After Crystal's departure, no one felt good about the experience, because all of them had really tried to make it work. But in the end, Crystal had failed at South Valley, and South Valley had failed Crystal. Crystal's mother was upset and angry that a new placement decision was made without her.

Recovering from False Starts

We all spent the two weeks after Crystal left trying to figure out what had happened and why. The various explanations that emerged seemed not only to renew the group's conviction, but also to provide some needed focus, especially around how things might be handled differently, who was in charge, and what they were really trying to accomplish.

How could we do this better? It didn't take long for the group to realize that Crystal's transition to South Valley could have been handled differently. Perhaps if Noble and the teachers had met Crystal the previous spring, it would have helped them to anticipate what kinds of capacities and resources they would need. More than one person pointed to lack of information and communication about Crystal and her needs as a major problem. In retrospect, it was clear that they had needed more time, more rapport-building, more structure, and more sensitivity and familiarity.

What are we really trying to do? Although Green River's central administration supported bringing students back home, there was no clear policy that students living in the district would go to school in the district. The long history of sending certain kinds of students away was not really replaced by a firm decision to bring back all previously exported students. The decision to send Crystal back had been possible in part because the option remained open. Crystal had never been a student in the district—she was an experiment. Crystal had a reputation and a history as an *out-of-district* student. Even when she returned, she was a "district-class student" earning her way back to her neighborhood school. Because she was a child without a school, the old assumptions and mechanisms remained available. It was a sobering realization. What were they really trying to do? Bring back students with severe disabilities? Build the capacity of the district to educate all students by letting South Valley remain "the special education school," or somehow help all the schools in the district manage a wider range of different students? The supported education project remained fuzzy.

Who's in charge here? It was becoming evident that there was really no clear leader for the supported education project and no mutual understanding about who was in charge of making decisions. Should the special education supervisor or the principal make decisions regarding Room 3? Were there different types of decisions that should be made by groups of people? This was going to be harder than they thought. Roles would change, and people would have to make decisions others had made in the past. Everyone would have to learn things that had simply not been part of their job descriptions. The definitions of roles, responsibilities, "ownership," and "support" would continue to change for the rest of the year and into the next. Three things about that first year stand out now as characterizing both the struggles and the accomplishments: Joni's lone crusadership, a small, quiet resistance that led to systemic inclusion, and the faculty's capacity to rise to repeated challenges.

Joni's lone crusadership. As soon as Crystal left, Joni threw herself into making sure Room 3's remaining students spent as much time as possible in their assigned general education classrooms. She and her two assistants swept through the school, crusading to "transform Room 3," to create "whole-building change, to have an impact on the whole district about how special education should be done." By the end of the year, the project had gained seven more students, each of whom was more severely disabled than any student who had previously attended South Valley, and all were assigned to general education classrooms.

Joni was a promoter and change agent in her own mind and in all her actions at South Valley. She personalized the district decision to "bring back kids" into a day-to-day crusade to "change attitudes" and to promote the images of her students. For a first-year schoolteacher, even an experienced

educator like Joni, the task set by the district's new commitment was formi-
dable and frightening. She was, in her own words, "petrified" in the beginning. Some, like Keith and Kelly, encouraged her to take a slow careful approach; but Joni was both eager and ambitious. In the end, she did everything
at once, calling this "a comprehensive approach." She was concerned about
building a good relationship with teachers, interested in laying a careful foundation so that the more severely disabled students to come would not "blow
everybody out of the water," and absolutely committed to providing teachers whatever supports they wanted: "The support will be there if the teacher
is feeling she needs it, and I will do everything within my physical capabili-
ties to provide that support, . . . because I think actions really do speak much
louder than words, and through our actions we've done a lot of education of
these teachers."

Her efforts took a toll, though, and she was often tired, frustrated, anxious, and confused. Of course, Joni wasn't the sole provider of support. She
managed, over the year, a growing staff of classroom assistants, assigned and
orchestrated to be at just the right place at just the right time so that teachers received the "support" required to make it possible for her supported
education students to be present and involved.

The scheduling complexity grew as the year progressed, requiring mas-
terful planning and management. In part this responsibility rested solely with
Joni, because she was always working with *her* students and *her* staff to effect a change in how "special education was delivered" in Green River. Within
the first few weeks of school she became a *teacher without a classroom*, as
her students moved out into general education classes, plying her teaching
skills almost everywhere but Room 3. While she sought to collaborate and
influence all levels of the system, from individual classroom teachers to building and district administrators and school board councils, she also struggled
to become a *member* of any team, at least until near the end of her tenure.

Joni and the existing resource room staff never joined forces, which created a good deal of confusion for others in the school. Why, for example,
should Joni's students be included during difficult academic lessons when
even more able, but still needy students, were being accommodated in the
Learning Resource Center? If seemingly more able students needed to leave
the classroom for necessary learning supports, and Joni's students did not,
did that mean they were not learning? Who was this special educator with
the message and approach completely different from all the special educators South Valley had known so far? For their part, the LRC staff simply continued on their way, not particularly objecting to her activities, but not seeking
to pull her into the existing special education team either. The contrast in
teaching philosophy and style was more obvious, and obviously confusing,
to the classroom teachers.

Joni devoted herself completely to her teaching and her mission at South Valley, often working long days, into the evenings and over weekends. She faced issues with energy and passion, though some would say, not always with tact and grace. Nevertheless, her uncompromising commitment to being the consummate *teacher without a classroom* created for others a context in which to question and learn just how to become teachers for these more diverse students. Her vision, commitment, and mission never faltered during her time at South Valley, even when challenged. In her words:

> I felt that I had been given this mission and I packed up my suitcase and I've been traveling this journey with the teachers at the school and with the parents and the kids and with my staff, and we've reached our destination, so to speak, of having the kids integrated. Now I'm looking back saying, "Well, what happened to the administrators and the support that needs to go along with this?"

"Support" for Joni meant, and continued to mean, more classroom assistants to be with *her* students in their general education classrooms. She was teaching South Valley's faculty that *person* support was the most critical variable in successful integration and inclusion. And many of the staff learned this lesson well. By March, teachers were enthusiastic about Joni's approach to support—at least most of them. One of the Grade 5 teachers reported that:

> I have had a really, really lot of success. I've had Mark and Jane. They've done really fantastically. . . really grown this year. It would not have been possible without the support from Room 3. Besides Mark and Jane, Pat Fredrick and Meg Vaughn [Joni's classroom assistants] have worked with five of my really low spellers and got them excited, working hard, and trying to do well. It's been really successful for my whole class.

Another teacher said, "It's been a great success. I definitely believe in this." A second-grade teacher found that her three students "worked magic in my room. It's hard for me to share the stories and the things that have happened. It's been wonderful." A third-grade teacher, just beginning to receive Room 3 students, decided:

> I'm the enrichment program for the third grade, and I just have to say I can't think of a better enrichment experience than the kids in the room. It's just wonderful. We're still at the stage where everybody is real helpful. I've never done this before, but somebody is always there when I need it. The transition into the room—the kids were really ready, really excited. The support's always been there.

Only one small voice reported a slightly different message. During the same meeting, Molly Nagel reported:

> Heidi functions so well. She doesn't really need to have somebody with her every minute. Whoever is in the room is taking groups and helping everybody. It's not like anyone's there helping Heidi. I almost feel guilty sometimes because I'm getting extra help. The model that we're using with Heidi is just that she's doing what we're doing, and that works.

A small, quiet resistance. Heidi had been in kindergarten last year, but spent most of her time in Room 3. This year she was assigned to Molly's first-grade classroom. On the first day of school, she spent one hour in Room 3 and never came back. But Molly had not felt prepared. She was operating on the same assumptions everyone held:

> "I'm happy to have her in my room for the socialization, . . . but I can't promise you that she's going to be able to read at the end of the year. . . ." I guess I didn't feel as responsible then. I felt like, "You guys are the special ed people. It's your job and if you decide that she's really not learning what she needs to be learning this year, then I trust that you're going to come in here and take her out and teach her, but it's fine with me if she's in here." That was my attitude at the beginning of the year.

What helped Molly change her attitude was her collaboration with Asta Thorsdottir, our Icelandic master's student, whose practicum involved helping to support Heidi at the beginning of the year. In her first days of helping in the classroom, Asta began to be concerned about the support the EA was providing:

> The assistant was sitting next to her, even supporting her arms and hands and telling her what to do . . . and trying to get her to look like all the other kids. In the very beginning I felt that this didn't look right. It looked so different from what all the other kids were getting. [I thought] Heidi was getting frustrated. . . . She didn't do the things she was supposed to do. She was hitting the assistant. When I was watching, I thought to myself, "She doesn't want all this support. She wants to do it by herself. She has a strong will."

Asta kept these feelings to herself for awhile, but eventually jumped into a conversation between Joni and Heidi's EA. "I just jumped in and said, 'I think she doesn't want this support.'" Asta's challenge created some tense times for the next few weeks. Joni and the EA were worried that things weren't working out well for Heidi and decided that they would pull her back to Room 3. Asta and Molly realized that they had been thinking the same things. Molly remembers:

> My style of working with [Heidi] was not as demanding, not as forceful —a little bit more letting her guide and show me what she could do. The EA was guiding her, not giving her much power. I think Asta can work beautifully with her because her teaching naturally follows [the child]. But if you think of her as this little special ed child that you have to control and boss and tell her what to do and keep her on task, she's going to get real stubborn, and you're not going to get much out of her.

Molly and Asta designed a different support plan that used the EA less and permitted Heidi more flexibility. Together they watched her begin to work and learn. She began to "look so different! Happier! . . . She was writing, working, sharing her journal with the other kids." Heidi mastered all the objectives on her IEP and more. She learned to write more than her name, not just to copy letters and numbers but write them in dates and little sentences. Molly was "blown away a lot of the time" about how well Heidi learned.

Asta realized that her years of experience as an elementary school teacher served her better with Heidi than she had expected, and better even than some of the special education she had learned in her undergraduate education program. By sharing their thinking and experience, Asta and Molly learned together that, as Asta said, "Heidi is not different. She's just like the other kids. We have to find out for each one what it is they need. Some of them are really easy and it takes you just a day to find out, [but] some of them are really tough." Molly added:

> If I hadn't had Asta in the room, I would not be nearly as far as I am. She and I have the same sense about how to deal with children and to have somebody else in the room that you can bounce ideas around with has just been really wonderful. I don't think I would have been brave enough to do some of the things that I've done if I hadn't had somebody I respected to [confirm] what I was thinking and seeing. A lot of the other teachers in the building are wanting and getting more support—more EAs or Joni in the room—helping out with the children or working one-on-one with that particular child. The other teachers have found that to be very helpful, but in my classroom it was detrimental. Heidi wanted me to be her teacher, and it was annoying Heidi to have somebody else bossing her around. It was annoying to me to have someone else talking in the room when [the class was] trying to listen to me and to have the

two of them fighting over whether or not she was going to do what she wanted to do. It was very frustrating for the EA, because she felt like she wasn't getting any respect. [But] I didn't really know how to say to her, "I'm the teacher here. I want you to do it the way I'm doing it."

The Schools Projects staff was learning some important things about inclusion along with Molly, Heidi, Asta, and Joni; but it would be well into the next year before any of us were really able to articulate these lessons.

Joni couldn't expect that Molly's willingness to take over being Heidi's teacher would be the general response from other classroom teachers, and she also felt the need to "take ownership as the special ed teacher," because it was her understanding that she was the one finally accountable to the system for Heidi's learning. What we could only see, from hindsight, was that two systems were meeting each other head on, and tension was a symptom of the beginning of a shift in thinking and practice for the general educators and for Joni and her staff. They were involved together in creating something new.

Molly started to see some of the special education practices—now so much more visible in so many more classrooms—as somehow keeping children dependent, teaching them to wait for adult direction rather than taking responsibility for some of their own learning. Other classroom teachers, assuming that "only the special educators knew how to work with these kids," or because of discomfort with what was so unfamiliar, were delighted to have Joni take primary responsibility for "her" students when they were in their classrooms. In these classrooms, Joni and her EAs did a remarkable job of supporting the teachers, helping with both designing and teaching lessons, until teachers felt more comfortable. An interesting twist was that this was also the first time any of Joni's EAs had worked with students with significant disabilities, and, in a few short months, their job had evolved from becoming familiar with the students themselves and learning how to support them to "letting them go." As time passed, they realized that the students should have a chance to be more independent some of the time: "Every minute doesn't have to be supported or supervised." They made a point of working with all students in the class instead of just the "supported education" students.

Rising to repeated challenges. Between New Year's Day and March, Joni had absorbed three students, but now three more were due, bringing her total to a dozen. She was working with three tightly orchestrated EAs. The three new students, all significantly more disabled than any before, were creating a good deal of anxiety, maybe because people were recalling their experience with Crystal. This time, however, some of the teachers had met the students and each student had come to visit several times. Fox was feeling the full responsibility for twelve students—without additional assistants. She worried about her EAs not having time for planning, or even lunch, and she was already working overtime: "I mean, I have three EAs who work six hours each. I have twelve kids, some of whom need six-and-a-half hours of support a day, and they are in eight different locations. It's a phenomenal task to take on. . . ."

On the second day after the arrival of the new students, while Joni and her staff were meeting with Assistant Principal Phil Bowers to discuss their problems, Joni's worst nightmare—what she had worked all year to avoid—happened:

> I sent Cindy [one of the new students] down to homeroom without support because I just wasn't thinking clearly. I messed up big time and I'm really sorry because Cindy was inappropriate. She was banging on the piano and it was very disruptive. This is every teacher's fear: that you're going to get kids that you don't know what to do with thrown [into your room] with no support.

The arrival of Cindy, Eliot, and Amy pressed everyone, not so much to do more with less, as to do something completely differently. Joni's model had reached its limit. "There were cost concerns," along with concerns for the level of stress, the need for some peacefulness, and an ending to the year. The supported ed teachers, Joni, Phil, and Keith met again. Joni felt more was being expected of her than the other teachers. Others may have felt the need to calm the situation. Still others may have begun to realize that they didn't need as much of Joni, her approach, and her staff as they had thought. "People started coming up with answers." Kim Black (the speech therapist) agreed to support several students on Wednesdays for a half-hour block. Phil agreed to support Marcie Graves in the morning for reading—a whole hour— as well as for the 40-minute-lunch for Cindy and Eliot. The crisis abated as others took on Joni's self-assumed tasks. To her, it reflected "how far they had come" in accepting her ideas about inclusion. To some it might just have been a way to get through the rest of the year with a little less drama and tension. Regardless of motives, everyone rose to the challenge of three new, even more disabled students in a way that would have been impossible six months earlier. Their experiences thus far had emboldened them.

The year wound down. Joni did less—"letting some things slide," such as being in teachers' classrooms and collecting data and managing some of the logistical details that others, especially Phil, picked up. And there continued to be new issues and projects: getting Amy on the "regular" bus and, with the PE teacher, creating a swimming program that could accommodate the supported ed students with the assistance of peer buddies, so they wouldn't have to retreat to a "disabled swimming" program. On the whole, everyone felt good about the success of the project.

What stood out for us at the end of the year was the small, quiet voice of Molly. Her words had something to teach us and her colleagues, but it would take most of the next year for all of us to realize the implications of her words when we asked her what she would say to other teachers:

> I really think that you need to give yourself and the child a little bit of time—just to let the child be in your room . . . see what's going on . . . get used to things. . . . I think that we tend to get these kids and we're all afraid of them. We just want to control them and make them sit still and be quiet, and we don't really know what to make them do. We cannot have support plans written in stone. Give us a month. Give us two months to figure out what we're doing. I would say, "Expect more than you expected. They can do more a lot of the time, if you just kind of give them the opportunity."

YEAR 2: REALIZING POTENTIAL

Year 2 was to bring quite significant changes for all of us. The year became one that explored new roles for university staff at South Valley, saw the faculty there take on more and more responsibility regarding both general and special education reforms, and resulted in some momentous decisions when South Valley was faced with significant staff cutbacks.

Efforts to "Build Capacity for Change"

At the Schools Projects, we were impressed and overwhelmed with what had occurred in just a year at South Valley. Looking so closely at the school's efforts validated and extended much of the data we had collected over the previous 2 years from 16 other schools. It also clarified our direction.

Most of our other experiences in schools had really centered on the perspectives of special educators. Our access had always been through the teachers of self-contained classrooms who were trying to move out into the school. What was different about this experience was our initial appeal to South Valley's full faculty. Though none of us realized it at the time, it was a critical shift in our own actions and thinking. It committed us to looking at the *whole* school through the eyes of all its members. For us it was a shift from *special education research* to *educational research*.

South Valley's faculty helped us access and understand the perspectives of general educators and to appreciate how much of a minority group special education teachers really are in schools—in terms of who they are and how they operate as professionals and also of how they think about what they do, about their roles in schools, and about the students they serve. We began to wonder what it would mean for inclusion to be part of an *educational* agenda to restructure schools rather than a *special* education agenda to reform a parallel service delivery system. It seemed to us that often the best efforts of very talented special educators still resulted in students being separated and even isolated to the point that they occasionally struck back—as Heidi had.

We began to realize that, if inclusion were ever to mean more than integration, we special educators would have to change our tactics. Resolving the debates about roles, ownership, accountability, student learning achievements, the meaningfulness of IEPs, and the achievement of genuine student membership required us to begin with the *majority* perspective and build tools and strategies "from the center out" rather than from the most exceptional student *in*. Devising and defining inclusion to concern only students with severe disabilities—indeed, any disabilities—seemed increasingly wrongheaded and quite possibly doomed. It continued to focus everyone's attention on a small number of students, and a small number of student differences, rather than the group with all its various diversities. We were learning to *respect* rather than to *defend* that diversity.

As we were learning these things during South Valley's first year, we were awarded a new funded project, beginning in fall 1992. The Building Capacity for Change (BCC) Project enabled us to provide "inservice training" in inclusion to school personnel by inviting them to participate in a four-course sequence that was also part of the initial teacher preparation for students seeking one of Oregon's special education teaching licenses. We knew that successful "inservice" really should be constructed as ongoing professional development and characterized by consistent involvement over an extended period of time. We felt this commitment to time was even more critical with inclusion. The issues were not only very complex, but frequently misunderstood. At least we realized that everyone—school personnel, policymakers, family members, and academic educators—seemed to have different definitions of both inclusion and the issues surrounding it. Resolving these differences would require the best thinking of all kinds of educators and community members as well as the time to learn how to communicate well with one another. So we constructed our "inservice" by inviting field-based school professionals to join our existing degree-oriented classrooms.

Sharing responsibility to teach. We began our second year of involvement at South Valley with new commitments and partnerships. We began to place our practicum students not only with Joni, but also with some of the classroom teachers who were working with quite diverse groups of students. Asta had taught us that our students needed to learn as much about working with "general" education students as with labeled students. Even more important, we believed that working closely with general educators would create for our students an ability to "talk education" rather than just special education.

Two graduate students, attracted by Mary's enthusiasm for teaching, asked about working in her fourth-grade classroom. Winter and spring terms saw the expansion of practicum experiences at South Valley and a whole new range of opportunities for learning, both for students and Schools Projects staff. The master's program students were challenged by the demands of teaching a class of 30 squirming youngsters who represented a broad spectrum of abilities. They worked to stay at least one step ahead of the students in their knowledge of art, the Oregon Trail, math, and rain forests. They struggled to find the balance in the lessons they designed and taught that would include the students with unique and diverse learning needs (not always the students with severe disabilities), yet still interest and challenge the other students. They enjoyed becoming part of the school staff, attending meetings, and learning more about South Valley and its operations.

As practicum instructors, Schools Projects staff began to access their own opportunities for professional development as *educators* with special knowledge of and ability to teach disabled learners. As they supported master's students in more and more general education classrooms, they solidified their own knowledge of cooperative learning, literature-based approaches to reading and literacy, activity-based math teaching, integrated curriculum approaches, and more varied strategies for evaluating and documenting student achievement. We also became more completely familiar with the limits of lecture, worksheets, and other forms of traditional, didactic teaching, not only for students who might be labeled and "included," but also for many of the "regular" students who were struggling to make sense of and use their schooling.

Sharing responsibility to learn. Our growing familiarity and fluency with general education curriculum and teaching overlapped well with the BCC Project and our shared responsibility for teaching aspiring teachers. It balanced our commitment to reinvent our own university classroom so it better mirrored the teaching we wanted to encourage. We had to incorporate more of all kinds of student differences and experiences, while at the same time sharing our own expertise about supporting the learning needs of "different" students. The invitation to include field-based professionals offered unique opportunities for our master's students to learn in the same classroom from, and with, the same teachers they were working with in practicum. The possibilities for breaking down irrelevant professional distinctions appealed to us very much. Our formal partnership with South Valley staff expanded when two Grade 4 teachers and a classroom assistant enrolled in the BCC sequence. All had been recipients of "supported ed" students the previous year and continued to welcome "inclusion" students into their classrooms.

Of course, we made mistakes. We lectured too much that first term, despite our commitment to do less of it. We probably got some of the content in the wrong order and we were dissatisfied with the linkage between our every-Tuesday-night class and everyone's day-to-day teaching. We needed better constructed assignments and activities to link the two.

Fortunately, our field-based participants were not at all shy with their constructive criticism. We adjusted, changed the sequence, and added more things in the second term. We created more ongoing application activities, attempting to tie all course activities to teachers' and students' work in schools better. We also began to demand more real collaboration in the design and sequencing of the courses from the participants. It was great to learn what hadn't worked when we asked at midterm and end of term, but class seemed to go better when the "students" became active participants in making decisions and adjustments as we went along.

By the third course in the sequence, we began to create some genuinely collaborative solutions to some of the curriculum and teaching issues the teachers were struggling to resolve. Our emergent Individually Tailored Education System (ITES) and all its planning and information gathering tools reflected the concerns, approaches, constraints, and work styles of both general and special educators trying to "do" inclusion as well as many components of broader school reform and restructuring. The ideas, the broad principles, features, and specific working papers of the ITES could not have been developed by either general or special educators alone.

Taking Full Responsibility

Two years earlier, Oregon voters had passed a property tax limitation measure. Like many states, Oregon funded schooling mainly with property tax revenues, and passing the measure meant that there would be cuts in programs and staff to meet the requirements of the new law. Green River and South Valley faced substantial cuts. The district considered closing a smaller elementary school and consolidating students and staff at two of the larger buildings, including South Valley. In addition, the process of "bumping" by seniority promised to affect South Valley's young staff noticeably.

Joni and her staff carefully orchestrated their support to their students and their teachers. The rest of the LRC special education staff continued their patterns of teaching, mostly by pulling students out to the resource room, but occasionally joining teachers in the delivery of some aspect of their lessons. Joni and the rest of the special education staff worked apart. In Keith Noble's mind,

> We still ended up with two separate programs. We had the self-contained room and we had the LRC program, and we still ended up kind of running parallel programs. We became very reliant on Joni and the two EAs, who basically handled the kids with the most severe challenges. That wasn't really the direction we wanted to head, but because of our history, that's what we fell into.

The classroom teachers were variously involved in the teaching, and "owning," of Joni's students. Some participated in the development of IEPs, independently adapted curriculum, or provided direct teaching. However, in most cases, Joni was still the "case manager" and took responsibility for the paperwork and progress reports. All but two of last year's students were still at South Valley (the other two had moved on to middle school), and most were in fourth grade. Mary Crane, one of the South Valley staff participating in BCC, had requested several of these fourth graders.

The distinctions between South Valley and Schools Projects agendas became harder to make. The researchers–subjects, instructors–students, general–special distinctions and roles all deteriorated. Our partnership was expanding.

Beginning to share. By February, staff at South Valley were beginning to realize that they were involved in something exciting and instructive for others. We nurtured that feeling by inviting quite a few of the South Valley staff, as well as staff from other schools we were working with, to participate in a day-long workshop on inclusion. The experience was affirming of both their past efforts and their future plans. The teachers in the BCC courses began to meet outside class to continue discussions and problem-solving. Sometimes other teachers joined, and a larger group shared their ideas and skills at planning curriculum, tailoring lessons, and figuring out how to manage a wider and wider variety of unexpected events.

February also brought another meeting, this one prompted by some of the classroom teachers, to talk about the supported education project. Keith arranged substitutes so that four classroom teachers and Joni and her staff could join him, Kelly, and Gwen Meyer from the Schools Projects for the afternoon. The agenda reflected continuing questions as well as feelings of accomplishment. Indeed, participants shared many positive comments. One of the EAs, who had worked in Room 3 before Joni came, said that, compared to including students in general classes, it had been much easier keeping them in Room 3, but that she had seen them make progress "by leaps and bounds" now that they were out, and she would never go back. Others reported that students who had previously needed support were operating independently and that, once the "novelty of their inclusion" had worn off, they were getting more peer pressure to conform. She said they had moved from the status of "pets to peers."

Joe Cooper, a first-grade teacher, wanted the whole school to be more involved and more teachers to be willing to include challenging students in their classrooms. While Joni reported feeling more unity with the teaching team, Meg Vaughn said she felt fractured—as if it were not a cohesive group. One of the EAs felt that existing resources were not being used well; this meeting was long overdue; and she personally had things to offer that were not being accessed. Clare Brown, another first-grade teacher, was trying to adjust to having another adult in her room.

When all was distilled, three themes emerged. First, there needed to be a formalized process and structure to help this "supported ed group" communicate. The group wanted more frequent meetings like this one, but just as important was regular planning time for teachers working together in classrooms. Second, the group felt that they needed to move away from labeling either students or teachers. They would close Room 3 and create the inservice and professional development opportunities for all teachers and EAs to work with previously excluded or "pulled out" students. Third, they wanted more ideas and tools to help them with curriculum development and teaching design, not just for the "included" students, but also for other students, including those described as talented–gifted.

The sharing produced some immediate decisions. They planned another meeting that would include the LRC staff. Keith agreed to use 2020 Grant money to support substitutes one day a week so that teachers would be freed for half-hour blocks to meet with EAs for planning time. A second decision was that Joni should begin immediately to dismantle Room 3 as the supported education classroom. The staff had other ideas for using the space, and the room's materials and equipment could be moved to a smaller room.

Deciding the Future

In the midst of all these welcome and celebrated changes, the gloomy specter of layoffs hovered over the school and haunted the staff. Joni—a second-year teacher—was expected to be one of the casualties. Knowing this, she began applying for jobs and found a new position in March. She would leave South Valley within the month. The staff began to get nervous as her departure approached. Who would replace her? Even a well-qualified new teacher would not know the students, staff, or what had evolved over the past year. In the interim, her assistants took responsibility for the students on a day-to-day basis and for talking to the families. Chuck Anderson, the LRC teacher, took over the paperwork. The LRC staff agreed to "shadow" the EAs and students for the time being. It felt, according to Noble, as if they "were patching things together." Chuck later admitted that he felt, at that point, as if he "was flying blind."

Once Joni left, the supported education project finally became a *school* project. Students previously discussed only among Joni's team were now discussed at staff meetings. Teachers not previously involved in the project began to talk to students in the halls. Generally, the shadowing by LRC staff was going well. Chuck's feeling was that for some staff, the shadowing did indeed work well, but for others, it was a problem. EAs were not always sure what they were supposed to be doing, and he didn't feel much more confident, in some situations, than they did.

Meanwhile, the small group attending the BCC courses talked about things they were learning with a new confidence. They had learned some new approaches to assessment, developing curriculum, and designing teaching plans that should meet the requirements of the IEPs without another person to write them. This small group of three began to attend special education team meetings and advocate more openly for changes in all South Valley's special education services, including the practices of the LRC. An emerging leadership pressed the Site Council and other schoolwide groups to commit South Valley to becoming inclusive without categorizing students or teachers.

Out of the challenge of Joni's departure, South Valley's faculty began to realize that they could accommodate new students by working together, without compromising the learning of other students. By the end of the second year, their processes for problem-solving and planning were more formalized and seemed to be working. The group had managed to solve some really tricky problems, and more and more staff were becoming involved and newly passionate about what they were creating for their students and the school. From our point of view, they had changed their question. Rather than asking "Will it work?" they were now asking "How can we best make it work?"

South Valley's staff began to appreciate their potential for flexibility, for learning to think differently, and for changing roles and relationships among themselves. They also could see that they'd begun to think differently about their students and schedules—and about change. Things that had seemed simply impossible only a year previously were now open for challenge and discussion. Finally, they learned about their capacity to survive major trauma.

Keith handed out 20 layoff notices and of those, only 5 staff were able to come back when the dust had settled.

Through it all, they had developed a reputation in the state for both "doing inclusion" and "doing restructuring." Our practicum students were accessing more and broader learning experiences than ever before. Working with the general educators in the BCC sequence had helped us create the first draft of a manual, the Individually Tailored Learning System. Despite the struggles and the loss of staff, those of us most involved in the supported education changes ended the year aware that some important and significant progress had occurred. At a final BCC class meeting over a potluck lunch, we learned recruitment by this year's team for next year's BCC sequence had already begun, and not just among South Valley faculty. Teachers have decided that it would be important in just another year that teachers at the middle school be able to support the continued participation of South Valley's students in the life of the middle school. We learned a team of five or six would enroll in the fall and offer their classrooms as potential practicum opportunities for our master's degree students.

YEAR 3: BUILDING FUTURES

In the end we began the BCC course in fall 1993 with five staff members from South Valley, four from the middle school, and one from the high school. We felt more and more at home, and the school staff were feeling more and more confident about the future and their ability to meet its challenges. The year was a building year for all of us that involved living the commitment to diversity and change and expanding our networks and resources.

Living Commitment

At South Valley. The third year presented its own unique challenges. In September, South Valley staff returned to a school short 15 adults from the previous year. The four classes per grade level (except for Grade 5) were reconfigured to three per grade level—all larger than before. The music and PE teachers were gone, leaving the classroom teachers to draw on their own skills. This loss also effectively cut out planning time the teachers had formerly enjoyed.

Chuck Anderson was the only full-time special education teacher who returned at the beginning of the year. He was joined by a part-time special educator, newly transferred from another school and hence unfamiliar with South Valley's changes, and by a substitute teacher who worked until November when the special educator she was replacing returned from mater-

nity leave. None of these teachers really knew the students they were supporting, and Chuck, feeling the responsibility of coordinating all of their
efforts, recalls how stressful that period was. He attributes much of the credit
for the continuing success of the students and the program in general to the
dedicated efforts of the entire special education staff. This included a large
group of EAs, who with little training, no concrete plan, and minimal outside help, became experts at supporting teachers and students.

The idea was still for all eight South Valley educational assistants to work
with all students, regardless of designation. However, the practical problem
was that only one of Joni's assistants had returned and no EA worked more
than a 6-hour day, leaving little time for sharing or planning. To further
complicate matters, two new students with need for extra supports had moved
into the area during the summer and arrived at the school unexpectedly. It
felt like the beginning all over again.

It was hard. Keith scheduled some meetings early in the year just to allow
people to vent—"to talk about how hard this is." That seemed to help and
"flexibility" became the new slogan. At the same time the principal tried to
help everyone support their commitment:

> It was really a stretch for people . . . we needed to "hang in there" until
> they [teachers and EAs] got over initial fears. It wasn't as though we had
> a lot of time to just go slowly. . . . It was "Okay, you'll learn. You'll study
> these children and learn their quirks and that's the way we're going to
> go about it."

The first priority was to support those students who required the greatest amount of support and to spread the capacity for that support among at
least three EAs and the three special education staff. Each classroom teacher
had a variety of students. The diversity and variety seemed to work, "sharing the load" as well as the "wealth." The press for time had never been
greater. Fortunately, a district policy that established early release on Wednesdays permitted the possibility of at least some extra time. On the other hand,
managing more with less created such stress and demanded such creativity
that it was well into October before the teachers with the "supported ed"
students were able to meet and compare notes. The first of these meetings
drew some 20 people, all struggling. Two themes dominated: not enough time
for meeting with all the "players" and too many adults in their classrooms.

Important to South Valley's commitment was the need to listen and af-
firm the feelings of those faculty and staff with growing concerns: "Here you
are trying to teach 30 kids a whole bunch of subjects and meet the needs of
TAG kids, medium kids, low kids—for every lesson. [Now there's] this other

child who needs something special and it sounds real easy, but I don't think it's possible to do."

Even teachers who had been feeling successful with the dismantling of Room 3 were pressed by the cutbacks and rising demands to wonder:

> Maybe they would be in the classroom part of the day with support and then maybe the other part of the day they would be in their own environment, with their teacher . . . having them all go to Room 3 like they used to. I know that's not ideal, but we don't have ideal situations for anybody else . . . that's what we have the time and the money to do.

The year proceeded. Keith and his faculty made decisions quickly and firmly because their "basic direction was set. You just shuffle what you have and keep going." Despite the new challenges, the overall commitment to the spirit of the original "supported education" project was strong, if not unanimously shared.

It was a delicate time. The future, which had seemed so secure before the cuts, was clouded by the dramatic cutbacks and increasing pressures. Living the commitment to systemic restructuring and maximum student diversity was much more difficult. Still, many seemed to share the sentiment of the teacher who admitted: "I like working here. It's a unique school with lots of different personalities. And yet, it's a school that's open to trying new things and really cares about what's going to be best for kiddos."

At the Schools Projects. Two years had taught us a good deal both about inclusion and teaching. Our effort to "build capacity" had become more of a collaboration, thanks to the contributions of the first year's participants, from South Valley and elsewhere. But the need for professional development among school personnel was dramatically underlined for us by teachers traveling more than an hour, and sometimes more than two, through treacherous mountain passes to come to class on campus.

We decided to increase our accessibility by broadcasting the class on one of Oregon's educational satellite networks, thus gathering an additional 25 students across the state and having our teaching skills challenged even more dramatically.

The first term was rough. It was hard for all of us to become comfortable enough with the technology to maintain our cooperative work group approach to teaching. The camera seemed to encourage the old forms of lecture and discourage either group activities or discussion. The logistics of managing handouts and assignments in nine locations were challenging and time consuming. There was not nearly enough time to plan, to coordinate, or to meet the needs of each of the students adequately, especially those of the distant students. Our efforts were further challenged by a studio classroom that was too small, in an area that was still under renovation and often without needed ventilation and air conditioning. Teachers and students alike struggled, after a full day of work and practicum, to stay focused and motivated.

Fortunately, the 10 participants from Green River School District contributed a critical mass of "general" educators in our studio classroom, putting us special educators finally in a "natural proportion." In December, the Schools Projects hired a former sixth-grade block teacher, who had been laid off from the middle school in Salmon Lake in the massive staff reductions of the previous spring. She had enrolled in the course in the fall, and we asked her to join our staff, attracted by her background in general education and the perspective she could bring to our work.

The final segment of the 4-course BCC sequence was a 2-week summer workshop, the focus of which was working with and including parents and families in the design and construction of inclusive schools and communities. As a result of its participation in the workshop, the group from South Valley is now adding the planning of family linkages to the agenda of the Site Council. By the end of the third year, our collaboration with South Valley through the BCC course and practicum allowed us to refine and crystallize the curriculum planning approaches that had been emerging through our classroom-based research; and it helped us to reconstruct for our graduate students practice teaching experiences that were more inclusive in nature and form.

Expanding Networks and Resources Into Year 4

It is difficult to capture a relationship with words, especially one characterized by rapid and dramatic changes over an extended period of time. Still, we have used words to describe specific, clear events, which highlight those changes and our learning, but, as we think back over the past three years, the details blur to create impressions and images whose boundaries are less clearly defined. Set against a background of time, these images take on new meanings and lend themselves to different interpretations, which were not possible at the time of their occurrence.

This has been a chronicle of how we all grew and changed. More than that, it's an account of how South Valley and the Schools Projects have influenced one another's growth. Certainly, we would have all grown without the benefit of the partnership, but in ways different from the way we did together. As a partnership, our experiences together have been unique. Yet, our partnership has not been particularly unusual or even one that we would hold up as a model to be emulated by others. The stimuli for growth will be different for others, the pressures to change emanating from situationally unique circumstances. What is special about this partnership is that it developed naturally over time, and that it continues to grow into its fourth year and even continues to expand and to strengthen speaks to its mutuality: evidence that as partners we provide important resources and support for each other.

We can't speak for South Valley, but we know that we now look at inclusive teaching and learning in a new way. We began watching, through the eyes of special educators, as South Valley embarked on a project arising from an infant vision shared by a limited number of people. We wanted to see how the school included the special students. In the beginning, we brought our special expertise with a small group of children with severe disabilities, some information about "bubble kids" and how inclusion didn't work in some situations, and ideas about how students might become members in truly inclusive schools. We started with lots of questions, a desire to learn more, and a growing awareness that it was only by understanding and merging general and special education that a school could become truly "inclusive." We realized that we were ready to move out of our own special education bubble.

We watched as the "project," with undeveloped guidelines and uncertain plans, matured into a fairly sophisticated "process" that merged with all the other processes at South Valley. The goal was no longer just "doing inclusion" for the special students, but to make it an integral part of South Valley's educational process for all its students. What we saw over the course of the three years was good teaching that got better in ways that created more meaningful outcomes for a wider range of students. We saw major changes in a school that was already well into restructuring itself and, by living together through all the crises and successes, we came to know many of the staff well. They brought their own questions, a continuing desire to learn, and some effective strategies for problem-solving that helped to carry them through the good times and the bad.

During these three years, the networks at both South Valley and the Schools Projects expanded—individually, jointly, and, then, in other directions. By the end of the third year, South Valley's networks within the school were not only characterized by more collaboration among EAs, general education staff, and special education teachers, but the numbers of teachers involved in the school's efforts to change had grown from a handful to most of the teachers in the school. This was part of the plan, according to Noble, "[It's] just a matter of time and exposure, because every year we try to include one or two more teachers who haven't been involved in the program before."

South Valley also forged new connections with the middle school. This occurred partly as a result of the BCC courses, but also because the fifth-grade teachers tried to create a new transition process to the bigger world of middle school. South Valley became more involved in community issues and projects, and it has recently taken on the sponsorship of multicultural family activities. As faculty from other schools and districts around the state come to visit South Valley, additional links are established.

Updating Year 1's emerging reforms reveals that South Valley has indeed accomplished much of its agenda. The following list summarizes the current status of reform at South Valley:

- *Chapter 1 services merged into general education classrooms.*
  Chapter 1 services are given as a pull-out computer class, along with pull-out small-group instruction.
- *Chapter 1 teachers replaced with more educational assistants.*
  Continues to be the case.
- *Two educational assistants assigned to each grade team.*
  EAs are assigned according to the need for classroom support (some classrooms are mixed-age, some have more need for support).
- *Additional time generated so assistants meet weekly with teacher teams.*
  This is still provided on Thursday afternoons and some Wednesdays, since the district has moved to early release on Wednesdays.
- *The Site Council, originally formed in 1988, beginning to manage more and more school operations and decisions.*
  The Site Council has continued to take on more governance responsibilities. The district has caught up, and now has a district council to to which South Valley sends a representative.
- *Pupil Assistance Team meeting to problem-solve with teachers about challenging students.*
  PAT has been discontinued, but South Valley has initiated a new prevention-oriented discipline program that will be meeting to problem-solve.
- *More involvement in community issues and projects by school faculty and students.*
  A new districtwide volunteer program has prompted South Valley's Parent Group to provide their own coordinator to manage volunteers involved in many facets of school–community activities. South Valley is also involved in sponsoring multicultural family activities.
- *Kindergarten teachers experimenting with "developmentally appropriate practices."*
  DAP has been embraced by kindergarten teachers and has spread into

implementing mixed-age classrooms. It also has impacted on the way South Valley is looking at assessment.

- *Curriculum–teaching experiments by Grade 1 team in response to new group of kindergarten graduates.*
  Some mixed-age classrooms have been implemented (1994–95 school year).
- *Some teachers combining classrooms and team-teaching units.*
  Teachers continue to work at this. It is happening with general ed–special ed and speech therapy–general ed. Planning time has been designated for teachers of mixed-age classes to collaborate.
- *Discussion about creating some "schools-within-a-school," using non-graded and mixed-age–ability groupings.*
  South Valley decided to initiate mixed-age classes first. They were reluctant to try the schools-within-a-school approach, fearing that it would alienate staff. It remains an option for the future.
- *Discussion about including parents on curriculum committees.*
  Parent participation is included in the Site Council. The Parent Club continues to grow at South Valley.
- *Discussion about exploring new student assessment options.*
  Teachers continue to experiment with portfolio assessment. As state-level reforms begin to impact on elementary schools, new assessment tools will continue to develop. South Valley collaborated with other district teachers to develop Curriculum-based Assessment, which they are currently using.

The Schools Projects networks have expanded as well. As we shared our learning through the EdNet classes, conferences, inservice slots and workshops, we established connections with others around the state and nation. Internationally, we entertained visitors who had learned of our work concerning reform and inclusion and came to see schools that were "reinventing themselves" and "including students with disabilities in general education classes."

As we all began the school year in fall 1994:

General and special education teachers [at South Valley] report that mixed-age classes are working out well. They seem to be starting the 1994–95 year with great attitudes. Now that classrooms are not overloaded with extremely challenging students, they are feeling very relieved. They have reviewed the needs for classroom supports and seem to feel at ease with keeping support fluid throughout the school year.

Last year, South Valley used a "floating sub" once a week to provide planning time for the classroom teams supporting students with more severe disabilities. The Site Committee has decided to provide the same support for this year. The approximate cost ($4,000) will be paid by the existing 2020 Grant and South Valley's professional development funds.

At the Schools Projects, two more teachers from South Valley have enrolled in the BCC class, one a special educator. One of the former supported education EAs who worked with Joni the first two years, and who now works at the high school as the transition specialist, is also a class member. Two teachers from another elementary school in Salmon Lake have also joined the class. We are beginning a new collaborative research project with both South Valley and the middle school, involving the site councils from both schools and two teachers from the middle school and one from South Valley. Three practicum students have been placed in classrooms at South Valley, two are in the middle school and one is at the high school, all working with teachers who are either graduates of the university class or are currently enrolled. One of South Valley's former special education EAs, who took the class two years ago, is now back in school at the university and works with us part time.

LAST WORDS

When people call us to ask if we know of schools they can visit to see "inclusion" or other innovative practices, we often mention South Valley, not as a school that has all the answers, or as a perfect example (because there really are none), but as a school that is active in its search for excellence. South Valley always graciously opens its doors to these visitors. A discerning visitor, sensitive to the complexities of educational reform, will look beyond obvious and unavoidable problems—the "warts" that are a part of every school—and not be put off by the imperfections they see. If they look beyond the surface, they will be rewarded with a view of the philosophy and the focus that makes South Valley a truly unusual and successful school. South Valley's goal is to be a school that, in the words of one teacher, "embraces all children" and provides them with a quality education. Visitors will give this statement their own interpretation and take away with them ideas influenced by their own experiences and agendas for change. What they see and learn will be translated into uniquely different outcomes in their schools, using different resources.

At South Valley, the vision, tailored to the culture of the school, has sustained the faculty and kept it headed forward. Many of the teachers give Keith a lot of the credit. "Keith lets you go and do. He is supportive and helpful. South Valley's the place it is because of Keith."

Of course, other staff members were frustrated sometimes by what seemed like his refusal to make "administrative decisions" on difficult issues. More often than not, even when he had a strong opinion and a good solution, he would bring the problem back to the staff and the Site Council. The problem, he would point out, was really not his to solve. They must "figure it out." This strategy, for some, was very disturbing, but it demonstrates Keith's commitment to sharing responsibility and control with the staff.

Perhaps it's Keith's quiet leadership—his support and encouragement with comments like "Go for it. Do the best you can. It's OK. You'll learn"—that creates an environment in which everyone knows that change does not come without problems and where it's all right to take risks and make mistakes. It's an environment that encourages the teachers not to be afraid to do new things.

In spite of the increasing attention that South Valley has received, the staff remain focused on their school and at times seem almost unaware of what they are creating as a natural outcome of their efforts. This past summer, a parent in the BCC class offered strong praise for South Valley's efforts and accomplishments. Taken aback, the South Valley participants wondered aloud, "Are we really doing things that are so different from other schools? Are we really that unique?" We look forward to the coming years, to the opportunity to continue our partnership as we work with them on the new project, and to the learning that, we are sure, will not only continue to expand our understanding of inclusive schooling and our ability to engage in more effective practices as educators, but will also undoubtedly generate new questions.

CHAPTER 5

Creating an Inclusive Community of Learners: Souhegan High School, Amherst, New Hampshire

Cheryl M. Jorgensen and Carol Tashie

AMRO'S STORY

Riding the school bus, selecting next semester's courses with your guidance counselor, going to a basketball game with a couple of friends, and participating in an all-day environmental summit at the conclusion of a unit on deforestation of the Brazilian rain forest—these are pretty typical activities for most high school students. Before the 1992–93 school year, however, they would have been impossible dreams for Amro Diab, a student with "severe disabilities," who has just completed his sophomore year at Souhegan High School in Amherst, New Hampshire.

Before coming to Souhegan, Amro was enrolled in a substantially separate special education class in a school district far from his home community. With the exception of "specials," Amro spent most of his day with other students who had disabilities. According to his teachers, "His peer relationships within the self-contained setting [are] good, but he doesn't intermingle too much with the students in the mainstream population."

From Special to Regular, From Ordinary to Extraordinary

When the district's inclusion facilitator, Marty Rounds, first attended a meeting to discuss Amro's transition from a self-contained, out-of-district program to ninth grade at Souhegan High School, Amro kept his head buried in his arms during the whole meeting. Amro's parents and all his teachers said that he was very shy, didn't speak beyond a muffled "yes" or "no," and was unable to read and write due to brain damage from seizures he experienced shortly after birth. Educational testing had labeled him "severely mentally retarded." Because Marty felt that Amro needed a peer group to help him make the transition from a very small and protected educational environment to a typical high school, he approached football coach, Jim Mulaney, to ask if Amro might join the team as an assistant manager. Jim, Assistant Coach Bobby O'Sullivan, and Amro became fast friends, and Amro worked out with the team during the last two weeks of August. Although Amro showed signs of coming out of his shell in response to the natural camaraderie of his football teammates and coaches, he had no effective means of communication other than an occasional "yes" or "no" and a set of increasingly demonstrative gestures. A visit from Carol Tashie, inclusion consultant from the University of New Hampshire, proved to be a turning point in Amro's ability to communicate, in the content of his educational program, and in others' expectations about his life goals. Carol had been exploring Facilitated Communication (FC) with a number of students around New Hampshire for the past year, and she and Rounds thought that Amro was a perfect candidate for FC (Biklen, 1990).

One hot August day, Carol was introduced to Amro and talked to him about FC as a way for people to communicate when they have trouble using their voice. With a laminated letter board in front of them on the table, Carol told Amro to point to letters to spell out the answers to some easy questions. She provided support and resistance under his wrist and began to ask him some predictable questions. Who do you want to do this spelling with? Amro spelled K-O-C-H. Someone ran to get Coach Mulaney! Who did we play last week in football? L-E-B-A-N (Lebanon). Did we win or lose? W-N. Who do we play next week? M-T-N (Fall Mountain). Who else do you want to do this spelling with? R-U-S-S-L (Russell had been giving Amro a ride home after practice). What position does Landry play on the team? T-A-K-L. What position do you play? M-N-G-R.

While Carol was accustomed to the emotional feelings generated when someone shows they are literate for the first time, the other people in the room were speechless. All of Amro's records indicated that he had significant intellectual disabilities and was unable to communicate using conventional spelling.

Throughout the remainder of the 1992–93 school year, Amro progressed to the point where he could spell on a letter board independently with only verbal encouragement from his peers and teachers. Because his native language was Egyptian, his teachers joked that Amro spelled in English with an Egyptian accent! When Amro was in a self-contained classroom, his language arts program focused on recognition and articulation of basic sight words from a standardized preprimer reading program for students with disabilities. Now Amro participates in a typical schedule of academic classes alongside his classmates. His educational goals include: (1) reading brief summaries of text prepared by classmates, (2) answering comprehension questions based on class discussion and reading, (3) learning the definitions of topical vocabulary, and (4) communicating within academic classes and informal settings using a laptop computer or letter board.

During a unit on the Civil War, Amro came to understand that the war was fought because the Southerners wanted to keep blacks as slaves and the Northerners wanted them to be free. Amro was able to identify situations in his own life in which he was not free or could not make his own choices and decisions. His final report at the end of the unit was a collage on which he grouped pictures of young and old people from different racial groups. Amro printed PEOPLE ARE FREE to caption his collage.

Identification of learning goals for Amro occurs during weekly planning meetings between the core academic teachers (English, social studies, science, and math), Marty Rounds, and Amro's in-class teaching assistant. The classroom teachers describe the topics and lessons that will be presented during the coming week, focusing on the major themes or "essential questions," which they hope all students will study. Within this major theme, a few concepts are identified for Amro. Adaptations to tests and projects are planned and criteria are determined for judging the quality of Amro's work. Amro is judged on these criteria and his grades are designated with an asterisk (indicating a modified curriculum) on his report card.

Amro completes his written work using a variety of strategies and technologies. Sometimes he uses a laptop computer in class and for homework assignments. Usually he spells out words on his letter board and another student or a teaching assistant scribes for him. Occasionally he will copy notes or assignments from the board. Although his writing and penmanship are not precise enough for these notes to be used as study guides later on, he gets valuable practice in letter formation and spelling. The teaching assistant uses a highlighter pen to mark important phrases or words on teacher-made handouts and oftentimes makes a study guide for him based on his learning goals for the unit.

Perhaps the most exciting development is that Amro now initiates the use of the letter board for communication—to converse socially, to ask questions, to provide others with information, to tell people that he isn't feeling well—and his team is exploring the feasibility of obtaining a communication system with voice output.

Social Relationships

Amro is probably the best known student at Souhegan High School. He has an infectious personality, is known for his punctuality, and serves as the school's informal peacemaker. If he sees two students having a verbal dis-agreement that looks as if it might escalate, he gets right between them and chastises them with a gentle slap on the hand or a quickly spelled N-O F-I-G-H-T-I-N-G. Amro has many students who enjoy spending time with him and providing him support in school and a few friends who visit him on the weekend. To expand that circle of "out of school" friends and to assure that Amro's summer will be full, a group of about 10 students met together several times at the end of the 1993–94 school year to talk with Amro and his support teachers about their summer plans and how Amro might be in-cluded in them. From these discussions, one student was identified as Amro's "bridge builder" over the summer. Amro's friend, Ryan, will be paid 15 hours per week to "connect" Amro to activities and friends throughout the Amherst community. For several hours a day, Amro will work with the maintenance crew at the school, supported on some days by Ryan and on other days by the maintenance staff. It is Ryan's job to find out how Amro would like to spend his free time and then to facilitate connections with his other friends for shared activities.

11th Grade and Graduation Planning

In the 11th grade at Souhegan High Schools, students begin to make their postgraduation plans. They meet with their guidance counselor, take their SATs, visit with college recruiters, practice completing job applications, and investigate postsecondary training and educational programs. Although Amro will be eligible for special education supports until he turns 21, it is anticipated that he will graduate with his class at 18 and then spend the next 3 years learning a job and independent living skills outside the school building. Amro's social relationships will be with his coworkers and with friends that he makes through community activities and organizations that all young adults join, such as town sports leagues, places of worship, and vocational training programs. Although Amro will be eligible for support from one or more adult service agencies, the quality of his life will depend on the richness of his social relationships. Being fully included in high school is the best investment in those social relationships, because the friends that he makes now will become his coworkers and neighbors after high school graduation.

THE STORY OF SOUHEGAN HIGH SCHOOL

Through Souhegan High School's commitment to full inclusion of stu-dents with disabilities, Amro's horizons have broadened to include the same range of choices for participation and membership as those available to his peers without disabilities. From the initial planning of his return from an out-of-district placement to the challenges of involving him in a typical schedule of academic courses, Amro's inclusion requires commitment to the vision of inclusion, ongoing communication and collaboration with classroom teachers, and most important, enlistment of classmates for problem-solving and support. Amro's story exemplifies the successes and difficulties of involving students with disabilities in an educational system that is wrestling with "excellence" and "equity" issues for all students.

Since Souhegan opened its doors in September 1992, one of the authors (Cheryl Jorgensen) has had the privilege of being "on the inside looking in" on Souhegan's day-to-day struggles. Through the University of New Hampshire's Institute on Disability, Souhegan is part of a 4-year U.S. Department of Education (DOE) research project designed to evaluate how students with disabilities can be included in systemic efforts to restructure schools. Two or three days a week, Cheryl provides technical assistance to teachers and administrators on inclusion practices while also documenting the inclusion and restructuring processes and the resultant student outcomes.

Prior to 1992, high school students from the towns of Amherst and Mont Vernon, in southern New Hampshire, attended the regional high school in Milford, New Hampshire. In the late 1980s the Amherst and Mont Vernon school boards began discussing the feasibility of building their own high school. They thought that Milford High School was getting too big and that control over educational decisions was too far removed from their communities. This chapter describes the process through which that new high school —Souhegan—was developed, with a focus on the practice of including all students with disabilities within heterogeneous, mixed-ability classes.

The Statewide and Local Context for Inclusion

Although some people believe that the creation of Souhegan occurred virtually "overnight," there was already considerable support for inclusive education in the state of New Hampshire and within the Amherst and Mont Vernon school systems. In 1989, the New Hampshire Department of Education (NHDOE) received a 5-year U.S. DOE grant supporting statewide training and systems-change activities, designed to increase the capacity of local school districts to integrate students with severe disabilities in their neighborhood schools. The Amherst and Mont Vernon school districts had participated in this project, and most of their elementary age students with moderate and severe disabilities had been integrated into general education classrooms in their neighborhood schools. In addition, members of the high school planning team were invited to participate in another grant application focusing on the inclusion of students with disabilities within systemic efforts to restructure schools. Souhegan is now part of a 4-year applied research project concerning the development and evaluation of inclusive educational practices.

Planning Team's Exploration of Educational Models

During the 1990–91 school year, Amherst's Superintendent Dr. Richard Lalley and the Amherst and Mont Vernon school boards assembled several working groups composed of community and school board members to research contemporary high school educational models. After reading hundreds of research articles and several books, the school board decided to approach the Coalition of Essential Schools (COES), founded by Theodore Sizer at Brown University, regarding the potential for the new school to become the coalition's next member. Coalition schools subscribe to nine principles, which guide school governance, organization, curriculum, instruction, and the relationships among teachers, students, and community members:

1. Focus on helping students use their minds well
2. A few simple but clear goals
3. Interdisciplinary learning
4. Personalization and interdependence
5. Students as worker
6. Teacher as coach
7. Diploma reflecting achievement of performance-based skills and knowledge
8. An ethic of growth, development and inquiry
9. A just community reflecting democratic principles

An administrative planning team was hired to work together for an entire year prior to the projected opening date (September 1992), and many meetings were held to develop a school philosophy, curriculum guidelines, hiring criteria, and policies and procedures. The planning team included Robert Mackin, principal; Cleve Penberthy, dean of students; Dan Bisaccio, head of math, science, and technology; Allison Rowe, head of the humanities; and Kim Carter, director of the Information Center (library). By the spring of 1992, the team had made a commitment to heterogeneous grouping, and, as Principal Bob Mackin noted, as the team considered further issues relating to students with disabilities and special education, "The clear commitment to [that belief] from the outset served as a prelude to being predisposed to thinking about inclusion."

The Souhegan High School philosophy developed by the team was:

Souhegan High School aspires to be a community of learners born of respect, trust, and courage. We consciously commit ourselves:
   To support and engage an individual's unique gifts, passions, and intentions.
   To develop and empower the mind, body, and heart.
   To challenge and expand the comfortable limits of thought, tolerance, and performance.
   To inspire and honor the active stewardship of family, nation, and globe.

A working group, chaired by Amherst's Director of Special Instructional Services Kathryn Skoglund, was organized to consider the "special education model" that Souhegan would adopt. Kathy Skoglund and other planning team members visited several New Hampshire and Vermont high schools to find out what models they were using. Staff from the University of New Hampshire's Institute on Disability gave a presentation to the planning team about the philosophy of inclusion and its best practices.

Then, in May 1992, an important meeting occurred between Souhegan's Dean of Students Cleve Penberthy, Marty Rounds, the Amherst school district's inclusion facilitator, and George Flynn, then superintendent of the Waterloo Separate School Board in Ontario, Canada. Flynn was in New Hampshire for a weekend doing inclusion training, and the three met for two hours to pick his brain about how Souhegan might address the learning and social needs of all its students. Flynn and Penberthy discovered that they held very similar views about the possibility that a public school could become a democratic and caring community and, in fact, that any school was in a unique position in the community for imparting the value of respect for diversity.

Afterward, the planning team decided to incorporate a full-inclusion philosophy into the school's policy foundations:

It is our strong belief that all students can learn and that, as much as possible, all students should be given the opportunity to stretch themselves academically across the school's curriculum. Mixed-ability grouping is utilized in most classroom settings. This means that students who have historically been tracked into lower-level courses and students "coded" with learning disabilities are also asked to meet high standards, but are given additional time and the support of a teacher when necessary.

An early idea for an "alternative high school" program at Souhegan for students with emotional disabilities was abandoned in favor of fully including those students and providing them with in- and out-of-school counseling services, in-classroom academic support, and the option of structuring an individualized academic schedule. Marty Rounds, as Souhegan's inclusion facilitator, worked all spring and summer to plan for the return to the district of six students with moderate to severe physical and/or intellectual disabilities, and, on September 1, 1992, Souhegan opened its doors to approximately six hundred students, all of whom would be fully included in the mainstream of general education.

Many of the values and practices that characterize Souhegan are inherently supportive of inclusion—the school philosophy speaks about nurturing each student's passions and interests, small student advisory groups meet with faculty every day for academic and social support, an innovative wellness program replaces the traditional sports-oriented physical education curriculum, and the school is governed by a democratic council of faculty, students, and community members. Inclusion is facilitated by five interconnected program components:

1. The innovative nature of the school structure and schedule
2. The use of essential questions to guide performance-based curriculum development
3. The evolving academic and behavioral support model that addresses the needs of all students
4. The empowerment of students to advocate for an inclusive school community and provide support for one another
5. The emerging model of supported graduation planning that is being developed for all students

A disclaimer here about "model schools"—there is no such thing! There are only schools that are trying their best to prepare students to thrive in an increasingly complex and difficult world. Although Souhegan has much for us to emulate, it is far from perfect. The challenges that faculty and staff face sometimes seem as weighty as the lofty standards they have set for themselves. These challenges and shortcomings will be described as honestly as their successes.

Souhegan's Community: Once Over Lightly

Demographics. Souhegan High School is located in southern New Hampshire in a picturesque New England town, complete with village green.

It is a fairly affluent community, and its per pupil cost for education (supported almost exclusively by local property tax revenues) is about two-thirds that of the communities in the state that spend the most on education. There is little racial diversity in the community—a small number of families are from Southeast Asia—but the community contains families at all levels on the socioeconomic scale. Perhaps the greatest diversity in the community arises from its members' political views, with both liberal and conservative voices actively involved in educational and local government issues.

Philosophies. As previously noted, Souhegan's general education and inclusion philosophy statements reflect an acknowledgment that students are different; that those differences are to be celebrated; that it is beneficial for students with differences to learn together side by side; and that all students need challenge, high expectations, and support. As a member of the Coalition of Essential Schools, Souhegan subscribes to nine basic principles that reflect their philosophy about governance, learning, and the purpose of the American high school as we approach the twenty-first century (see the previous section). "A few simple but clear goals" sounds like the process of identifying priority learning goals for students with disabilities as part of an Individualized Education Plan. "Interdisciplinary learning" certainly benefits students who have a hard time generalizing skills they learn in one area (such as reading or math) to other applied situations (e.g., science class or working at an afterschool job). The "personalization and interdependence" principle seems to indicate a realization that all students are different and that, although they ought to learn together, the means through which they demonstrate what they know, and their learning outcomes themselves, might be different from one another's. And a "just community" implies that this school believes in the right of each student to take advantage of all the learning opportunities that the school has to offer. The foundational COES principle, however, is that the high school diploma (the community's judgment that "you've achieved what we wanted you to—we've done our job well") is granted on the basis of students being able to demonstrate what they know and can do in observable, authentic ways that go far beyond the ability to pass a paper and pencil test.

Enrollment. Next year (1995–96) Souhegan will house 750 students in Grades 9 through12. The 9th and 10th grades are organized like a middle school—teachers and students are on teams (2 per grade, with 100 students to a team). The 11th and 12th grades are organized very much as is the traditional high school.

Advisory groups. Every day, groups of about 10 students meet for 30 minutes with a staff member (faculty, administrators, teaching assistants, custodial staff) for "advisory." Advisory is a time for students to talk about academic, social, school, and world issues. Advisors work closely with the guidance staff to monitor and support students to prevent problems with truancy, academic failure, substance abuse, and other school youth issues. Students with disabilities benefit from this system because they have more people looking out for them than just their "special education" case manager.

Senior seminar. All seniors are enrolled in a double period for "senior seminar," which is taught collaboratively by an English and a social studies teacher. Senior seminar is comprised of units that integrate English and social studies through the examination of current national and international problems. The final exhibition for the two-semester course is the presentation of a "senior project," which represents each student's culminating demonstration of how he or she can integrate the knowledge and skills learned throughout the previous 12 years into the investigation of a new problem. One student built a rocket while another started a cake-decorating business. The choice of topic is made during the first semester in consultation with the student's teachers and senior seminar project advisor. Students with learning difficulties have the same range of choices for doing a senior project as their classmates. Two years ago, a graduating senior with significant learning difficulties made a videotape on fishing with the assistance of a local fish and game warden who served as his mentor.

Governance. Although the local school board (elected) has the responsibility and power to make final decisions about personnel, budgeting, curriculum, and policies, it is advised by the school's Community Council. Community Council members are elected for one-year terms and represent students, administrators, faculty, school board, and community. The council's various committees receive input from small schoolwide working groups formed around such issues as smoking, absenteeism, discipline, celebrations (graduation and Fang Fest), and they forward a consensus recommendation to the school board for approval.

Wellness. Three components comprise Souhegan's Wellness Program: physical education, outdoor education, and health. All of the wellness teachers are extremely supportive of diversity and the recognition of individual student talents. Sports and physical education instruction focus on lifetime sports and games. The outdoor education program includes indoor wall climbing and "challenge by choice" on the outdoor ropes course. The health curriculum features making healthy choices in the areas of nutrition, sexuality, substance use, and personal safety.

Community service. In order to graduate, every Souhegan student must perform 40 hours of community service sometime during the high school years. Examples of service activities include organizing an Earth Day walk to raise awareness and money for local environmental activities, working in a battered women's shelter, developing a curriculum for a local day care facility, working in the school store during free periods with the profits going to a local homeless shelter, and serving as a candy striper in a hospital. In some schools, only students with disabilities leave the school building to "learn in the community," but at Souhegan all students receive exposure to the world of work and community responsibility through this community service requirement.

Creating Collaborative Planning Time

> But when do you have time to plan? All those great interdisciplinary curriculum units sound wonderful, and I'd like to have time to find multilevel materials for my students, but how am I supposed to do that when I teach six periods a day and have meetings during lunch and my planning period. Help!

Time to talk, debate, plan, find materials, and evaluate one's own teaching is essential in order for inclusion to work for all students. At Souhegan, the structure of the 9th and 10th grades provides that time and opportunity. In 9th- and 10th-grade math, English, science, social studies, and special education, teachers share two academic blocks of time each day— a two-and-a-half hour block in the morning and an hour-and-a-half block in the afternoon. During these times, the teachers may organize instruction in any way they wish. Often students spend about an hour in each class (with no bells!), but sometimes the teachers schedule longer blocks for a particular subject area, or interdisciplinary teaching, or for work on a comprehensive project.

Although there are two math tracks throughout the grades, the majority of other classes are heterogeneously grouped. In other words, in the 9th and 10th grades, all students take the same English, social studies, and science classes—there is no "honors English" or "college prep science." In the 11th and 12th grades, there are some choices in the curriculum, based more on differentiation of subject matter (environmental science, Biology 2) than on a judgment of the difficulty of the material or a desire to sort out students. Advanced placement classes are offered in several areas, and they are more homogeneous.

Each day the 9th- and 10th-grade teachers have a one-and-one-half-hour block of time for planning while the students are in two elective classes. Special education teachers and teaching assistants participate in the Monday, Wednesday, and Friday meetings. Team 10D elects to use its planning time in the following manner: Monday's block is devoted to team and school business, Tuesday's and Thursday's to individual planning time, Wednesday's to curriculum planning, and Friday's is devoted to guidance and individual problem-solving.

Despite a school's philosophical commitment to inclusion and heterogeneous grouping, long-term success is only possible when school structure and the schedule support collaborative planning time. The talents of special and general education teachers are needed to plan curriculum and teach diverse groups of students.

Essential Questions Guiding Curriculum Development

When students with widely varied talents, interests, learning styles, and support needs are fully included in content-driven high school classes, developing curriculum and instruction can be extremely challenging. Traditional responses to this classroom diversity have included:

1. Within-class grouping (reading groups)
2. Cooperative learning (all students working together to solve a common problem while still focusing on individual and group learning goals)
3. Project-based learning with skills and knowledge interwoven throughout the project
4. Individualized curriculum and learning pace (with a teacher-developed sequence of learning "packets" that students progress through at their own speed)
5. Some combination of these strategies

At Souhegan High School, "essential questions" are used to guide curriculum development that takes diversity into consideration. This process can create a unified curriculum in which all students will learn from a variety of materials, allowing different demonstrations and personalized outcomes within a broad, common course of study. Some characteristics of essential questions are: (1) there is no one right answer; (2) they help students become investigators; (3) they involve thinking, not just answering; (4) they offer a sense of adventure, are fun to explore and try to answer; (5) all students can answer them; and, (6) they require students to connect different disciplines and areas of knowledge. Examples of essential questions which have guided Souhegan curriculum for the past two years and two examples of curriculum units follow.

From the Civil War to the Rights of People With Disabilities

Cathy Fisher, a 10th-grade social studies teacher at Souhegan, has proved to be a "natural" at designing curriculum units in which all students can learn. She says:

> I was very nervous at first about having all students—students with severe disabilities and all students really, . . . they're all different—in my room. How could I pick material that they all could understand and connect with? I've found out that creating questions that all students can answer is the key. When I did a unit on slavery and the Civil War we used the question "Can you be free if you aren't treated equally?" Some students in my class could answer by using information from their Civil War reading and by thinking about the progress of civil rights in the United States. One or two students in my class had to approach this question from their own personal perspective first. Amro knows that he is treated differently from his brothers and he has a strong opinion about that. If we start with his personal experience, it's a little bit easier for him to make a connection with the Civil War.

> The questions for this unit are:

> - How will the face of America change in the next century?
> - What is your sense of place?
> - What does having money do to people?
> - If we can, should we?
> - Is the world orderly or random?
> - The more things change, the more they stay the same?
> - Can you be free if you aren't treated equally?

For a final exhibition in this 10th-grade Civil War unit, many students completed a written assignment such as researching the *Brown v. Board of Education* case or writing a letter to a student 30 years in the future describing the progress of civil rights in the United States over the last two centuries.

What were the outcomes for students with significant disabilities in this unit? Amro learned about the Civil War for the first time in his life. He learned of racial diversity and the history of slavery. He gained an understanding of slaves by comparing their loss of freedom to some of his own experiences as a student who was once segregated in a special education class. Amro produced a collage showing that he understood that there are people all over the world who look very different from one another but who all have the right to and desire for freedom.

Brandon, another Souhegan student with significant communication, behavioral, and physical challenges, chose to write a letter to a student 30 years in the future. He wrote about the progress that had been made in full participation and opportunities for people with disabilities. He talked about his own frustrations and the efforts that schools are making in the 1990s to include all students.

Who Started the Fire?

These were the essential questions facing 89 ninth-grade students on team 9A as they arrived at their team meeting on Monday morning. They knew that something would be different about the upcoming week. On Friday, Billy Joel's recording of "We Didn't Start the Fire" had greeted them as they began each team-block class in English, social studies, science, and math. Teachers involved in this unit were Gary Schnakenberg, social studies; Kris Gallo, math; Jessica Forbush, social studies intern; Bruce Shotland, science; Sally Houghton, special education support teacher; Jack Mattke, audiovisual specialist; Kim Carter, Information Center director; Lynn Mauro, Information Center assistant; and Peggy Silva, English.

The teachers' goals for this week were simple. They wanted to work on a project that would cross subject boundaries. They had all identified research and cooperative learning skills as common goals. Kim Carter, the Information Center director, suggested this song as a research vehicle. Based upon biographer–historian William Manchester's *The Glory and the Dream* (1974), the lyrics offer a capsulated look at the last 50 years of our cultural history.

The questions for this unit are:

- What is the fire?
- Who started the fire?
- Have any fires been put out?
- Are any fires still burning?

As the week's activities were planned, the teachers thought they were providing an opportunity for their students to choose work partners, to engage in some research, to share knowledge with their peers, and to have a good time. It turned out, however, to be a pivotal experience for all of them. The teachers saw overwhelming evidence that when careful attention is paid to students' individual learning styles and talents, all students can not only succeed, but even thrive in a rigorous academic environment.

For their final exhibition, students were told to "wow us" with a 5- to 15-minute presentation that would address at least two of the essential questions, explain a portion of the lyrics, and educate and entertain their peers. They were allowed to group themselves and plan their work time. Team classes were canceled for the week; students were encouraged to use all available school resources. Each student maintained a learning log, a research record, a self-evaluation, and a group evaluation. Each group submitted a project proposal, outlining plans for the final exhibition. Student work was assessed in 11 different categories ranging from "demonstration of preparation time" to "effective use of selected medium." The grading scale included "distinctive," "effective," "acceptable," and "ineffective" designations. Teachers reserved some grading points, which were referred to as the "wow" factor.

The students were told to have fun since they were in total control of their week. They could plan work time, free time, and homework. One very angry student stormed into the classroom on the second day of the project, fuming that her teachers were crazy to use the words "teenager," "work," "research," and "fun" in the same sentence. Two days later, she burst into the room exclaiming that she had finally "gotten it" and was having a great time.

Final exhibitions ranged from a "Saturday Night Live" skit, in which Davy Crockett and Albert Einstein visited *Wayne's World*, to a demonstration of a cycle-theory model, in which every person or event is identified as either a problem, an inspiration, or a solution. The explosion of the bridge over the River Kwai was recreated, and footage of Egyptian President Nasser's funeral was shown to the accompaniment of music by Sergei Prokofiev. One group of students performed a powerful theater piece incorporating the tensions of the 1960s, from birth control to Vietnam. The class learned about Joseph Stalin, Sputnik, Juan Perón, the Bay of Pigs, Princess Grace of Monaco, the Suez Canal, James Dean, Dien Bien Phu, Sonny Liston, and Syngman Rhee. The influence of television and video was apparent on this generation of students as they performed live skits and video skits, gave lectures and played music, and even took a turn at the "Wheel of Fortune." The students and teachers learned together and had fun.

Student evaluations and a debriefing demonstrated that students had mastered both content and process. They were able to reflect on what they had learned and how they had learned. They outlined their frustrations and suggested refinements for future activities. Above all, they wowed us with their commitment to learning and to the task assigned.

RESPECTING STUDENT DIVERSITY

"Honors Challenge"

Currently, Souhegan accommodates high-achieving students by offering an "Honors Challenge" within each major unit's final exhibition. Any student can accept the challenge for one unit or for every unit throughout the semester. Students who get an A or B in the honors work for one or several units receive a designation of "Distinction" on their report cards along with their grade for the semester. Students who get an A or B in the honors work for *every* unit receive the "Honors" designation along with their grade.

Students With Learning Challenges

A school is not truly inclusive unless every student, including those with significant learning, behavioral, and physical disabilities, can participate in learning and strive toward challenging outcomes. For these students, a framework of curriculum adaptation must be used to identify how students will participate in lessons and the support they'll need to do so. The following questions form the basis for this curriculum adaptation model (Tashie, Shapiro-Barnard, Schuh, Jorgensen, Dillon, & Nisbet, 1993a & 1993b). The first question is, Can the student participate in this lesson in the same way as all other students? When a student with significant disabilities first enters a general education classroom, teachers may believe there will be very few parts of the day that will not need to be modified. After teachers get to know students well and have some experience observing the student working with the curriculum, they usually find that there are many times during the day when students can participate without additional support or modification.

Amro was able to participate in his chef's class with very few modifications and earn an A. Brandon is able to participate in cooperative activities on Souhegan's ropes course, because support and choice for all students are built into the activity.

If students are unable to participate fully *without* accommodation, the second question becomes, Which supports and/or modifications are necessary for the student's full participation in this lesson?

Some students may not be able to participate independently but can participate with *support* from classmates or an adult. Brandon has visual impairments and must have most print read to him. Amro benefits from sitting next to another student who rephrases questions for him during classroom discussions.

For many students, *modifying the materials* used in the classroom is necessary for full participation. One student's lines in theater class are tape recorded by a classmate. During the class performance, she leans her head against a pressure switch connected to the player, which plays her lines at the appropriate time. This student needs to have materials and technology *added* in order to participate. Another student completes multiple-choice tests by pointing to the letters *a*, *b*, *c*, or *d* written in four quadrants of a portable white board. A teaching assistant reads him the question and the answer choices, but the answer sheet needs to be *adapted* so that he can participate.

And finally, a *substitution* for the regular classroom materials may be needed so that some students can participate. Amro uses a calculator to solve addition and subtraction problems in a 10th-grade integrated math class while the other students are working on 2-step equations.

The third accommodation that may be required to assure some students' participation is *modifying expectations*—changing how students demonstrate what they know, the quantity of work that they are assigned, or the priority of learning objectives of a particular lesson. Several students built picnic tables to be used at the high school. They demonstrated their knowledge of mathematics by following a blueprint, using measuring and cutting tools accurately, and assembling the table in the correct pattern. Another student was expected to use just three sources for his history research assignment. Instead of turning in a paper written in the usual narrative style, he was allowed to hand in his note cards with his summaries of the information he had gleaned from his source books.

Although Gwen participates fully in the same 10th-grade classes as every other student, her priority learning goals do not include the content of science, social studies, English, and math. In science, students categorize plants by species, kingdom, phylum, and order. The names of plants in the same species are mounted on red poster board, same kingdom on green, same phylum on blue, and same order on yellow. Gwen's goals are to sort the plants by color. She has numerous opportunities to use her fine motor skills in this activity and sometimes needs to ask a table mate for assistance if she can't reach a card. She works on this at the same time that her group is studying for a test on the plant classification system.

Figure 5.1 illustrates the interrelationship among the different curriculum-modification questions and options.

EVOLVING SUPPORT MODEL FOR ALL STUDENTS

Another Souhegan practice that supports inclusion is its model of collaborative planning, teaching, and academic support. When the school first opened, the academic support and case management responsibilities of special education teachers were a blend of a traditional categorical and noncategorical models (described in Table 5.1).

This meant that teachers with training and certification for working with students labeled emotionally handicapped managed the educational programs for those students, while teachers with learning disabilities certification worked with classroom teachers to support students with "LD" labels. In addition to

FIGURE 5.1. Curriculum modifications and student supports.

1. Can the student participate in this lesson in the same way as all other students?
      If YES—stop here.   If NO—go on to question 2.

2. Which of the following (one or more) supports and/or modifications are necessary so the students can participate in this lesson?

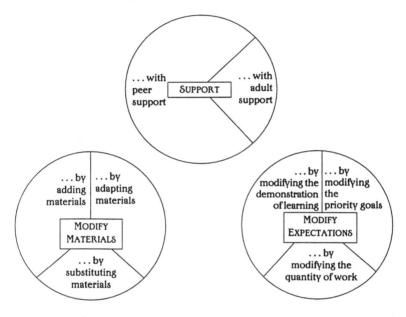

having case management responsibilities for students in the 11th and 12th
grades, three of the LD teachers were also members of 9th- or 10th-grade interdisciplinary teaching teams. This meant that, for most of the day, they were in
class "on team," but had to spend all of their planning time trying to meet
with 11th- or 12th-grade students on their categorical caseload. Marty Rounds,
as school and districtwide inclusion facilitator, supervised four teaching assistants who worked with the six students with moderate and severe disabilities.

Neither the special education teachers nor their general education partners felt that this model was truly supportive of Souhegan's heterogeneously
grouped classes. Everyone voted to change to a noncategorical model, so that
teachers were permanently attached to a teaching team or a consistent group
of teachers. A noncategorical support model was adopted for the 1993–94
school year (Table 5.2).

Regardless of area of certification, each teacher was responsible for supporting all students on the team or in the class that she or he cotaught with
a general education teacher. Thus, Bill Chouramanis (the EH [emotional

TABLE 5.1. 1992–93 Souhegan High School support model.

	Total Students	Special Education Support
Team 9A	88	LD teacher
Team 9B	88 (Including four students with moderate and severe disabilities)	LD teacher .5 Inclusion facilitator 2 1:1 Teaching assistants .5 Teaching assistant
Team 10C	88	.5 LD teacher
Team 10D	88	.5 LD teacher .5 Teaching assistant attached to a student
11th Grade	175	.5 EH teacher .5 Teaching assistant
12th Grade	175	.5 EH teacher .5 Teaching assistant

handicap] specialist) and Linda Stewart (teaching assistant) worked with all students in the 11th and 12th grades, regardless of their label. Similarly, Sally Houghton, the team 9A special education teacher, supported all students on the 9th grade team, 9A—those with EH or LD labels.

At a review meeting in the spring of 1994, every teacher expressed a clear preference for this model. They all felt that it allowed them to be involved in curriculum planning with their teaching team. Curriculum could be developed with student diversity in mind, and classroom teachers grew to know and understand the learning styles and needs of all of the students in their classes through the constant presence of the support teacher.

Out-of-Class Academic Support

"Academic support" for students occurs through the development of inclusive curriculum and cooperative teaching as well as within the Academic Support Center, the Writing Center, or classrooms not being used for whole-class instruction. There are no programs or rooms or classes in the building utilized solely by students with disabilities. All students are encouraged to utilize the school's Academic Support Center to receive individualized tu-

TABLE 5.2. 1993–94 Souhegan High School support model.

	Total Students	Special Education Support
Team 9A	88	LD teacher
Team 9B	88 (Including four students with moderate and severe disabilities)	LD teacher .5 Inclusion facilitator 2 1:1 Teaching assistants .5 Teaching assistant
Team 10C	88	.5 LD teacher
Team 10D	88	.5 LD teacher .5 Teaching assistant attached to a student
11th Grade	175	.5 EH teacher .5 Teaching assistant
12th Grade	175	.5 EH teacher .5 Teaching assistant

toring from a subject-area or special education teacher. The center is staffed all day by both general and special education teachers. Students who have incomplete or below C-minus work are referred to the center by their classroom teacher, and a plan of support is developed by the center's coordinator, Ellie Bosman. The center is also used by students for small group meetings, for one-on-one tutoring, for chess club meetings, and as a general "hang-out" during their free periods.

Role of Special Education Teachers

At Souhegan High School the discussion about the most effective support model for students with disabilities extends far beyond the question, What is the role of special education teachers? Teachers and administrators are asking, What are the essential knowledge and skills that high school graduates ought to demonstrate? How must curriculum be developed so that all students can participate and learn at high levels? When students are not succeeding, who's responsible for intervention? How much individualization in both demonstration of learning and learning outcomes is possible without compromising excellence in standards?

Because the answers to these questions and associated policies and practices are still being developed, the role of special education teachers is uncertain and undefined. In some situations, special education teachers function primarily as "accommodation and remediation teachers." After the general education teacher develops curricula and selects learning materials, the special education teacher adapts those materials to the learning styles and reading levels of the students in the class with learning difficulties. The special education teacher works with those students in and outside the class to help them understand the material and helps them prepare for the final unit test or exhibition.

In other situations, special education teachers participate in curriculum development right from the beginning so that accommodation to students' interests, learning styles, reading levels, and so forth, is built into the unit and final exhibition. This accommodation to student differences is made for *all* students, not just those with identified learning difficulties. Students may still need assistance in understanding readings or preparing for a final exhibition or test, and this is often provided by special and general education teachers both in and outside class.

Two areas are likely to provoke confusion or outright disagreement among teachers. The first area of possible dissension is over who has *control* of curriculum design. The second concerns who is responsible for actually *managing* interventions for students who are not succeeding—meeting with students to determine what is causing the difficulty, dealing with troublesome family situations that are negatively affecting the students' ability to learn, working with students who have lost their motivation to come to school or complete their work, and facilitating problem-solving meetings among the students, their families, and the various school and nonschool staff involved in the students' life.

The issue of control over curriculum design is founded in the continuing uncertainty about exactly what the model of curriculum design is at Souhegan High School. All the teachers and teams have their own views about how this process is supposed to proceed, although there is general understanding about the value of using essential questions to design learning units. Nevertheless, the strategies for designing curricula that reflect student differences and challenge for every student have not been clearly debated, identified, or adopted. There is also still some confusion and debate about who has responsibility for students with learning difficulties—the general education teacher, the special education teacher, or both.

Schools that have had the most success at including students with learning difficulties fully within the mainstream of general education have not resolved these concerns by simply defining the *roles* of general and special education teachers. Instead, they have implemented a collaborative problem-solving team *process* as the tool for identifying options, selecting courses of action, assigning responsibility, evaluating results, and resolving conflicts. For example, the Winooski School District in Vermont resolved the whole debate regarding the roles of general and special education teachers by developing one job description that applies to all teachers and by providing extensive training in the problem-solving process to teaching teams. While the clarification of roles for general and special educators may help resolve this current uneasiness, two additional steps will be critical to moving beyond a paper-and-pencil solution to better learning outcomes for all students.

First, teachers and administrators need to develop some *guidelines for curriculum design that make accommodation of student differences obligatory*. These guidelines should be written not only to address the needs of students with learning difficulties, but also to accommodate the needs of students who are bored, students who already know much of what is traditionally taught in schools, and students who are disenchanted with life in general and school in particular. Supporting a common curriculum design process requires the systematic acquisition of multidimensional learning materials and technology in the school's information center (library). If teachers are going to be expected to provide a variety of challenging materials for a diverse classroom of students, they need articles and movies and reference materials to support that expectation.

Second, adoption of and staff development relative to a *collaborative problem-solving model* is an essential next step. Regardless of the roles that teachers have or the curriculum design model that is put in place, there will always be differences of opinion, a myriad of equally valid curriculum choices from which to select, and a variety of experiences and beliefs within teaching teams. Some approach is necessary for helping teachers make decisions and resolve differences for the collective good of the students.

EMPOWERING STUDENTS TO ADVOCATE FOR INCLUSIVE SCHOOLS

While typical students have been involved in supporting their peers with disabilities in both informal and formal ("circles of friends") ways since inclusive education began, the empowerment of students to go beyond personal action to making changes in their and others' school systems is new (Forest & Lusthaus, 1989).

In New Hampshire, the first students with severe disabilities to be included in general education classrooms were those whose parents had attended a Family Leadership series sponsored by the Institute on Disability in 1988. Using a similar training and empowerment model, the institute sponsored the first Youth Leadership Conference in June 1993; it was designed to help high school students experience firsthand the challenges of creating an inclusive, supported community (at the conference itself!) and to help them develop and implement action plans for influencing their schools over the inclusion of students with disabilities.

In the spring of 1993, students from four different high schools were recruited for the Youth Leadership Conference by their teachers. Two or three students with significant physical and communication disabilities from each high school were asked by their teachers if they wanted to participate in a three-day leadership conference at the University of New Hamsphire. Students' friends and acquaintances were then asked if they would like to learn about advocacy, social change, and community organizing around issues of diversity, specifically the issue of disability.

Getting to Know One Another

On the first day of the conference, students were introduced to the concepts underlying the retreat; and they were allowed plenty of time for unstructured socializing and participation in several noncompetitive games designed to help them get to know one another. As observers noticed, as long as the activities were structured, everyone was included and supported. When there was a break, however, students with disabilities were often off to the side in the gym or assisted only by the adults who accompanied their school team. It was clear that creating an inclusive community among the student conference participants was going to be a challenge in and of itself. Moreover, unless students could experience firsthand the rewards and difficulties of this task, they would not be fully informed about the job that lay ahead in their home schools.

Several students with disabilities had never been away from home without the support of familiar teaching assistants or their parents, and they experienced serious homesickness. Some students were separated from the people who were experienced in facilitating and interpreting their communication and thus were unable to make their needs and wishes easily known. Some students were comfortable with friends who had physical disabilities but uncomfortable with students whose behavior was unpredictable or challenging. Each activity or initiative led by the Project Adventure instructors offered potential lessons in cooperation, support, and problem-solving, and this diverse group of teenagers experienced them all.

Watching students approach students from different schools was illuminating, offering a glimpse into each student's mind and heart. Students from Souhegan High School seemed the most willing to pitch in to lend a hand to students from other schools. They were eager to experiment with students' communication devices or provide personal assistance during meal-time, and they often went the extra mile to involve these students in the ac-tivities and games. Was it a coincidence that these students attended a fully inclusive school?

Learning to Support One Another

On the second day of the conference, the students were involved with the Ropes Course. During the morning students experienced the low elements (i.e., those close to the ground) of the course, working together to cross pre-tend "rivers," to maneuver through obstacles, and to walk on elevated bal-ance beams. Although each school group included two advisors, teachers or teaching assistants, they were asked to stay as far away from the student groups as possible, for it was hoped that the students would rely on one another for support and problem-solving.

Most of the groups supported their members naturally and easily. How-ever, when a problem arose with a student with disabilities in one group, the student's teacher was sought out to solve it. In frustration, this teacher told the group that they should "solve it themselves." The group then spent some time processing this issue and concluded that the "sink or swim" method was not conducive to making people feel comfortable with providing sup-port to someone they didn't know. They discussed the need for education and support in order for all students to feel at ease with one another.

Learning What Inclusion Really Means

On the third and final day, the students processed what they had learned throughout the conference. The previous day's problem became a catalyst for a lively discourse on inclusion. When one student expressed concern that some students were being held to a different standard of behavior than other students ("I thought inclusion meant that people with disabilities could be included in everything but that you didn't make allowances for them"), the group learned that inclusion meant that everyone belonged *and* was provided with the support that he or she needed in order to participate fully in the activity. For some students, that support might be physical. For others, it might be adapting the explicit rules of a game or the unwritten rules of being part of a group.

When the time came for final goodbyes, there were hugs all around and promises to keep in touch. Students expressed that they had learned that cre-ating and sustaining inclusive communities was hard work—but worth it—

and pledged to go back to their schools and try to make a difference for all students in their schools. Each group left with a "plan for action" for their schools.

Back at Souhegan High School

The Souhegan High School group made great progress toward implementing their action plan. Twelve students made a videotape about inclusion and shared it with participants at an international inclusion conference held in Colorado in 1994. Throughout the course of the school year, different members of the group gave presentations at a statewide inclusion conference, a legislative forum on education held at the state capital, and various other conferences. Transcripts of two students' presentations follow:

The Gift of Believing
by Brad Fach

September 1, 1992 was the start of a new school and a new friendship for me. The new school was, of course, Souhegan. This school was different from the rest. The biggest difference I noticed was heterogeneous classes. Classes where all students were given an opportunity to learn, no matter what their learning capability was. I clearly remember the first day of school and my fellow students taking turns introducing themselves. All except for one large but shy-looking boy. There was a woman sitting with this boy who introduced herself and then the boy, as Amro Diab. She said that this student will be in all of our classes and please don't be alarmed if he doesn't talk because he is very shy.

When Amro first started in our school he wouldn't look me in the eye and he certainly wouldn't talk to anyone. This made it hard for some people to accept and communicate with him. I, on the other hand, found it quite easy and normal. The first real contact I had with Amro was on the football field. At that time Amro had chosen to become the assistant manager for our school's football team. I was also on the football team. One day before practice I felt a tap on my shoulder, and there was Amro. Amro pointed at me, and then at him, and then at a football. I soon caught on and started tossing the football with him. I didn't realize until later that he wasn't dumb or stupid, he was the same as me, he just communicated differently. That was the beginning of a new friendship.

The whole school began to realize that these few students we had at our school weren't different or dumb. They just needed a chance to prove to us and to themselves that they were as capable of doing everything you or I could, just in another way.

After Christmas that first year, I guess you could say Amro came out of his shell. He was participating in class, working in the school store, and managing to squeeze in a game of hoops from time to time. I remember picking Amro to work with me in a social studies exhibition. We were doing a skit in front of the class and I was worried that he wouldn't remember his lines. I was very wrong. He said his lines perfectly and he still remembers them correctly to this day.

I feel that everyone has a special gift to share. Amro gave me his gift that year, and it was the gift of believing. I never would have thought that I would have the opportunity to become close friends with someone who talks to me through a keyboard but it happened. I am amazed at how our whole school accepts and respects those students who are different from themselves. I have been over to Amro's house many times. I can't describe the great feelings that I get when his parents see that their child has a friend over. They make that apparent by spoiling me with seconds on Nona's broccoli burgers. I feel like I have finally done something good when I see Amro waiting at the end of his driveway pointing to his watch as I arrive. I feel good because I know that I have given him something he has wanted for a long time, something that everyone needs, a sense of belonging and more importantly, friendship. But I know now that he has given me much more than I could ever give to him.

Take the Time to Talk
by Brandon Worster

Q: What would you like to tell everyone about your experiences at Souhegan High School?

Brandon: I want to tell them that I don't belong. I think the kids try real hard to accept me.

Q: Why don't you feel like you belong if the kids are trying to accept you?

Brandon: Because I'll never believe them.

Q: What would they need to do in order for you to believe them?

Brandon: If they really wanted to be my friend, they need to try to know me.

Q: What do they need to do to get to know you?

Brandon: Take the time to talk.

Q: Do you mean you want them to learn to facilitate with you or that you want them to spend time talking with you?

Brandon: Both are important.

Q: Are there things about being here at Souhegan that you like better than your other school?

Brandon: Everything.

Q: Can you be a little more specific?

Brandon: I can take any classes I want to.

Q: What are some classes you can take now that you couldn't take at your other school?

Brandon: I had to take what they decided.

Q: What do you like about your classes here?

Brandon: Learning like everyone else.

Q: Do you have anything else you'd like to add or are you finished?

Brandon: Help me and everyone keep moving ahead.

Souhegan students continued to provide support for students on a very personal level. They listened to 10th grader Brandon talk about his dissatisfaction with his bus routine. While Brandon rode the usual bus to school, the driver insisted on dropping him off closer to the school door than the other students because she thought Brandon "had a hard time walking." Brandon hated the special attention, didn't like walking into school with a teaching assistant, and felt babied. The members of the Youth Leadership group made an appointment to talk with the bus driver and the bus aide and presented a proposal for assisting Brandon off the bus and into the school building. Starting the next day, Brandon and a friend walked off the bus together and into the school building. It was not a hardship for Brandon and he felt more like the other students.

PLANNING THE FUTURE: A HIGH SCHOOL GRADUATION PLAN

We have described a school in which all students are fully included in a typical schedule of high school classes and extracurricular activities. What about community-based instruction? When do students learn "functional" skills? What about preparation for the world of work?

For the past several years, the Institute on Disability has been teaching students, parents, and teachers about the importance of students with disabilities learning in general education classrooms during the school day, not out in the community. There are both philosophical and practical rationales to support this practice.

Access to all school and community opportunities should be independent of a student's abilities and/or disabilities. Whether a school requires all students to spend their entire school day within its walls or embraces a free-flowing partnership with community businesses and organizations, expectations and access should be the same for all students. Disability or label should neither increase nor decrease access and opportunity. As schools throughout the country develop philosophies and policies that merge the dual systems of education for students with and without disabilities, some still continue to perpetuate the existing separate system for secondary students with significant disabilities. Secondary students with disabilities, even those who have been fully included in elementary and middle schools, are expected gradually to move away from their peers during their secondary school years and enter a daytime community void of others their age. By leaving the school building—when all others remain—students with disabilities become physically segregated and potentially socially isolated from their peers. Typical relationships are impeded, peer contacts are minimized, and the stereotypes of separate and different are reinforced. Certainly, these are not the desired outcomes for instruction designed to prepare students for life after school.

The segregating outcomes of community-based instruction during the school day for students with disabilities is but one—albeit a very significant— reason to discontinue this standard practice. However, this social inequality is coupled with academic inequality as well. As many schools move toward a belief in the ability of all students as learners and the disability field is challenged by increasingly frequent reports of literacy and competency in individuals with labels of mental retardation, it is remarkably clear that students with disabilities can and should have access to the learning that occurs in typical high school classes. Limiting a student's time in the school building limits the number of classes that constitute a student's school accomplishment. A society that values a well-rounded, liberal arts education for its students cannot exclude students with disabilities from this tenet. Long-held belief that students with disabilities could not learn or benefit from the knowledge and skill imparted in high school classes sets up an endless cycle of low expectations and minimized outcomes. High school classes offer all students opportunities to gain knowledge that assists them in making present and future life choices as well as in developing interests and community connections. These same classes provide students with life skills such as communication, cooperation, problem-solving, initiative, and leadership, skills and qualities valued by teachers and employers alike. It is this knowledge and skill, coupled with strong social networks, that help to prepare a student for a well-rounded life after school.

If Not Community-Based Instruction During School, Then When?

There certainly is value in teaching students—all students—in real community environments. With that stipulated, the question then becomes when and where do students with disabilities gain experience and skill in areas not traditionally covered in high school classes or curriculum?

The answer to this question lies in the basic principles of inclusion. Students with disabilities must have access to the same opportunities as their peers to develop skills and experiences in relationships, the community, and on the job. Traditionally, students without disabilities venture into the community, not during the school day, but after school, on weekends, and in the summer. Students explore the full gamut of community resources (e.g., shopping malls, movie theaters, recreation centers) as well as work at a variety of jobs when school is not in session. Students combine their school day with a rich array of out-of-school experiences.

This knowledge allows us to determine where and when students with disabilities should have access to this array. Community instruction and experiences can occur at the times—and places—where other students are also pursuing such goals. A student who wants job experience can be supported in an afterschool, weekend, and/or summer job. A student who needs experience in ordering and purchasing in a restaurant can be supported to join peers at the local "hamburger joint." Support for this instruction and experience occurs in the typical places that students use for recreation, social connections, and work experience. For schools that embrace the value of community connections for all students, this support can also occur during student apprenticeships, community service projects, and school-supported cooperative work experiences.

At Souhegan High School, teachers are striving to make all students' education "functional." All students, including those with significant disabilities, take a full schedule of academic classes, have the opportunity to gain job skills through apprenticeships within the school environment (office, Information Center, school store), have the choice of working at afterschool and/or summer jobs, and receive support to engage in comprehensive decision-making about post–high school plans.

Implications for "Transition" and Graduation Planning

In high schools throughout the country, educators are discussing the "transition" needs of students with disabilities. In response to federal and state legislation, "transition plans" are being developed and implemented for all students with disabilities.

There are several major problems with the traditional view of "transition" for these students. First, many high school students with disabilities are not included in typical school experiences—classes, extracurricular activities, and graduation planning. They are not supported to become fully participating and valued members in the experiences and classes that can assist them in the development of their future goals. As mentioned earlier, many students with disabilities progress through their school careers spending less time in the school building with their peers and more time in the community. This not only prevents students with disabilities from taking a full schedule of classes, it isolates them from the very peer group they need to be successful now and as they enter into the world of adulthood. It also serves to negate the valuable learning—academic, life skills, and social—that occurs for all students in high school

Second, the traditional "transition" process tends to perpetuate the notion that "special" paid people are the only ones who can support students in school, at home, in the community, or on the job. Many professionals see "transition" as something that happens to students with disabilities to help them move from special education into the world of adult services. Depending on the community, this can mean making the transition from "school to work" or "school to sheltered work" or "school to day-habilitation" or even "school to waiting lists for services."

Third, only students with disabilities make a "transition," all other students "graduate." This system itself implies a separation between students with and without disabilities. With a strong emphasis on the merger of the separate systems of education, it seems counterproductive to maintain, or develop, a separate system of "transition."

When viewing students with disabilities as members of the whole community, it becomes clear that "transition" must fit into our concept of quality inclusive education for all. Efforts must not be targeted at developing a different, special system of high school education and "transition" for students with disabilities, but rather on making the typical educational experience and graduation planning process open and meaningful to all students. The following questions can be used as a graduation planning checklist:

1. Does the student have a typical daily schedule—all age-appropriate, regular education classes in the neighborhood school—and the supports provided so that he or she can be successful?

2. Does the student move through the grades in the usual fashion (9th through 12th) and participate in all grade-related activities (move-up day, graduation planning, etc.)?

3. Does the student use natural environments and people to gain supports (study halls, guidance, nurse, lockers, etc.)?

4. Is the student valued for his or her participation in school, and do grades, transcript, and diploma reflect this?

5. Is the student involved and supported in desired extracurricular activities?

6. Is the student supported to have friends and meaningful relationships in and out of school?

7. Does the student have an afterschool, weekend, and/or summer job, if desired?

8. Is the student supported to participate in "community-based instruction" only during times when other students are engaged in such activities (afterschool, weekends, summers, after senior year)?

9. Is the student supposed to develop the usual connections within the community?

10. Is the student supported to develop meaningful skills and knowledge through participation in typical classes?

11. Is the student regarded with respect for her or his gifts and abilities and supported with the highest of expectations?

12. Is the student involved in typical career–futures planning courses?

13. Does the student have regular contact with the guidance counselor?

14. Is the student the leader in planning present and future choices as demonstrated by choosing classes, choosing extracurricular activities, choosing career paths, leading the team?

15. Does the student, after graduating from the high school in the senior year, continue to receive supports in the community via the school system?

16. Is the student supported to pursue career, continuing education, housing, and recreation choices after completion of senior year in high school?

Changing Job Roles

Changing the perspective about high school education and the "transition–graduation" process requires a change in some of the ways that people have traditionally viewed their job roles and responsibilities. A shift from a model of direct professional or paraprofessional support to a model of encouraging and nurturing natural supports in the school and community is essential. School and community members must provide support to students with disabilities in much the same ways that support is provided to others—employers to new workers, churches and service organizations to new community residents, and so forth. In addition, the hours that school personnel work may need to change in order to support students beyond the school day.

Changing the Educational Timetable

The traditional way of educating students with disabilities was full time in the school building through elementary school, community-based instruction through middle and high school, development of a job by the age of 20, and finally, "transition" compressed into the last few months of school. A student with disabilities might have to repeat the senior year two or three times in order to "exit" school at the age of 21.

To accompany and guide the new vision of graduation planning, a new timetable—a typical educational timetable—must be embraced. The sequence of moving through the grades, taking required courses, choosing electives, participating in extracurricular activities, and then graduating into adulthood upon completion of their (first and only) senior year is important for all students.

Graduation and Beyond

What about graduation? New Hampshire's state regulations, and those of most other states, are interpreted to mean that a student's eligibility for special education services and supports ends on receipt of a standard high school diploma. For this and other reasons, many schools have presented students with disabilities with alternative diplomas or certificates of completion (or in the words of one parent, "a certificate of occupancy") in order to continue services through the age of 21.

Today, schools and communities that embrace the more typical timetable of education for students with disabilities are struggling to match regulations with effective education. These schools have acknowledged the need for a compromise until policy catches up with practice. They believe that support must continue after the formal graduation ceremony (after senior year) to young adults in jobs, colleges, or technical schools, adult education classes, community activities, and so forth. In many of these schools, students with disabilities participate in all the ceremonies and activities of senior year, including graduation, but do not receive their standard diploma until they are 21 years old. While this compromise is not ideal, schools and communities recognize the need to move forward with practice, as one way of changing policy and regulations.

And after graduation? High school students make a variety of choices. They go to college part-time or full-time, they work part- or full-time, they live at home or find an apartment with a roommate. Students with disabilities need the same choices. School districts must work in close collaboration with the young adult and the family, and with employers, college officials, and community organizations to determine what supports will be needed to assist the individual in achieving goals and dreams.

Restructuring as Help or Hindrance?

The school restructuring movement offers some opportunities and raises some cautions regarding the graduation process. Souhegan High School does not award a high school diploma on the basis of Carnegie units, credits, or accumulated "seat time," but rather on the student's demonstration of mastery of a body of knowledge and a set of performance-based skills. The diploma can be awarded to a student at any age and at any time during a high school career. Some students may leave school when they are 14 years old, while others may not leave until the age of 23. This increasingly flexible system for all students can certainly benefit students with disabilities. A strong note of caution, however, is in order. Students with disabilities must not be overrepresented in the group of students who stay in school beyond the age of 18. Students with disabilities must be fully included in all reform and restructuring efforts and must share equitably in the rewards of the educational experience.

CHALLENGES FOR SOUHEGAN HIGH SCHOOL

Factors that operate to initiate a major change in an organization are sometimes different from those that are necessary to sustain change and weather adversity. In Souhegan's instance, thinking about the differences between those sets of variables helps us understand what Souhegan must do in order to continue to grow and change for the benefit of all students.

There were six conditions that predisposed Souhegan to establish its philosophy of full inclusion right from the start and to experience early success. Although these are not prerequisites for inclusion, they have assisted Souhegan High School in its journey toward excellence and equity. The conditions were:

1. The district had had success with inclusion at their elementary schools for several years before Souhegan opened.
2. Marty Rounds' presence in the school as a committed supporter of inclusion and his skills at supporting students and teachers were essential.
3. District Superintendent Rick Lalley and the members of the planning team believed enough in inclusion to be willing to take the risk of "just doing it" at the beginning.
4. The planning team heard from strong inclusion supporters—including George Flynn and the Institute on Disability staff—during their critical discussions prior to Souhegan's opening.
5. The district received constant support and direction as it made the small and large decisions that impact teachers' values and resources relative to inclusion.
6. Everything is new at Souhegan—nothing is "carved in stone"—and most teachers who have chosen to work at Souhegan are willing to take risks,

experiment, admit that they have lots to learn, and go the extra mile for each and every student.

The strides made at Souhegan during its first two years of operation are nothing short of remarkable. Most students with disabilities are doing well socially and academically. Most of their parents are thrilled with the quality of the education being offered their children. They see perceptible changes in their children's self-esteem and learning as a result of the confidence being expressed in their ability to succeed in a rigorous academic program. New and veteran teachers are experiencing success in developing teaching strategies for heterogeneous classes, and many have expressed a new respect for the value and abilities of students with disabilities. Teachers are developing mutual respect for one another's experiences and perspectives and are looking forward to working even more effectively on interdisciplinary teams next year.

The challenges that lie ahead are clear:

1. How can the community be invested and involved in the school in a way that respects the diversity of values and opinions in that community without forcing the school to adopt policies and practices that are so bland—so nonoffensive to anyone—that teachers lose the willingness to take the risks that lead to more creative teaching for all students?

2. Not all students with disabilities who live in the Amherst area are attending Souhegan (three are currently in out-of-district programs). As long as some students continue to be placed outside the district, teams must be extra vigilant about building supports into the current system and not relieving the pressure on the system by sending students away from the school.

3. The support model and the respective roles of special education and general education teachers are still confusing to many teachers. Although efficient use of the district's financial resources dictate that the highest level of special education support be placed in those classes in which more students with disabilities are enrolled, classroom teachers need support for challenging all students in the classroom. This implies a new role for special education staff who must also serve as curriculum resources for all students.

4. Few of the members of Souhegan's exemplary teaching staff have experience working collaboratively with their general education colleagues, much less those in special education. Everyone in the school feels a need to improve the group process and their problem-solving skills.

5. Can or should outcomes be expressed in such a way that all students have a chance to achieve them? How can differences in talents and interests be accommodated without sacrificing academic rigor? Even though some teachers are comfortable and skilled at challenging each and every student

in the class, some high-achieving students say that they are bored, and their parents may be encouraged to send them to a private school that does not have Souhegan's diversity. What are effective instructional models when abilities and interests are so diverse?

6. And, finally, the responsibility for decision-making and the process of communicating those decisions to staff and the community is perplexing even to Souhegan's own staff. Who makes decisions about curriculum: Teachers? Grade-level teams of teachers? Administrators? The Faculty Steering Committee? The Curriculum Committee of the Community Council? The Curriculum Committee of the school board? The Division I Outcomes Committee? the humanities teachers? The math, science, and technology teachers?

Despite these ongoing challenges, Souhegan is well on its way to becoming a school that is truly a place where all students belong, are valued, and can achieve excellence.

ANOTHER HIGH SCHOOL STORY

When Robert Pedersen, principal of Pelham High School, was recently asked about the major restructuring efforts underway in his school, he cited "inclusion" as one of the reasons the faculty and community are committed to and energized by these changes. "When we began including students with disabilities in our regular education classes, teachers began to take a look at the ways in which they taught all students," says Principal Pedersen. "Inclusion helped teachers realize that there were strategies they could use to ensure that all students could learn. This eased the way to implementing major restructuring in our school and district."

Pelham High School, located in southern New Hampshire, is home to over 400 students. In 1989, Pelham High School, along with the elementary and middle schools in this district, became a fully inclusive school—all students with disabilities were returned to their neighborhood schools and began attending all regular education classes. Teachers received training in how best to educate all the students in their classes, families received information on the best practices in education and community living, and students received all the supports necessary to be successful in those regular classes. Pelham was viewed by many as a school worthy of replication for its success with inclusion.

Today, Pelham is still viewed as a model of a fully inclusive high school, but people are also taking note of the numerous changes in curriculum, scheduling, support, and community involvement that have occurred since 1989. For example, the high school has recently converted to block scheduling and has plans underway for a four-block schedule beginning in 1995. Pedersen states that having students and teachers spend longer periods of time together allows for a more comprehensive and hands-on approach to the curriculum. "All students benefit from a schedule that allows for practical applications of the material being covered," Pedersen believes. He is also excited about the increased flexibility in support services that will begin with the next school year. In addition to the support that is now given to students and teachers in the classroom and during students' study periods, the school will offer support to students before and after school.

Many of the changes in the basic structure of the school are guided by the School Council, a governing body made up of representatives from the student body, faculty, administration, school board, and community. The School Council meets on a monthly basis to propose changes and support ideas. One of the latest proposals to the council is the development of a comprehensive career–future planning process for all students. Pelham High School is developing a planning system for its students that involves career portfolios, community service, and the development of strong school–community partnerships that would support apprenticeships and internships. All of these opportunities would be available to all of the students, with additional support provided to any student who requires it. As the principal said, "Students with disabilities are a part of our school and, of course, they are included in all typical career and futures planning processes. The only difference is in the amount of support that an individual student might need."

Pelham High School is but one example of schools throughout New Hampshire that support restructuring and inclusion. It is significant that these schools are not engaged in school restructuring efforts separate from inclusion. Instead, they are asking themselves the question: How can our school be restructured in order to support the best education for all students? It is this question that will lead us into the next century.

ACKNOWLEDGMENT

Preparation of this chapter was supported by grants (H023R20018 and H158A1003-94) from the U.S. Department of Education, Office of Special Education and Rehabilitative Services. The opinions expressed in this article are not necessarily those of the U.S. Department of Education or the University of New Hampshire. The University of New Hampshire is an equal opportunity employer. We would like to thank all the students and staff at Souhegan High School for sharing their thoughts with us. We are especially grateful for Peggy Silva's impassioned and comprehensive description of the "We Didn't Start the Fire" unit.

REFERENCES

Biklen, D. (1990). Communication unbound: Autism and praxis. *Harvard Educational Review, 60,* 291–315.

Forest, M., & Lusthaus, E. (1989). Promoting educational equality for all students: Circles and maps. In S. Stainback, W. Stainback, and M. Forest (Eds.), *Educating all students in the mainstream of regular education* (pp. 47–57). Baltimore: Brookes.

Manchester, W. (1974). *The glory and the dream.* Boston: Little and Brown.

Tashie, C., Shapiro-Barnard, S., Schuh, M., Jorgensen, C., Dillon, A., & Nisbet, J. (1993a). *From special to regular: From ordinary to extraordinary.* Durham: Institute on Disability/University Affiliated Program, University of New Hampshire.

Tashie, C., Shapiro-Barnard, S., Schuh, M., Jorgensen, C., Dillon, A., & Nisbet, J. (1993b). *Changes in latitudes, changes in attitudes.* Durham: Institute on Disability/University Affiliated Program, University of New Hampshire.

CHAPTER 6

Environments for Everyone: Community Building and Restructuring

Peter Knoblock

The search for community is persistent and elusive. Its perceived benefits compel many of us to persevere in our efforts to create learning environments with others as a way to maximize the benefits to the children and adults working within these settings. As a young professor at Syracuse University in 1962, I quickly became involved with the local schools and community agencies, but my involvement was the result of relationships with a group of mental health workers interested in creating an innovative classroom program for students labeled emotionally disturbed.

This collaborative effort was exhilarating to me at the time. To find like-minded colleagues with a shared sense of purpose was a heady experience, particularly in the context of our interest in fostering changes in the programming for these students and in the attitudes of teachers toward them. Our ideological position was secondary to the forming of a network of adults as a small community to examine student needs. From that beginning, we pursued a multidisciplinary model of staff functioning in an effort to harness human resources to maximize student functioning. By today's standards, there is nothing very innovative about special class programs for students labeled emotionally disturbed; however, it was progress in the context of what existed at the time and it reinforced my belief that school change can be facilitated by group efforts.

A few years later I helped form Jowonio School. This chapter celebrates the vision of the teachers, parents, and students who came to value the community-building begun at Jowonio. Their efforts are illustrative of the good things that can happen when people with a shared vision come together to create a learning environment that is responsive to all the participants.

Despite the idiosyncratic nature of Jowonio School—an alternative school created to include students with moderate and severe disabilities—there are lessons to be learned from its 25 years of experience. I spell them out in some detail here in the hope they will help others; however, it is equally important to recognize the unique challenges each school district and community faces and the importance of adopting a school restructuring agenda that addresses local needs.

When a small group of parents and educators came together in 1969 to consider children's needs, its focus was clearly on general education, despite the realization that several of our own children were perceived by the schools as "special needs" students. We assumed that all children could profit from a learning environment that viewed all participants as equally valued—including the adults.

The educational ferment of the late 1960s and 1970s reinforced our belief that it was possible to structure such an environment. We also recognized that what we were planning fell outside the existing educational structure of the Syracuse public schools. The implications of this distance became apparent later, as our "experiment" became more acceptable within the school system. I trace these implications as I recount one school's reaction to what was missing in children's schooling and its gradual evolution into a more planful and self-conscious school restructuring effort to reconceptualize education.

Early work at Jowonio led me to define "alternative education" broadly —as neither inside nor outside public schools. In fact, many school districts then began thinking of alternative classroom architectural designs to accompany curriculum changes. We saw schools without walls designed to facilitate social interaction among students and the use of collaborative projects involve students at different ages and ability levels. When we developed the interdisciplinary team approach and merged it with a special class program in the Syracuse City School District, we were, in effect, creating an "alternative" to what existed. Jowonio School was initially conceived as an alternative to public education, but, in truth, we were never far from the public school orbit.

As the "free schools" of the early 1970s became the "open education" classrooms in public schools by the end of the decade, schools like Jowonio were always within reach of public education. For example, in order to gain a charter as a school from the New York State Education Department, we needed the Syracuse City School District's approval of our curriculum as equivalent to that of the public schools. When we began the transition of our students from Jowonio School to the public schools, we placed our staff members in the schools and worked out salary arrangements with the school district.

Thus we hoped to demonstrate a "newer look" for classroom instruction and organization. This chapter traces the implications of presenting a different philosophy of growth and development, classroom organization, and parental involvement. Indeed, these developments created some profound school restructuring for certain schools and, to a lesser extent, for some schools across the district. On the other hand, starting outside the formal structure of the public schools and then attempting to reconnect undoubtedly contributed to tensions among people and systems. I hope a creative tension was the norm, but these tensions are also examined here as one aspect of how our efforts influenced general education.

BUILDING COMMUNITY

I hope it is now clear that Jowonio was not begun as a planned social change effort; however, it evolved into precisely such an effort, thanks to the community-building efforts of scores of parents and educators. Today, in Syracuse, we have a network of inclusive classrooms located in preschool, elementary, middle, and high schools. They are taught by teachers originally prepared as general educators or special educators and some who were dually prepared in our new Undergraduate Inclusive Teacher Education Program at Syracuse University. These classrooms are supported by a school district administration that recently passed a districtwide inclusion policy developed in collaboration with parents of disabled and nondisabled students. Visitors from far and wide travel to see Jowonio School (Knoblock, 1983), Edward Smith Elementary School (Fenwick, 1987), and other emerging models that address the diverse needs of students.

Twenty-five years is a long time to plan for change but each time we reached one of our goals, the next set of challenges surfaced. Just identifying young children with autism who had no school program seemed like a big step; however, once having taken it, we had to develop meaningful programs for those children. Gaining confidence in our ability to individualize instruction for each child, disabled and nondisabled alike, encouraged us to plan a transition into the neighborhood elementary school for our "aging out" students. The decision to transfer children from Jowonio School into the Syracuse public schools was one of our strategies for pushing the issue of integration (as we called it then), but the move triggered a host of immediate and long-term issues and questions. Where would the teachers come from to teach students previously considered uneducable? And in general education classrooms! Is there a curriculum approach responsive to such a range of students? When would teachers find time to plan—if they knew what to plan for? The list goes on, and some of the major questions, along with our answers, are highlighted in this chapter. My hope is that others can profit from our experiences and that readers will gain the confidence to find local solutions for the problems of bringing all students together in general education.

One reason for the lengthy change process in Syracuse was our gradual recognition that we were actually aiming to reconceptualize the educational process. It took time to practice what we preached: that students with autism, for example, were indeed capable of learning and changing. Once we began to see the results of orchestrating classrooms for success, we turned our attention to school and systems change. All of this has taken time, and we have no end point in mind. Our solutions to the issues posed here in this chapter are certainly specific to our community in many ways. Yet it is this very notion of community, and community-building, that has guided our accomplishments.

A Tale of Two Communities

Several years ago a 5-year-old child was kidnapped by her father and murdered. She had been missing from home over a long holiday weekend, and the child's teacher—a personal friend of mine—was obviously distraught. Of necessity, she had no more information than others, and on Monday morning when the newspapers reported the sad event, she faced the children who had also just learned of their classmate's death. Some of their parents had come to school that morning, too, and together they shared the range of feelings and concerns expressed by children and adults. They hugged, wept, talked, and even undertook some activities together that reminded them of how such time spent together could be healing. My friend told me that very few other staff members approached her and the students that first week. She realized it was necessary for her to help the school recover from a trauma of this magnitude. It must have taken all of her emotional reserves to reach beyond her classroom to address others' unspoken needs. That she did it is a tribute to her basic decency, but also a serious indictment of most schools' inability to respond systematically to predictable emotional fallout.

The mother of a high school senior from a neighboring community told me that after her son was injured in an automobile accident in which another student was killed, the junior high school observed a "minute of silence," as the only organized effort to address the emotional contagion spreading throughout the small district.

The lack of any sense of community is amply demonstrated by these two examples. In the first, the teacher found the emotional resources to reach out to her students while feeling isolated from her colleagues. She alone seemed to recognize the potential benefits of pulling together as a school at a time of crisis. She related to me how many other children and teachers would be affected by this tragedy, but that there was no history in the school of shared support and problem-solving. Similarly, the lost opportunities for grieving and healing among the junior high school students remind me of the "teachable moments" lost to the distance between individuals in schools.

When our small group of parents and educators came together to create Jowonio School, we, too, grappled with this dichotomy of individualism and community. We were concerned about our individual children, their need to feel good about themselves and to feel competent as learners. Our group also recognized that what was missing in the existing school programs was a sense of community. Once we were together, we felt exhilarated by the resources within our group. We had all the curriculum specialists one could hope for: reading teachers, graduate students majoring in mathematics and anthropology, parents interested in science, several school psychologists, and on and on. This reminded us of the value in working together as a group and of how scattered these people–resources seemed to be when we were navigating the system as individual parents and educators.

Along with seeking a balance between individualism and community, we sought to change the system. We wanted to create an alternative. Early on, we lacked the rhetoric to describe what we were doing, but we knew, on a values level, that we were participating in an educational change process.

Even then, we recognized that connected participants in a learning environment are vital—that what happens for one impacts on many others. This "social systems" viewpoint is one we are much more articulate about now; then, we simply sought ways to communicate caring and concern to each member. If someone either stood apart from our learning environment or was pushed aside, we felt committed to examining our part in the exclusion.

We began to recognize the limited view of children with autism held by most professionals. Our students were forming relationships with their teachers and learning to play with their peers. Our observations contradicted the prevalent view of children with autism as neither interested in nor capable of such behaviors. Parents helped us recognize the potential they had observed in their children. Together teachers and parents structured learning experiences to elicit conceptual and relationship interests within the children. Gradually, this partnership between parents and teachers empowered both and led to the children's growing skills. With the encouragement of parents, many teachers expanded their repertoires, the better to foster a communication environment within their classrooms—a major need of children with autism. Parents would often report discrepancies between their children's language performance at home and in school, and teachers became intrigued with finding ways to systematize language use in both environments. The ongoing communication between home and school encouraged teachers to become more knowledgeable about communication interventions. In turn, this led to a more functional curriculum approach—one in which teachers made more realistic suggestions for generalization of skills to home, because they had learned more about the routines and demands at home. Our sense of community was growing because of our interdependence. This reliance on one another directly supported the ongoing development of both our students and our adults.

We Start With Ourselves

One must want to reach out to include others *and* to be touched by others. Self-interest certainly plays a part in the development of a person's seeking to be with others. Personally, the extent to which I seek out others and make decisions about how and with whom I spend my time and energy has much to do with finding ways to meet my perceived needs.

At the beginning of the alternative school movement in the late 1960s, I was confronted with the realization that my oldest son's school experience was contributing to his diminishing feelings of self-esteem. If his school experience was unresponsive to his needs, then how was one to go about changing it? Attempts were made within the existing school structure (e.g., meetings with teachers, participation in the school as parent and professional, etc.), but the cultural press that was developing at that time to examine alternative school approaches and structures was very appealing to me. Frankly, I did not have the experience, and perhaps the courage, to strike out on my own. Instead, I joined a small group of parents with similar concerns for their children to explore the creation of an alternative school. My personal need to find a way, through schooling, to act upon my values and beliefs coalesced around my son's particular situation. A small community of interested parents and professionals developed Jowonio School, the first school program in the United States to include young children with severe disabilities in classrooms with their nondisabled peers.

Within five years, Jowonio School expanded its focus to include young children who were "clinically homeless"—a term coined by Burton Blatt to describe children who were not served by existing services. Certainly, in 1975, children with autism were not very visible in community schools and services. Institutional placement or home teaching were the prevalent options. With the encouragement of several graduate students enrolled in master's degree programs in special education at Syracuse University (Susan Gurry, Madeline Stoner, John Henley) and Jowonio staff members, the parents of two children reached out into the community for the financial support to include their children. They recognized the need to involve representatives of community agencies to help build a broader base of support for their children. Their political activity with community mental health administrators was responsible for the allocation of teaching personnel to Jowonio and for helping us recognize the value of reaching out and embracing other service delivery systems that were impacting on children.

Four years later, the same parents provided further leadership to Jowonio staff by paving the way for the integration of their children into their neighborhood school. After an agreement was obtained with Syracuse City School District administrators to develop an inclusive model, a lengthy planning process began among all parties concerned. Almost two years later, a combination third and fourth grade taught by both a general and a special educator included three children with autism, two of whom had been clinically homeless only four years earlier. They had a home now in the public schools, and so did those of us who had earlier left the public schools to develop an alternative model outside the system. Once we implemented an ecological model that incorporated more people and systems, we could find a place back in the system.

My personal odyssey to inclusion is linked with the journey of others. Our collective efforts helped me accomplish personal goals unattainable without the contributions, leadership, and visions of others.

RESPONSES TO BARRIERS

We knew from our early efforts to include our students in public school programs that there was no consensus on the issue. Some school districts did not believe that students with severe disabilities belonged in their school buildings, while others sought to design special classroom options for them. Except for us, no one had visions of what it would be like to design classrooms for these and all other students. We saw only lack of vision. Public Law 94-142 came the closest with its rather ambiguous statement that students should be educated in "the least restrictive environment." While scholars and practitioners sought the meaning of "least restrictive," teachers struggled to construct Individual Education Plans (IEPs), and parents and lawyers battled with schools over due process clauses.

Increasingly, however, small integration and mainstreaming victories occurred, but often the emotional and financial cost to parents, teachers, and schools was high. Each effort toward inclusion experienced false starts. Each family felt like a pioneer, and each school district had to find the comfort zone that allowed them to envision just how students could be accommodated within classrooms that had never before included them.

In Syracuse, we faced all the same concerns. The difference for us, however, was that we had created a school with inclusion as the centerpiece. We realized that, in order to communicate with others about our beliefs, we would have to be clear about them, which led us to construct this statement of philosophy:

- All children, regardless of severity of handicap, are capable of growth and change and demonstrate normal developmental characteristics.
- The structure of the learning environment exerts a powerful influence on the rate and direction of a child's growth.
- Receptiveness to instruction is initiated and maintained through warm, positive, accepting responses by the teaching staff.

"There Are No Experts Here"

We learned the importance of minimizing the expert role. Special educators initially flourished because we all believed they were the clinical extension of general education and had the answers. They also flourished because others relied on them to take over and find answers to all teachers' elusive problem situations. Whatever the motivation, our behavior as special educators became increasingly regal. We came to believe and assume the lofty position ascribed to us. Yet there are no experts at building communities able to respond to diversity. When we initiated our inclusion efforts we did not imagine we were dealing with clinical cases that lent themselves to prescriptive solutions. Rather, we quickly realized that building a sense of community meant including others.

Armed with the belief that process and content needed to go together—that we needed to practice what we preached—we sailed forward. Fortunately, we had the good sense to start with ourselves. Ours was no missionary effort, but rather an attempt to gain our own sea legs, to determine what an instructional program might look like, given our assumption that all children learn and can learn most meaningfully when they do so together in a caring environment.

Starting with ourselves was painful for it meant clarifying our own beliefs. Was it possible to espouse a point of view that called for celebrating diversity and still find difficulty practicing that viewpoint? Yes, it was—and that realization should come as no surprise. Nothing is as practical as a good theory, my colleague David Hunt (1974) tells us, and we all must learn firsthand when faced with the uniqueness of each situation.

Putting Beliefs Into Practice

How to explain the awkwardness we felt when the hiring committee was divided on hiring a teacher with spina bifida? We felt challenged to put our emerging beliefs into practice. If we truly believed in a diverse learning environment, then why were we raising questions about this candidate's ability to do all the things other teachers did? Exactly what is it that everyone did? At one point, a member of the committee asked if we were questioning whether she could take the students out on the playground and play basketball with them. Finally, after much soul-searching, we acknowledged the fact that not all teachers need to do the same things and that we were interested in this woman for the things she could do, not for what she could not undertake.

This example illustrates how complex it is to bring diverse people together in an inclusive classroom, and saying that does not reduce the concerns that may attach to each situation. Does this mean that constructing a classroom community is unique so that no guidelines can exist? And that each teacher or staff will have to reinvent the wheel, so to speak? Not really. It does mean, however, that we need to work from a base of values. In the case of the new teacher, we learned that belief in valuing differences in staff, as well as in students, can be tested. We needed to be open to such tests. It is only within the crucible of responding to real people in real situations that we come closer to understanding how complicated it is to act on our principles. Hence the guideline "Thou shalt not behave as expert" was etched into our consciousness early on.

The question of how much reinventing must occur within inclusive learning environments leads to another potential barrier. Few of us are prepared to deal with conflict situations where our strongly held beliefs are challenged.

We assumed that others shared our commitment to parents. After all, we were a group of parents and educators committed to all children's development. What a shock it was for us when we were confronted by a parent who did not agree with our decision to teach her child sign language as an alternative form of communication! The confrontation was an early wake-up call for us on the importance of listening to others. We hoped the parent would listen to us because of our obvious concern for her child and our expertise. Instead, we learned that while concern and expertise are necessary, they are not sufficient.

We needed to listen more carefully to the mother's concerns, including her struggle to set reasonable expectations for her child. Were *we* assuming too much, the mother asked? She did not then share our belief that her daughter would change dramatically if we could offer her an alternative form of communication. In fact, she understood her child to be severely disabled and envisioned her remaining that way. Once we were able to hear the mother's concerns and accept her position, while not necessarily agreeing with it, we could negotiate a compromise. The teachers agreed to use those signs that would allow the child to accomplish such basic needs as requesting food, using the toilet, and similar functional tasks. The mother agreed to use the same signs at home, and we all agreed to reevaluate the child's progress periodically.

Responding to Everyone

The experience with the mother and signing was a painful and important reminder of the need to pay attention to everyone in the learning environment. In our zeal, and perhaps frustration, to offer the child a more functional communication system, we neglected to bring the parent along with us. By the time we eventually shared our perspectives, there was already a strong tone of "You need to trust us, we're the experts" about the conversation. Yet, we realized that no one is truly the expert, or perhaps everyone is. If one person needs to be so designated, perhaps the parent comes the closest to it.

Our biggest challenge was to find ways to reduce the distance between participants. With this mother, we had retreated to our "professionalism" line when we felt defensive about our position. Another way of thinking about the importance of what we have to offer as educators, however, is to recognize the need to pool our collective wisdom. When we truly listen to each participant in the learning environment, it is easier to recognize the resource each person represents.

I recall a 4-year-old girl who continually reached out to her classmates, especially those with disabilities. Her degree of empathy was breathtaking at the time and included situations in which she actually resolved conflicts. For example, her friend Sam was having a particularly bad day. He was continually upset and would approach other children in an apparent effort to bite them. At one point, it was necessary for a teacher to hold Sam to help him achieve some control. The little girl approached the teacher and asked if she thought Sam was hungry. Without waiting for a reply, she retrieved her own sandwich and thrust half of it into his hand. He took it, ate it, and calmed down.

The next year, the little girl's needs had changed. Rather than being the "assistant teacher," she needed assistance herself. Family life was changing for her and she was feeling vulnerable. Instead of reaching out to others, she required holding and support from us. Her teachers "heard" her and adjusted their behaviors so that she could count on our support and would not be expected to resolve classroom conflicts.

We also observed many significant interactions among "typical" children. For example, Laurie was designated child of the week but felt shy when everyone focused on her. She brought in pictures of her family, but retreated to a corner of the room where she was obviously uncomfortable. Her friend Carl observed this and approached her eagerly, asking if he could see her pictures. Once relaxed by sharing with Carl, Laurie could approach the group. In an environment that is structured for everyone, we can readily identify each person's strengths and needs and try to address them in constructive ways.

Using the Potential for Friendships

In many classrooms, the common oversight is our bringing children together, but failing to focus on their relationships. When building a sense of community, an emphasis on making friendships is central. Providing children with such friendship-making opportunities complements all other aspects of a broadly defined curriculum. Skills of sharing, communicating, using language, and negotiating conflicts all "rise to the instructional surface" when friendships become an integral part of classroom life and curriculum. Children naturally pursue their interests and concerns about making friends, and it is to our advantage as adults to participate in this process.

Two of the children at Jowonio became close friends. One of these friends arrived at school one day very upset about his friend after viewing a television program on spina bifida. Apparently the program made the observation that children never recovered from the disability, but could only make adaptations to it. Roger had assumed that his friend would grow out of his spina bifida despite having a teacher in his classroom with spina bifida who used a wheelchair and "crunches" (as some children called crutches). He had not made the connection between his friend and his teacher, or perhaps he didn't see the teacher as having a particular disability. Nevertheless, he was distraught and inconsolable.

Yet, embedded within Roger's concerns were marvelous opportunities for friendship-building. Roger was obviously struggling to gain a clearer image of the friend he cared a great deal about and thought was just like him. Could Roger, his friend Hank, and the teachers all work together to maintain the friendship and still address Roger's concerns? Maybe doing so would allow Roger to develop an acceptance of differences on a conscious level. He already prized his friend and wanted him to be well. By gaining a realization of the complexities of physical differences he would be in a better position to make the relationship even more reciprocal. After all, we want our friends to accept us for who we are, not for who they need us to be.

Roger achieved just this kind of growth. He learned a great deal more about spina bifida and hence more about his friend. The teachers helped him confront his feelings and anxieties about his friend's future, and Hank gained a friend who could accept him as he was—and would be.

Establishing a Local Presence

Our most successful efforts to educate ourselves and the larger community depended upon collaboration between parents and professionals. One of the early community initiatives came from staff members at the Center on Human Policy at Syracuse University and parents of children with disabilities. Together they formed a parent hotline and an information and support network. From that small beginning grew Exceptional Family Resources, a major resource in our community that offers a wide variety of services and programs to families of children and adults with disabilities ranging from respite care to recreation opportunities, job training, and advocacy training. The organization's strength relies on maintaining strong ties with professionals from many other agencies, networks, and the university community.

A later initiative of families and professionals occurred as the students grew older, and the relevant adults came together to brainstorm ways to handle their future needs. For several years, Parents for Positive Futures spearheaded local efforts to draw attention to issues of adequate programming for high school students, supported work, and community living. Impetus for the group's formation came from close working relationships between faculty and doctoral students in the Division of Special Education and Rehabilitation at Syracuse University and the families of adolescents and young adults with whom they worked. As local options became available, the group became less active.

Despite increasing community options, the impetus for creating inclusive classrooms remained. Again, several years ago a coalition formed to address requirements for program development, parent advocacy, and community education. Parents and Educators for Inclusive Education reaches out to parents and the professional community in a variety of ways. One example was a conference, attended by more than 500 people, which consisted of presentations by teachers and parents working in and advocating inclusive programs. The group holds monthly meetings attended by a range of parents and educators who come to learn about topics as diverse as "parent advocacy" and "initiating an inclusive classroom in a school district with only segregated classroom options."

Our community-building efforts in Syracuse are part of a larger national effort to make schools a welcoming place for everyone. Syracuse and other communities and some national groups such as Schools Are for Everyone (SAFE) and The Association for Persons with Severe Disabilities (TASH) recognize that the national debate on the crisis in education cannot continue emphasizing separate strands of educational reform. Figuring out how to make schools safe, how to make teachers integral to the decision-making process, and how to improve the literacy skills of children from economically impoverished backgrounds, however, can all be addressed within the context of creating communities that maximize the learning and participation of everyone involved. In other words, the schools we have been reaching for may not be achieved by improving only parts of school organization or curriculum. Instead, we must put our energies into creating communities of learners that include children, parents, teachers, and the broader community.

Spreading the Word

As we gained experience with inclusion, we regularly produced materials for professional journals and books. I find the growing trend to encourage the participation of classroom teachers and school administrators in writing projects most interesting. An invitation to write a chapter for an edited volume on inclusion also urged me to invite one of my colleagues from elementary education to be a coauthor. What an interesting notion: to practice what we preach! If inclusion is the topic, then it is useful, perhaps even necessary, to model the process by including both general and special educators as contributors.

Another aspect of our sharing has been to present our approach, experiences, and continuing issues at national meetings. At first, those of us at Syracuse University were the ones to carry the good news about inclusion to the larger professional community. Of course, we were careful to express our indebtedness to the classroom teachers who did the actual teaching and from whom we were learning about all the complexities involved in including all children in general education classrooms. As with our writing, we now support and encourage teachers and parents to present their experiences directly at national meetings. What a marvelous development! It shows how all of the constituents have contributions to make. Some conferences also invite people with disabilities to present keynote speeches, further emphasizing how much there is to learn from one another.

Videotapes of ongoing classroom programs and teaching approaches have also made perspectives on inclusion available to the wider parent and professional communities. Producing the videotape, *Regular Lives*, was a complicated matter, and Douglas Biklen found it necessary to involve many groups in its funding and production. This process of seeking federal and foundation funding, enlisting the support of professional organizations such as TASH, and involving school personnel, parents, and students further expanded our partnership and collaboration. Making a videotape in this case was a community-building effort.

HOW FOSTERING COMMUNITY
FACILITATES SCHOOL CHANGE

Reducing Isolation

Proponents of inclusion now recognize the importance of addressing the isolation that teachers and students may feel within schools. By turning to ways to bring school participants together, we can move closer to valuing the diversity among staff and students.

A number of years ago, a colleague and I brought together a small group of teachers who were working with students labeled emotionally disturbed to discuss their relationships with their students (Knoblock & Goldstein, 1971). As the group began describing their work situations, their feelings of isolation became clear. They were working hard—but in virtual isolation from other staff members. They felt positive about their students, but they were not fully gratified by working only with them. They spoke eloquently about wanting to spend more time with other teachers and wished they felt more central to the overall mission of their school. Several spoke of missing talk time with other adults and expressed dismay when they recognized how all-consuming their work with a small group of students had become.

We had not begun this study as an exploration of inclusion, but that is what it became as teachers shared the many ways they felt cut off from their colleagues and the daily flow of school life. We recognized how damaging it is to isolate teachers *or* students. Competent and effective teachers working with a complicated student population reported subtle and not-so-subtle ways their functioning was impaired by such exclusion. Their discontent was not with their students, but with their lack of involvement with other adults in the school. Not feeling connected to the human community, they did not feel whole. These feelings propelled some of them to reach out to others in creative ways. Their goal was to help others see them and their students as valuable members of the school. It was no small task, given how often others devalued students with challenging behaviors. This basic view of the students often extended to the teachers who became much like their students in the eyes of potential colleagues. These all-too-common perspectives certainly complicated the teachers' task. Over time, the group of teachers shared all the various strategies they had tried to become part of the life of the school. Most reported constructive efforts to reach out to others. When rebuffed, however, some resorted to a grown-up version of acting out—including expressions of alienation and anger toward students and staff. In some instances, however, the status of "deviant member" of the school remained the role of both teachers and students. Which came first, students' and teachers' inherent deviant nature or the dynamics of exclusion expressed by the school or district human community? Our conclusion was that it was the processes of exclusion and isolation that created the negative images of those excluded. Children who are labeled have their behaviors evaluated as part of their label. A child's behavior becomes "aggressive" because he or she is labeled emotionally disturbed, while a student without such a label might be only "active" or "boisterous."

An alternative perspective views a child's or adult's behaviors within the context of environmental dynamics. We believe this ecological viewpoint provides a useful explanation of how teachers in this study behaved. They were excluded, they felt excluded, and so they attempted to the best of their abilities to find a way back into the fabric of daily school life. Any measure of success they achieved depended on their skills as well as the willingness of others to see them and their students as valuable members of the school community.

Minimizing the Two-Tier System of Education

Students and staff members experience a lot of undue pressure when they struggle to join the school community. Others in the school, including teaching assistants, instructional specialists, resource teachers, and office secretaries may feel similarly pressured and excluded. By creating one community with a sense of shared mission, feelings of alienation might be lessened for everyone.

Currently all school personnel in Syracuse who are not assigned to classrooms with the designation of "teacher," are referred to as "related service personnel." The superintendent of schools recently asked all staff members with that designation to prepare a statement detailing the extensive nature of their jobs despite the fact that they are not in a classroom. Faced with budget constraints and the need to justify a school budget to the city's Common Council, the superintendent is marshaling support for school personnel who, less recognizable to the community-at-large perhaps, are, nevertheless, essential to the maintenance of a responsive program for a diverse group of students.

Our experiences with this group of teachers taught us that the controversy over inclusion of students with disabilities and the creation of a single system of education is really a larger question about who is central to the educational enterprise and who should be excluded. Rather than having to marshal support for nonclassroom staff, we should be doing a better job of informing all parts of the larger community about what school personnel do. In a similar way, our special education teachers and their students need to become valued members of the school community.

To accomplish this level of inclusion, all adults and students within a school building need to feel a sense of belonging. To the extent that numbers of participants in a building feel left out, including others becomes more difficult. It is reasonable to assume that in schools that have segregated classrooms for students with disabilities there might well be other students and adults there who are also excluded, perhaps in a variety of subtler ways. When we convince ourselves that there is nothing "regular" about a "regular" classroom, we will be closer to acceptance and community for everyone within the school building.

Teachers as Community-Builders

Many of our teachers define their role more broadly than a typical classroom teacher. Before Rochester, New York, gained notoriety for reconceptualizing the role of teachers to include case management and other outside-the-classroom duties, our teachers were experimenting with a broader role definition. For example, our teachers became involved with their children and their families. They recognized that the child standing before them was part of a larger social system—the family. Once they spent time with families, they recognized even larger systems surrounding and influencing the family and children's needs.

Teachers worked with families in large and small ways. Some provided respite to families by allowing them to spend time together away from their child—a need expressed by many parents. When teachers take a child for an overnight or a weekend, they inevitably gain a more comprehensive understanding of the child and the management tasks addressed by the family on a daily basis. This kind of information can improve the accuracy and functionality of any tasks or interventions teachers suggest parents try at home. Families greatly appreciate teacher input, especially if it is realistic with regard to their particular routines and lifestyle.

In addition to time outside school hours, teachers and schools can provide support to families in many other ways. At Jowonio School, for example, teachers lend children's favorite school activities and materials over vacations, thus helping parents continue to work on learning tasks when school is not in session. Edward Smith School teachers helped initiate and staff an afterschool program for students that allowed some children more time with friends and offered working families another option for relevant childcare.

Participating with parents in organizations addressing inclusion can also reduce the psychological distance between teachers and families. Sari Biklen, a professor of education at Syracuse University, writes of the potential conflicts between middle-class teachers and middle-class parents, many of whom speak the same educationese! Teachers may feel threatened by a parent who is aware of the special education regulations and the recent literature and research (Biklen, 1995). We know from research on relationship-building that ongoing contact is necessary for enhancing relationships. When teachers and parents collaborate in all these various ways, we often see positive effects.

Teacher Preparation and Community-Building

The above examples depict teachers who are "alive and growing," to borrow a phrase used by Clark Moustakas (1959) to describe an authentic teacher. For many years, my colleagues and I at Syracuse University have grappled with how best to prepare individuals for real-world teaching, how to help them to engage in many of the behaviors described here. Basically, our goal is for teachers to participate as partners with parents and other citizens to celebrate the diversity that exists within a classroom. We can move closer to this goal by finding ways to structure schools and classrooms to address the individual and collective needs of students and adults. At present, our preparation programs at Syracuse University are in a state of flux, as we attempt to reconceptualize teacher education for community-building and participation.

Replacing the two-tier system. We are striving to move away from preparing general educators and special educators separately, much as we are attempting to bring together special and general education in the schools. We combined the undergraduate preparation programs that trained elementary education majors in one department and special education majors in another. Now there is one teacher preparation program located within the Department of Teaching and Leadership in the School of Education. This Undergraduate Inclusive Teacher Education Program breaks new ground for us and the nation. Students now entering as freshman can graduate dually certified in elementary and special education, not because they have met the requirements of each program, but rather because they have been exposed to one model of education that addresses the needs of all students in regular classrooms.

An important goal of our Undergraduate Inclusive Teacher Education Program is to provide future teachers with opportunities to build positive relationships with parents, and in turn, form positive attitudes toward families. In their sophomore year, student partners provide respite to a family with a child with disabilities. Trying to become companions rather than teachers, they enter into the life of the family in ways that are comfortable for each party. Some of our college students have reported a sense of belonging, of becoming part of the family. Others feel they are used as babysitters and "are only providing time-out for parents." Still others express confusion about why they have been assigned a child who "only has a learning disability and doesn't seem very involved at all." Nevertheless, each experience provides students and faculty with marvelous opportunities to explore perspective-taking. The majority of our students consider the respite experience one of their most significant opportunities to become acquainted with youngsters and their families.

Despite their youth, these college students appear to have the maturity and life experiences that allow them to value the families and children with whom they work. Some experiences do not begin positively, yet, with support, students persevere in their efforts to engage family and child. Support comes from working with Exceptional Family Resources, the parent-organized community agency discussed earlier. The agency identifies families requesting respite support and matches our college students with a family. Working in pairs (another beginning way to foster teamwork), our students are introduced to each family by a staff member of Exceptional Family Resources, who continues to be available by phone as needed. When conflicts arise, as they inevitably do, we encourage our students to problem-solve with us, with staff at the agency, and with their partner to seek a resolution with the family.

Providing respite is only one experience within the inclusive preparation model that addresses our belief in a social systems approach to understanding the needs of children and families. We also begin with the person of the prospective teacher. The attitudes and experiences students bring with them are revealed early in the program, as they are exposed to real-world opportunities to examine their own behaviors and ideas as well as the interests of others. We ask students to first examine themselves, then to shift their focus to their respite companion and his or her family. One college student angrily stated: "I'm not going back in that house, it's dirty." We had to help her understand her reaction as a value position. We accomplished this through discussion with the staff members at Exceptional Family Resources who explained the life forces impinging on this particular family.

Molding mature minds. We began reframing teacher education at Syracuse University by changing the nature of the undergraduate program. Many of us were dissatisfied with our special education program. That general dissatisfaction, coupled with the national controversy generated by the Holmes Commission's examination of the viability of undergraduate teacher preparation, motivated us to explore change.

This was not the case with our master's-level preparation programs in the Department of Education. For many years, we believed our graduate preparation of teachers—working with infants and young children, students with learning disabilities or autism, and other students with challenging behaviors—to be exemplary. Once again, however, the impetus for change arose from both internal and external forces.

Internally, several faculty members felt that, since we were already preparing special educators to ply their skills within a general education context, we should take the next step of combining with elementary education to create a single preparation program for all teachers. Externally, the New York State Department of Education was planning to abolish the single certification in special education. This meant that teachers would be required to possess certification in elementary and special education. We reasoned that it was time to rethink graduate teacher education at Syracuse rather than splice two models together.

I suspect this confluence of factors can be found at the heart of most change efforts, including those that occur in the public schools. Sometimes we push for change, or are pushed into a process. Sometimes we are willing followers of others' initiatives, sometimes we may initiate the effort. There are many instances of mixed motivations for change; change of any significant magnitude rarely occurs in a pure form. It is this interweaving of motivation and outside pressures and opportunities that make change so perplexing.

The complexities are palpable for us right now, as faculty from the Department of Special Education and the Department of Teaching and Leadership negotiate. For example, we are challenging ourselves to act on the basis of our beliefs. It is no small task to persuade college professors, or anyone else for that matter, to practice what they preach. Since we support inclusion of all students in general education, we are inclined to create a single structure for teacher preparation as well. This leads to abolishing special education as a separate entity and shifting our faculty resources to the Department of Teaching and Leadership, the program housing the preparation of elementary education teachers. Like public schools, we are struggling to abolish our two-tier system of education.

INCLUSION AS THE SEARCH FOR COMMUNITY

There is no conclusion to our accomplishments in Syracuse, because the process of inclusion for students with disabilities continues as part of the larger search for school community. We do know, however, that each inclusion change strategy has been effected in the spirit of fostering a sense of relatedness, a way of staying connected to the people and ideas we valued.

Many of those early change efforts continue to reverberate within the Syracuse City School District, and perhaps, from them, we can learn much about where we need to go from here. For example, when students from Jowonio School "aged out" at 8 years old, they made the first transition to their neighborhood elementary school, then on to the neighborhood middle school, and eventually to the high school. It just so happened that this cohort of students lived in the same geographical area, making it possible to use the feeder school approach to achieve change across the system.

Today in Syracuse, an array of inclusive classrooms exists at various schools at different grade levels. A policy commitment to placement of students with disabilities in their neighborhood schools is less clear. This may reflect our history of using the schools in one geographical quadrant of the city to cluster programs for students with a particular disability. Thus, students with autism tended to cluster in one quadrant and students with physical disabilities in another. Gradually, proponents of inclusion have lobbied for neighborhood school placements regardless of disability category, and the placement picture is changing as a result.

In hindsight, we learned several important lessons from our experiences, although there were good reasons for proceeding as we did at the time. Anticipating the importance of making each neighborhood school inclusive and avoiding a single-disability focus is essential to our thinking now. Historically, we were forging new territory. There we were, with a small group of children with autism who had never been in the public schools. Supporting their collective careers through a group of schools in one quadrant of the city seemed feasible and appropriate. Nevertheless, there have been lingering consequences for those early decisions. For one, the inclusive model was thought of as viable only for students with autism. Eventually, this led to some conflicts with parents who wanted a similar option for their children with other disabilities.

Today Syracuse public schools reflect the early decisions and models we created. Certainly, there are things we would do differently now, but that doesn't mean it is too late to change. In actuality, that is precisely what is happening in our district. The challenge is to move forward based on what we have done and learned—not to wait for a crystal ball to anticipate the future.

We now know what a luxury it is to work from principles rather than in reaction to children's immediate needs. Our growing focus on attendance in neighborhood schools is just one example, but it is an important one. This change strategy helps avoid the clustering of large numbers of students with labels in one classroom or school. As we move toward inclusive schools, the issue becomes less one of placement and more of accommodation to each classroom's student diversity.

In some of the classrooms at Edward Smith Elementary School, we included three children with autism, violating the principle of natural proportions. At that time, we were scrambling to assemble a team of willing and able teachers. The sense of urgency to meet all students' needs kept us from recognizing how unlikely it would be to find three children with autism in a single classroom in one school.

Then, what are we learning about inclusion and the change process? We are learning that:

- It is easier to ask others to make changes than it is to change ourselves.
- Planning for change is very time consuming. It means, among other things, a commitment of time and energy over many years.

- The very process of negotiating with others around change means that individuals and groups must clarify their positions. What is important and what is open to negotiation?
- When we truly listen to others' perspectives, there is much we can learn and profit from.
- Planning for change is ongoing. Each decision should have room to flex and grow.

When we first planned the undergraduate inclusive program at Syracuse University we set up so many course requirements that the students buckled under the demands of the program. We are now back at the drawing board, revising the requirements in light of the student feedback and of our growing awareness of what it means to combine rather than add on.

Do you have a list of your own?

REFERENCES

Biklen, S. K. (1995). *School work: Gender and the cultural construction of teaching.* New York: Teachers College Press.

Fenwick, V. (1987). The Edward Smith School program: An integrated public school continuum for autistic children. In M. S. Berres & P. Knoblock (Eds.). *Program models for mainstreaming* (pp. 261–286). Austin, TX: Aspen Publishers, Inc.

Hunt, D. E. (1974). *Between psychology and education.* Hinsdale, IL: Dryden Press.

Knoblock, P. (1983). *Teaching and mainstreaming autistic children.* Denver: Love Publishing.

Knoblock, P., & Goldstein, A. P. (1971). *The lonely teacher.* Boston: Allyn & Bacon.

Moustakas, C. (1959). *The alive and growing teacher.* New York: Philosophical Press.

Epilogue

Connie Woods

More than a year has passed since the editors of this book first met to discuss their personal journeys toward inclusion. Each of us is convinced that the journey has been worth the effort. We remain strong in our beliefs and committed to this philosophy of education. We have learned a great deal about ourselves, our colleagues, our students, and the process of change. We would like to believe that we are wiser now than we were a year ago.

The daily business of implementation is wearing on all of us, in different ways. There is seldom enough money and never enough time. Key personnel leave at critical moments. Individuals feel poorly prepared to take on the challenges presented by an ever more diverse group of learners. Some believe the expectation that they accomplish these challenges is unreasonable. We acknowledge that there are no experts, while trying to convince teaching teams that they are the experts. Only recently have we understood the resource and retraining issues of inclusive schools.

We find ourselves part of an evolving cycle of education, retraining, and community-building. It sometimes feels that we repeatedly fight the same battle. This feeling is shared by many parents of children with disabilities. They have learned that they can never relax and assume that each new teacher, each new principal, or each new school district will welcome them and their children. The faces change with every new college class we teach, inservice training session we conduct, school staff member or superintendent we encounter, but the issues largely remain the same. As one group learns from the lessons of the past, has value-altering experiences, and broadens its definitions of school and community, another group full of questions, doubts, and issues replaces them—and we begin again. Because there is no final degree of inclusion to strive for, the work is never finished.

The editors of this book have different perspectives on the cycles of change and improvement, based on our various roles in the process. For some of us the change has been extremely positive. We see that individuals and teaching teams who have chosen systemic change rather than mandated "add on" change are hard at work in their communities, schools, and classrooms. They are changing the face of public education.

The schools portrayed here provide all of us with examples of what is possible when committed staff and families work together to improve the way a school serves all of its members. They act as models and sources of inspiration for others who are not so far along in the restructuring process. We are constantly awed and humbled by what such places have to teach us.

For those of us involved in inservice training, these "early adapters," with their enthusiasm for new ideas, excitement about change, and willingness to engage the issues are frequently being replaced by other, more cautious individuals. More frequently now, as someone involved with mandated change, I see individuals who are coming reluctantly to the table. These teachers are being told to change their practices without being given the opportunity to evaluate and change their belief systems. They are angry at administrators whom they do not trust to support them and "experts" advocating ideologies that they view as unrealistic, inappropriate, or just another "passing fad." Others are simply confused by how the rules of the game are changing. They are trying to update their skills without truly understanding the reasons for change. They are unsure of why they are being asked to teach a broader range of students. They lack the shared vision of need and the personal experiences that would enable them to open their minds and then their hearts to this fuller approach to the restructuring of educational service delivery. Not yet having had those personal experiences that can change old belief systems and attitudes—yet being expected to implement changes they do not see the need for or believe in—these individuals frequently ask the wrong questions and make the wrong decisions. Some are trying to implement change while personally still believing that the changes may be harmful to "their kids." Others drag their heels, hoping that if they just wait long enough—as with so many educational innovations before it—"inclusion, too, will pass."

Often these same educators work for principals or administrators who do not understand the philosophical nature of the changes they are asking their staff to make. Too many administrators view inclusive education merely as a placement issue. Hence, they ask teachers to run dual systems simultaneously, with inclusion as a placement option for some students. They report that they have an "inclusion program" at their school much as they laud the school music program or afterschool daycare option. Frequently, they do not understand the resource issues, time demands, and retraining needs that must be addressed if the implementation of inclusive education is to be successful. Often, administrators have mislabeled an integrated program as inclusive. Because they consider inclusion a program placement option, they assume that offering "pretty good integration" to a few students is the same thing as having an inclusive school. Because many principals and administrators do not possess the value base to support these kinds of changes, I find a great number of odd and inappropriate things being done in the name of inclusion.

The odds against success would seem high for those schools and teachers beginning their journeys toward inclusion with such attitudes and deterrents, and yet, a fascinating and encouraging phenomenon is at work in schools. Quite often, these same teachers, having been required to accept a previously excluded child into their classrooms, undergo a truly heartwarming transformation. They frequently become the strongest, most vocal advocates of inclusionary programs. Such statements as, "A year ago I would never have believed this would have worked," and, "It didn't matter what I was told, nothing could have prepared me for this, I had to experience it for myself," or, "After 20 years of teaching, this is the most rewarding year I have ever had" are not uncommon. These teachers talk with other teachers in their buildings, encouraging them to take the risk of including a child. Then, their personal experiences and their credibility with their colleagues drive further change in their schools. No amount of inservice training can accomplish this alteration in attitude and outlook.

Many principals understand the issues, appreciate the benefits of having a diverse, accepting school community, and advocate strongly to build inclusive school environments. They do so in spite of the fact that such advocacy adds another complicating aspect to the myriad school reform issues already facing their schools. Developing a new school program is challenging and demanding. It is a living, fragile entity. Many principals find themselves in the position of beginning programs in which they believe strongly, maintaining those programs for a period of time, then moving on to new challenges. Sometimes these moves are on their own initiative; at times they are the result of district policy. Sometimes the programs they helped create thrive and grow stronger. Other times the programs slowly crumble, or are gleefully dismantled by people who did not support them. These moves are always undertaken with a certain emotional and personal cost to those leaving and to those left behind.

Michael Berres, the principal of Lawton Elementary School, has recently accepted a position as principal of a school in another district. Berres believes that the strength of inclusion comes from its centrality to the school's daily focus. As a principal, he has worked to entwine inclusive philosophy into the core of Lawton's daily practice. His belief is that, only when inclusion is intertwined in the daily school covenant, will it survive beyond particular personalities or the departure of the "early adapters," along with their strength and advocacy. Only when safely woven into the fabric of school life will inclusive practices be safe from the budget-cutting that usually works against the edges of a program, but not against its core parts. He feels that Lawton has reached this level. Although it makes him nervous to contemplate leaving, he has faith that "we have created a value around inclusion that will hold, and that the real strength of a program is best tested when the early adapters or a strong principal are actually away from the scene." He views inclusion as an evolutionary set of cycles. He knows that the new principal and the Lawton staff "will have to address new issues of inclusion, but they will never go back to the beginning."

There are a myriad of advantages for schools fortunate enough to be associated with a university teacher preparation program. Two of our editors have learned that there are also advantages for the university faculty in being closely associated with schools.

Dianne Ferguson, professor of Special Education at the University of Oregon writes:

> Our relationship with South Valley Elementary School continues to grow. This past year, the staff joined with us in a new collaborative research project. Our efforts so far have focused on creating a profile of the entire school, sharing that information with the staff, and helping them to use it to guide their planning as the school makes a transition to a new principal. Our endeavors have a new feel for us. South Valley staff ask us directly what we think and acknowledge our possession of a good deal of useful information about the school that few of its individual members have. We are feeling a bit more like ex officio members of the faculty and staff.
>
> South Valley faculty and other educators from Green River School District have continued to be involved with us through our continuing professional development course sequence and working with our master's degree students as cooperating professionals. Two or three of our graduates are now substitute teaching in classrooms of some of the teachers they met first in work groups and study groups during the university classroom activities. We feel we are learning more and more about this district and its schools and look forward to an increasing number of roles and linkages with this educational community.

Ferguson notes that experiences with Green River schools have "strengthened our resolve to keep changing our own teaching practice at the university." Her staff is currently reviewing the last year's course sequence, hoping to improve the experience for next year's participants. She realizes that "not all our tactics have worked. Some simply bombed, leaving students and instructors frustrated. Others 'worked' for some, but we never managed to succeed in tailoring everything for every learner, despite our continuing efforts." She thinks that sometimes "students were too challenged by the different activities we proposed. They seemed to bring their own set of expectations and 'rules' for college classrooms that we were not always able to quickly 'revise.' Still we are optimistic that all the teachers thus far, and those we will encounter next year from Green River and other parts of the state, will continue to teach us how to improve our practice."

Ferguson shares with Peter Knoblock, professor of Special Education at Syracuse University, the experience of helping to bring change to their own departments at their respective universities. She writes,

> We will soon find ourselves in the role of trying to share some of what we've learned with other colleagues at the College of Education as we restructure the entire college to renew all of our teaching programs. We'll look forward to the challenges and opportunities that this adventure promises.

Knoblock's experiences this past year have been of a highly personal nature.

> Collaborating on this book project has forced me to confront the kinds of personal changes I have been asking classroom teachers and their administrators to make for years. Specifically, I am reminded of the harsh reality that, once we move beyond the contemplation stage and into an action phase in which change is attempted, one must practice what one has been preaching!
>
> On some level I have always known how wrenching it has been for some school persons to embrace inclusion. That realization may account for my moderation the last few years as I encouraged others to proceed slowly, if needed, but proceed nevertheless. Perhaps I was preparing myself for my own inclusion.
>
> In our School of Education at Syracuse University, the faculties in special education and elementary education have been exploring a merger of the two separate programs into one. That may still happen in the next year or two. In the meantime, we are moving our offices into the same building as a way to enhance communication and pave the way for the eventual dissolution of separate teacher preparation programs.
>
> Does this first step sound familiar to those of us who once recommended moving special education classrooms out of the basement and onto floors and locations adjacent to other classrooms? For me, it means

leaving the Special Education Building and my office of 33 years. More important, does it mean losing my identity as a special educator? And what about the integrity of our training program that has existed for so long and prepared a generation of teachers who paved the way for inclusion?

Again, the questions sound remarkably familiar to what our colleagues in the schools have been saying as we marched forward in our rhetoric about the merits of inclusion. I can now confront these concerns more personally, and in the process I am examining my own beliefs in ways I may not have had to in the past.

What "conclusions" have I reached? For one, I experience how personal change is, along with the political and programmatic dimensions that come with it. For another, I am slowly telling myself that the move does not necessarily mean I will lose my identity as a special educator. It may mean that I can extend my view of the educative process, and do so in collaboration with others. Some faculty are not well known to me, others are colleagues with whom I feel closely aligned. And together, we may be able to construct newer ways to think of teacher preparation. If this happens, I may be prepared for the next step: the merger of our graduate teacher preparation programs.

How bravely I say this, knowing what I am experiencing about the change process. After all, it's a year or two away, plenty of time to ponder the questions and concerns. However, a voice tells me it will never be easy.

The editors have learned many lessons from our cumulative experiences of the last year—and the past two decades. We will no doubt learn many more lessons in the years ahead. Conventional wisdom has a way of changing as systems evolve. As educators continue to examine their practices, what is considered best educational practice is redefined based on new experiences, insights, and research. We work to build better systems of education based on the continually changing needs of the students in our care. There is every reason to expect that the future will hold many changes we have yet to envision.

We have learned that the skills required to develop an inclusive school are not necessarily the same skills required to maintain that program over time. People have talents and interests in different parts of the long-term change process. We must somehow tap into those talents at the appropriate times. We know that attitude is critical to success. Those individuals who see challenges rather than barriers and who have a "can do" approach to problem-solving are much more likely to surmount difficulties, find creative solutions, and experience success than those who do not.

We are learning that the familiar continuum of placement options may need to be replaced by a continuum of support service options that can be provided primarily in the general education classroom. We know that change takes time. What we may not have wholly appreciated is how frail the entire process is, how the process must be systematically managed and nurtured if it is to flourish, and how very long a time we face before the changes can be fully instituted.

The process of change is delicate, and yet we know and believe it can happen. Can inclusion really work for all students? We believe that, when properly understood and implemented, it can. However, one of the most critical lessons we have learned is that children's needs are more important than our ideology. If circumstances truly indicate that something other that an inclusive educational environment would best meet a child's needs at a given time, we are prepared to accept that. We must, however, be absolutely certain it is the child's needs, rather than ease of service provision or the adults' biases, reservations, or reluctance to change, that are motivating our placement decisions.

So why, in spite of all the difficulties, do we advocate so strongly for this change to inclusive education? Perhaps because, in all our years as "education professionals," we have never been part of an innovation that has touched us so profoundly and on so many levels. This journey has required that we grow professionally and personally. We have felt better about ourselves for being part of this process. We have seen children and their families blossom, as they are accepted and made part of a larger, enriched school community. There is something compelling about being involved in a process in which no one loses, in which there are benefits for everyone. We want others to experience these benefits and to share in the positive outcomes of inclusion. There are many areas of debate, many issues left to resolve, but there is one thing upon which we wholeheartedly agree—this is the right thing to do.

About the Contributors

Michael S. Berres is principal of Skyline Elementary School in the Ferndale (Washington) School District. He has previously served as principal of Lawton and Decatur Elementary schools in the Seattle Public Schools. He has also worked as a special education administrator, as a Washington State regional technical assistant for special education programs, as an administrator at Jowonio School (described by Peter Knoblock in Chapter 6) in Syracuse, New York, and as a teacher in mental health and school settings in Philadelphia, Washington, D.C., and Santa Barbara, California. His educational background consists of degrees from Syracuse University (PhD), American University (MEd), and the University of California at Santa Barbara (Teaching Certificate and BA). He is the editor of *Program Models for Mainstreaming* with Peter Knoblock (1987).

Dianne L. Ferguson, PhD, is Associate Professor at the University of Oregon, where she has been exploring school reform for all students, including those with disabilities. She manages a program that prepares teachers to work with students who have disabilities in restructured public schools. Dianne also directs several research and development projects that depend upon close collaboration with teachers in designing systems that will improve the quality of schooling for all students. As a parent of a young man with severe multiple disabilities, Dianne also brings another perspective to her work with teachers and schools. This perspective is further aided by her ongoing research and involvement with families, especially families of youth and adults who experience developmental disabilities.

Cheryl M. Jorgensen, PhD, is Project Coordinator and Associate Research Professor with the Institute on Disability at the University of New Hampshire, a university-affiliated program. Since 1985, she has worked with public school teachers, parents, and administrators to increase their commitment and capacity for including students with severe disabilities in regular education classes. For the past several years, her work has shifted to the design of schools, curriculum, and instruction that naturally facilitates inclusion and learning for all students. Cheryl has presented at conferences and workshops and edits the *Equity and Excellence* newsletter. She co-authored the book *Including Students with Severe Disabilities in Schools,* and authored several chapters in other inclusion texts. She is currently writing a book focusing entirely on restructuring and inclusion at the high school level.

Peter Knoblock, PhD, is Professor Emeritus at Syracuse University. Since 1962 he has taught in the Division of Special Education and Rehabilitation and most recently in the Teaching and Leadership Programs. By working with colleagues, he has helped develop a dual certification program in elementary and special education at the undergraduate level and prepared graduate students for inclusive classrooms. He is one of the founders of Jowonio School, the first school to include children with autism and other developmental disabilities in classrooms with their nondisabled peers. He is the author or co-editor of *Understanding Exceptional Children and Youth, Teaching and Mainstreaming Autistic Children, Teaching Emotionally Disturbed Children,* and *Program Models for Mainstreaming.*

In addition to having taught at several colleges and universities, **Judy W. Kugelmass** has been a special education teacher, school psychologist, and administrator of early intervention programs. She received her PhD from Syracuse University in the areas of Special Education/Emotional Disturbance and Educational Administration and an MA in Counseling Psychology from the University of Oregon. She is currently Assistant Professor and coordinator of elementary education programs in the Division of Education, School of Education and Human Development at SUNY Binghamton. Her teaching and research interests focus on developing inclusive, learner-centered, experiential pedagogies in general and special education. She has worked in the United States, Canada, South East Asia, and Europe. Publications include *Behavior, Bias & Handicaps: Labeling the Emotionally Disturbed Child* (Transaction Press), an ethnographic study of the classification of Black, male children for special education. Dr. Kugelmass served as the Coordinator of the Network of Empire State Teachers, the Foxfire Teacher Outreach program in New York State from 1990 through 1994.

Gwen Meyer, MEd, has been a long-term collaborator with the Schools Projects at the Specialized Training Program in the College of Education at the University of Oregon. She has participated on several design groups for project products, previous research projects, and has contributed as an instructor in preservice courses and as a practicum instructor in a personnel preparation program. She coordinated a project focused on helping teachers form collegial work groups as a context for adapting and using information acquired through more traditional inservice experiences to change educational outcomes for students with disabilities. She is currently a member of a qualitative research team at the Schools Projects which is working with several schools to develop and implement school improvement plans to benefit all of the students in their schools. Ms. Meyer has 15 years experience working with persons with low incidence and severe disabilities in school, residential, and work settings. As a teacher she developed and implemented systems and plans that supported her middle school students' participation in general education classrooms and a range of community contexts as well.

Carol Tashie is a Project Coordinator with the University of New Hampshire's Institute on Disability/UAP. Trained as both a regular and a special educator, Carol taught children with and without disabilities in a variety of school settings for many years. In 1987, Carol became one of New Hampshire's first inclusion facilitators and worked in a small rural community, supporting students with severe disabilities in becoming full members of regular education classes. Carol has worked for the University since 1989, and is the co-author of several books, including *From Special to Regular, From Ordinary to Extraordinary*; *Changes in Latitudes, Changes in Attitudes*; *Lighter Side of IEPs*; *Dare to Dream*; and *Treasures*. Carol provides training and technical assistance throughout the United States, and has consulted to the Czech and Slovak Republics on issues relating to inclusive education and community support.

Connie Woods received her master's degree in special education from the University of Oregon. She taught students with significant developmental disabilities for nine years before accepting a position with the Washington State Office of the Superintendent of Public Instruction. While employed by SPI, Connie coordinated the federally funded Washington State System Change Project. This multiagency project assisted school districts across the state in developing inclusive education programs. She is currently working as program consultant to school districts and professional associations in the area of inclusive education.

Index